The Greatest Game

*Golf is deceptively simple and
endlessly complicated,
A child can play it well, and a
grown man can never master it.*

*Any single round of it is full of
unexpected triumphs
and seemingly perfect shots
that end in disaster.*

*It requires complete concentration
and total relaxation.
It satisfies the soul and
frustrates the intellect.*

*It is at the same time rewarding
and maddening—and it is,
without a doubt, the greatest
game mankind has ever invented.*

—ANONYMOUS

ARIZONA'S GREATEST
GOLF COURSES

BY BILL HUFFMAN
FOREWORD BY TOM WEISKOPF

NORTHLAND PUBLISHING

TITLE PAGE: *The signature par-5 hole at Phantom Horse.*
PAGE V: *The 18th hole at Desert Forest.*
PAGE VI–VII: *"Hole in One" by Russell Houston.*

The text type was set in Monotype Janson
The display type was set in Bauer Initials
Composed in the United States of America
Art Director: David Jenney
Designer: Trina Stahl
Editor: Brad Melton
Production Supervisor: Lisa Brownfield
Editorial Assistant: Kimberly Fox
Map Designer: Kevin Kibsey

Printed in Italy by Artegrafica Srl.

www.northlandpub.com
FIRST IMPRESSION
HARDCOVER ISBN 0-87358-766-9
PAPERBACK ISBN 0-87358-774-x

Library of Congress Catalog Card Number Pending

140/2.5M/8-00 (HC)
140/5M/8-00 (SC)

Photographs by: Ken Akers/ Arizona State University Sports Information Office xvi (middle); Courtesy The Arizona Biltmore 2; Arizona Historical Foundation xiii (right); Arizona Historical Society/ Tucson xii; Arizona Sky-Cam 26, 27; Dick Atkinson 173 (both); Matt Barsema 138; Paul Barton 82; Mark Boisclair 49; Courtesy Johnny Bulla xvi (left); Courtesy Golf Club at Chaparral Pines 69; Chip Shots Photo 18, 19 (middle); Courtesy Concho Valley Country Club 134, 135; Conley Photography/ Arizona State University Sports Information Office xvi (right); D2 Productions Murphy/Scully 7, 8, 9, 63, 145; L. D. Darnewood 98, 99; Courtesy Desert Hills Golf Club 137; Courtesy Desert Mountain 77, 78; Courtesy Bill Dickey xvi (right); T. Doak 132, 133; Joann Dost x, 89; Chris Duthie 36, 37, 38, 39 (left); Dynjan & 116, 117; Courtesy Elephant Rocks 139 (top); Courtesy Emerald Canyon Golf Course 140, 141; Courtesy Estancia Club 82, 83; Pete Fontaine xi; Rob Griffin xvi (left), 96, 97; Norm Hall 100, 101; Courtesy Hassayampa Golf Club 90, 91; Henebry Photography 12, 130, 131; Robert Herko 136; Ken Howie 158, 159; Bill Huffman 19 (left and right), 39 (right), 49 (left), 65, 94, 95, 102, 103, 104, 105 (both), 106, 107, 115, 118, 119, 123 (bottom), 124, 125, 129, 143 (top), 146, 147, 148, 149 (both), 150, 151, 156, 157, 164, 165, 172; Courtesy Hyatt Gainey Ranch 86, 87; Courtesy Las Sendas Golf Club 16, 17; Courtesy Los Caballeros Golf Club 22, 23; Lucky Dog Graphic Design 4, 5; Lori Kavanaugh 50, 51, 54, 55, 153, 160, 161; Klemme/ Golfoto ix, 13 (top), 43, 48, 66, 67, 68 (both), 74, 75, 81, 108, 109, 112, 113, 116; Richard Maack 76, 128; Ed Masterson 3 (both); Courtesy McCormick Ranch Golf Club 24, 25; Brad Melton 139 (bottom); Courtesy Oakcreek Country Club 154, 155; A. F. Payne Photographics, Inc. viii, 64; Pamela Piper 58; Courtesy The Phoenician Golf Club 33; Courtesy Pointe Hilton Resorts iii, 31, 34, 35; Kathy Reed 10 (both), 11; Courtesy Rio Rico Resort and Country Club 163; Tony Roberts 72, 73, 85, 120, 121; Keiichi Sato 13 (bottom), 47; Courtesy Sedona Golf Resort 40; Sharlott Hall Museum xiv; Don B. Stevenson 169; Courtesy Troon Golf 14, 15, 20, 21, 44, 45; Courtesy Tubac Golf Resort 170, 171; Lonna Tucker 42; Courtesy Tucson Country Club 122, 123 (top); United States Golf Association/John Mummert xv (right); Courtesy Ventana Canyon Golf Club 52, 53; Courtesy Vistoso Partners 111; Lissa Wales xv (left), xvii, xiii (left), 28, 29, 70, 71, 142, 143 (bottom), 166, 167; Courtesy Westin La Paloma 92 (both), 93 (both); Courtesy Wigwam Golf Resort 56, 57; Frank Zullo 41. These photographs are copyrighted to the individual photographers or the institutions they represent.

This book is dedicated to
my children—Kristen, Sky, and Meghan—who are the
driving force in my life.

— B.H.

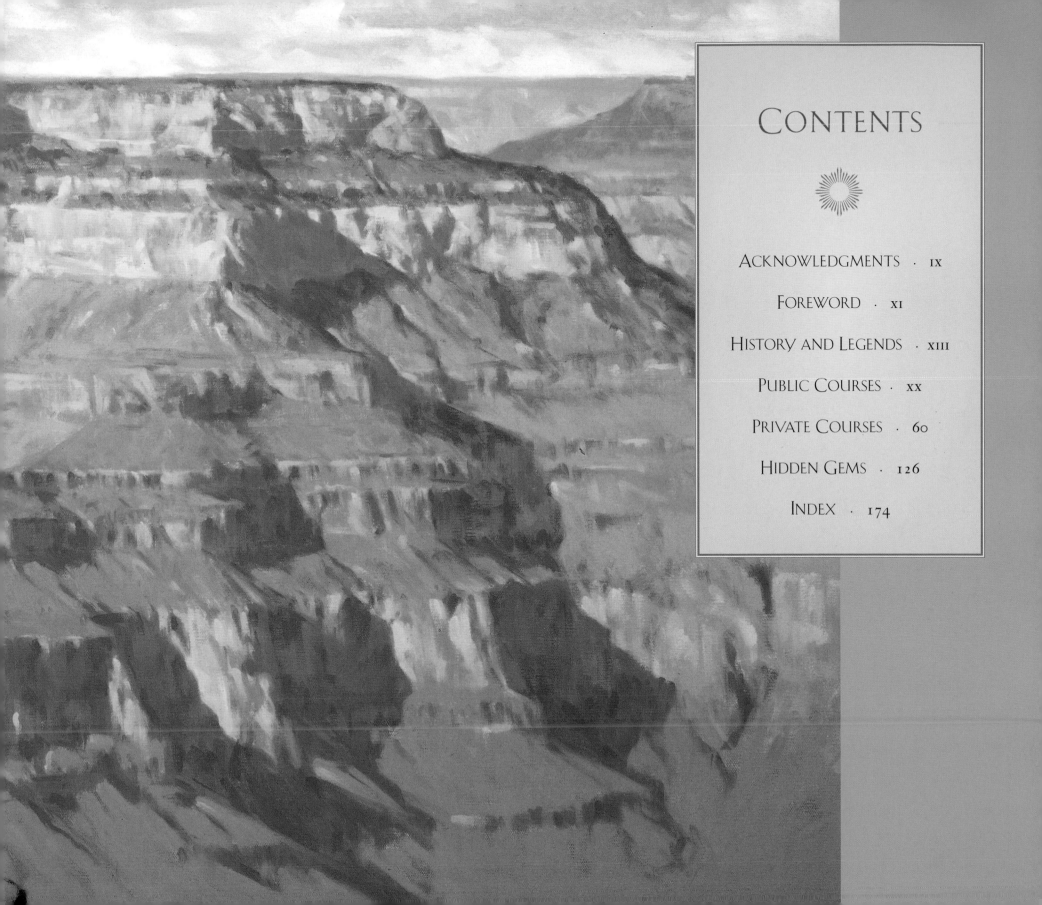

CONTENTS

ACKNOWLEDGMENTS

· ·

Arizona's Greatest Golf Courses was a dream I had as far back as the early 1990s. I talked about it, others talked to me about doing it, and because my work load was always heavy at *The Arizona Republic*, I put it off. Sound familiar?

Fortunately, the winds of fate sort of swept me down this path. After leaving *The Republic* in August of 1999, I was determined to write this book. Why? Well, it was my strongest area of expertise, having played at least 90 percent of the 300-plus courses in Arizona. What I tried to do in almost every case, was present an inside story about the golf course that would go beyond the obvious. Luckily, I found enough insiders at the various clubs whose courses were selected to help me along the way. In many cases these were the hard-working pros that make up the backbone of Arizona golf.

How did I choose which courses made the book and which did not? This was not an easy task, obviously. Arizona has so many terrific tracts, and those not found inside these pages perhaps will be included in future revisions of the book. But mostly, the criterion was based on visual appeal, challenge, fairness, design, condition, tradition, history, and impact. All of the 101 layouts found in *Arizona's Greatest Golf Courses* are blessed with these characteristics.

Naturally, there were a lot of people that helped to produce *Arizona's Greatest Golf Courses*. First and foremost, I would like to thank the many photographers who contributed their fantastic images. It goes without saying that Arizona's golf courses are an extremely photogenic subject, with all of that desert and forest and rock outcroppings and green grass providing an array of color and shapes. At the same time, it takes a keen eye and skills based on years of snapping pictures to put all of those elements together in a powerful photograph. In the following pages, you will find many of these.

The author has played 90 percent of Arizona's courses, including Desert Highlands (above) and Arizona Country Club (opposite).

I'd also like to thank my publisher and editor, Dave Jenney and Brad Melton at Northland Publishing. I thought I was picky, but Dave took the level of quality a step further, and because he did, this book is better-looking than even I had hoped for. Perhaps he did not reject more photographs than he approved, it just seemed that way. Well, being a nongolfer perhaps Brad's editorial eye was just what I needed to make these stories clearer and more precise. After all, golfers tend to have their own language, and sometimes others can't relate. But thanks to Brad, anyone can pick up *Arizona's Greatest Golf Courses* and come away with something, even if it's not hard-core golf.

I also would be remiss not to mention my good friend Russell Houston, the amazing artist from Eagar, Arizona, who paints the fabulous cowboy golf art. And, of course, I must acknowledge the driving force in his life, Kristi Houston, who I've also worked with on several projects including this one.

Finally, I'd like to acknowledge my friends and family who helped keep me on course during this nearly yearlong project. Among them were the "road warriors" who accompanied me on numerous trips around the state to revisit courses. They included Jim Austin, Tim Gates, Frank Macioce, Ruth Feldman, and Lori Kavanaugh, who also took many of the finest photos in this book. There were also dozens of other golfing buddies over the years that played significant roles in the book, and they know who they are. Then there was my editorial support on the homefront, which included Gail Baker and Beth Morris. There were others who played important roles, such as my parents, Bob and Martha Huffman, and my kids, Kristen, Sky, and Meghan. All of these special people, or forces, helped me get the job done.

So here we go with the first edition of *Arizona's Greatest Golf Courses*. In coming years, we plan to update and revise it with many new courses. Remember, there has been no attempt on my part to rank these courses in terms of stature, only present to you what I believe are truly *Arizona's Greatest Golf Courses*. ✿

— BILL HUFFMAN

FOREWORD

As a kid growing up in Ohio, I always thought of Arizona as a desolate desert full of cowboys and Indians, rattlesnakes and cactus, home of the Grand Canyon and—of course!—the Lone Ranger. To me, it was the wild, wild West, where guys wore cowboy hats and boots, and everybody traveled by horse or Jeep. Never in my wildest dreams did I imagine Arizona to be the mecca for some of the greatest and most dramatic golf courses in the world.

But that is exactly what our state has become. If you don't believe me, just read on in *Arizona's Greatest Golf Courses.* My good friend Bill Huffman, whom I have known for years, has done a marvelous job of putting together the inside story on each of the state's top layouts. The awesome photographs that accompany his keen observations offer further proof that Arizona is home to the finest fairways and greens on Earth.

How did we become a golfing paradise? Well, it's been a slow and steady growth process marked by an immense variety of courses constructed through quality design and workmanship. All the variables have been mixed to perfection in an extremely sensitive environment. First and foremost, the desert is misunderstood. The truth is it provides a beautiful backdrop of vegetation and mountains, and when contrasted with emerald green turf, the results are simply stunning, especially the way our courses are so immaculately conditioned. We've also been fortunate enough to attract the top architects in the world—the likes of Pete Dye, Jack Nicklaus, Tom Fazio, and many others. I feel very fortunate to have been involved in the design and construction of 10 courses in Arizona. I think the clincher is that each year we can bank on over 320 days of sunshine to enjoy these wonderful golf courses.

For me, the love affair with Arizona golf began in 1965. I remember my first trip West vividly. At the time, I was 22 and never had been beyond St. Louis. I drove nonstop all the way from Dallas to visit a couple of friends and play a little golf. I remember that the stars were shining brightly when I arrived in Phoenix,

Tom Weiskopf (above) has designed some of Arizona's finest golf courses, including the Canyon Course at Forest Highlands (opposite).

and the next morning I went out to get the newspaper and came back into the house in total amazement. I said something like, "Can you believe the thunderstorm we had last night? I must have slept right through it." I was so puzzled. I had never seen a front yard flooded by irrigation.

It was January, a month I normally spent indoors, and there we were playing golf on this gorgeous course called Desert Forest, the true forerunner of desert golf as we know it today. The sun was beaming down, the grass was so green, and I was having the time of my life. I knew nothing like this could ever happen in Ohio this time of year. Later in the day, we drove up to Pinnacle Peak Steakhouse, and I could hardly eat lunch because I was so busy gawking at those stately saguaros with their big, long arms. I loved the desert,

and I knew that someday I would end up here.

Back in those days, the roads were mostly dirt beyond Shea Boulevard, and the area was designated as open range. It is unbelievable what has happened in Scottsdale in terms of growth, and for that matter, all throughout the Phoenix Metropolitan area. We have almost 200 golf courses in Maricopa County alone—the highest density in the country—and another 100 courses and counting in Tucson, Flagstaff, Prescott, Payson, as well as the rest of the state. Our different types and styles of golf courses—we've got them all!—are overwhelming for the average golfer. We have low desert, high chaparral, and mountain golf. To put it in perspective, you can play golf in the state of Arizona from the elevation of 8,200 feet down to sea level.

I have lived here since 1973, when we first bought a home, which we still own, at White Mountain Country Club, a serene summer retreat. I've never regretted for a minute leaving Ohio. Living in Arizona is the best, and being able to fly all over the world and build courses is a dream come true. But I'll tell you, quite frankly, I always look forward to coming home to Arizona and playing a little golf. The sunsets are so awesome, the lifestyle is heavenly, and even the summer heat doesn't bother me anymore. In fact, I like it!

As Arizona's premier golf writer, Bill Huffman also has watched our state become a golf haven, and he has chosen some terrific tracts to write about. I think you'll find Bill's experiences and recommendations, as well as some of his subtle tips and tales, to be quite enlightening. In every way, Bill has given the reader an insider's perspective on what it's like to play our desert gems and mountain treasures, as well as some wonderful history on how each course was conceived.

So, read on, my friend, and enjoy *Arizona's Greatest Golf Courses!* ☼

— Tom Weiskopf

Golf came slowly to Arizona, at least in the beginning. In fact, the sport actually missed the Grand Canyon State on several occasions before a group of the game's pioneers put together Phoenix Golf Club in 1900, the course that eventually became Phoenix Country Club.

For the record, the first official round of golf in America took place in 1888, and the first club was formed later that year. That it came via two transplanted Scotsmen, Robert Lockhart and John Reid, should come as no surprise. That it took nearly 12 years to arrive in Arizona, also is no shocker. A lack of water and the presence of an intense summer heat seemed contrary to the conditions of the game.

Phoenix Golf Club on "Yuma Road" during the Flood of 1905.
OPPOSITE: *Arizona cowboys enjoy a round of golf in 1901.*

But golf eventually spread west, and by 1898 there was a belt of about 15 golf courses that ran south from San Francisco all the way to San Diego. Eventually enough Arizonans witnessed the game being played on the West Coast, as well as in such locales as Denver, Colorado Springs, and Salt Lake City, that interest was piqued. "Phoenix, Arizona, is also about to spring into the arena," Thomas H. Arnold wrote in his book, *Golf: A Turn-of-the-Century Treasury.* "A professional has already been engaged to lay out a course there and to 'start the ball rolling.'"

It wasn't easy. The first attempt at organizing what was to become Phoenix Country Club was defeated at the annual meeting of the Phoenix Athletic Club in the fall of 1899. But even back then wannabe golfers had a sense of resiliency, and the proposal was passed at the club's next meeting. On February 22, 1900, the little nine-hole dirt course known as Phoenix Golf Club debuted on the corner of Central Avenue and Roosevelt Street. "This little links kept the golfers of Phoenix happy, but it was obvious that a new location would soon be needed," wrote the late Barry Goldwater, senator from Arizona, in his compilation of Phoenix Country Club's history.

Less than a year later, Phoenix Golf Club had pulled up the pins and moved to Yuma Road, which today would be near the corner of 17th Avenue and Van Buren. Ten years later, the club again was on the move, this time to the north end of Central Avenue, where it changed its name to the Country Club of Phoenix. It was there that Goldwater and his younger brother, Bob, played their first rounds of golf.

It might be said that this initial experience was, if not typical, then indicative of the newness of the game in Arizona. "I think I was 10 years old, and Barry was 12," said Bob Goldwater of his very first round in 1920. "I remember my mom [Josephine], who was the state women's champ, had wanted us to learn the game, and so she dropped us off with some clubs and balls just beyond the Arizona Canal, and we had at it."

Not knowing the rules or proper etiquette,

Barry and Bob set out on one of the merrier rounds of golf ever played in Arizona. "We thought it was like croquet, and that we supposed to take turns, so we kept yelling, 'It's your turn! . . . It's your turn!'" Bob recalled. "Well, that went on for a couple of holes, and then after awhile, Barry was a hole or two ahead of me, and we couldn't hear each other yelling anymore."

During the span, several other courses arrived on the Arizona scene, including one near Bisbee. Turquoise Valley Golf Club opened in 1908, serving as the links for what was the state's biggest city at the time, as the copper mines of Bisbee ruled commerce.

Josephine Goldwater, one of Arizona's first women golfers.

The following year, Ingelside Golf Resort became Phoenix's first winter resort near 56th Street and Thomas Road. If that location sounds familiar, it presently is the site of Arizona Country Club. One other club of note came on board in 1912, when Dr. Alexander J. Chandler built a small course and resort called San Marcos in the Valley community that still bears his name.

All of these original Arizona offerings were nine-holers with dirt fairways and sand greens. Golfers would reach the green, sweep it with a broom-type apparatus, and putt out. What some might find hard to imagine is that grass greens were still years away. In fact, the evolution of greens in Arizona included the cottonseed variety, which first popped up in 1919 at Prescott's Hassayampa Country Club. The two early types of putting surfaces were a vast contrast.

"Sand greens were oiled black sand that were pretty easy to play, because they were small and smooth," Goldwater explained. "You always got a good roll because you could sweep the path down from your ball to the cup. You might say that the USGA would frown on such a situation today. Cottonseed greens were made from the seed [pockets]. After the cotton was removed, a lintlike substance was left, and that's what the greens were made of. When you would hit a ball real high, it would bounce, and when you would hit it low, it would spin. The way you putted was by tapping down the lintlike material all the way from your ball to the cup."

It wasn't until 1927 that the first grass greens were introduced, and as might be expected, Phoenix Country Club, which had moved to its present location of Thomas Road and Seventh Street in 1919, again led the way. But this time, PCC hired a well-known Scottish architect, Harry Collis, to build its 18-hole course. Three years later, Collis redesigned San Marcos, which also received grass greens and the full 18.

Naturally, a lot of other elements were at work during the first 20 years of Arizona golf. The sport was still very much a novelty, as even range-hardened cowboys occasionally teed it up. Pictures from the Arizona Historical Society show cowpokes on

Golf at Hassayampa Country Club in the 1920s.

the open desert near Russellville in Cochise County playing a five-hole golf course with niblicks and cups marked by branding irons. There were others, which is no doubt how Arizona humorist Dick Wick Hall got his idea to write his comical "Greasewood Golf Lynx" piece in the *Saturday Evening Post*.

According to Hall's fictitious account, golf came to the outpost of Salome, Arizona, around 1907, when a tourist heading to California hit a bump in the road, causing a set of clubs to fall by the roadside. Nobody in Salome knew what the clubs were until another tourist saw them hanging in the town's gas station, then drew up a map of what a golf course should look like while explaining the principles of the game to the locals. How Hall's Greasewood Golf Lynx came to be was a major miscue, as the locals thought the abbreviation for yard was "rd" instead of "yd," and laid out in rods rather than yards. As Hall pointed out, such oversight led to a course that was "just a little over 20 miles long."

"They say some folks play golf just for fun and exercise," Hall observed. "It's exercise all right, but I wish I could get somebody that thinks it's fun to come and do a few days' real work for me, if playing golf is their idea of fun. . . . The only time I ever did get clear around [the 18 holes], it took me three days and a half, and I used 31 balls."

Hall ended his story of early golf in Arizona with this colorful account: "The other day, a Missus Delaney from Maine en route to California stopped

over to rest, she said, and play a little golf. The first day she was playing along in the afternoon out between the third and fourth holes, and she stood on a lizard hole while she was swinging her club, and the lizard crawled up her knickerbockers just as she was making a big swing. She missed the ball, but she knocked the caddy off his horse, and when she started running towards Mexico the war whoop she let out was heard in Buzzard's Roost, and the caddy had to chase her three miles on horseback to catch her and then wrap her up in his saddle blanket to get her home again. She went on to Pasadena the next day." The article was signed, "Dick Wick Hall, editor and garage owner, and lately long-distance amateur golfer."

But according to Goldwater, most early golf was played on real courses by those fortunate enough to get on one. "In the early days, you had Phoenix [Country Club], San Marcos, the Arizona Biltmore, and Arizona [Ingelside] around the Valley, and there was El Rio in Tucson, which was known as the only course in the United States to be completely surrounded by outhouses," Goldwater recalled. "Up north, Prescott had Hassayampa, and there was a Flagstaff Country Club on the way to the ski area [Snow Bowl], and that was about it."

But there were enough golfers and courses to get organized, and in 1923 the Arizona Golf Association took root in a small alcove at Phoenix Country Club. The Arizona Women's Golf Association followed in 1924, also with strong ties to Phoenix Country Club. The first AWGA tournament was held later that year, with Lorraine McArthur defeating Josephine Goldwater in the championship match.

What is interesting about the AGA's inception is that nobody alive can remember just how one of the country's most influential golf associations came to be. But the purpose was clear: To establish an Arizona State Amateur golf tournament, which debuted at El Rio later that year. The first champion was Louis Curry, followed by Charles McArthur and Dr. Kim Bannister. That Bob Goldwater won the 1926 event at the tender age of 16, the youngest champion in the history of the tournament, should also be duly noted.

It was in the 1930s that Bob Goldwater established his other legacy—the Phoenix Open. The first tournament was held at Phoenix Country Club in 1932, and Ralph Gudahl was the winner. The following year, Harry "Lighthorse" Cooper was champion, and then interest waned until Goldwater resurrected it in 1935. "I went down to Caliente [Mexico] and talked 13 or 14 pros into playing [for money]," Goldwater recalled. "It was a pro-am, and I remember that I called Barry, who was working at the office, talked him into playing, and he and Ky Laffon won it."

Bob Goldwater is "the Father of the Phoenix Open."

Reflecting the sport's slow start in Arizona, the Phoenix Open was a tough sell, and the next tournament was not held until 1939. Once again, Goldwater got the ball rolling through a Chamber of Commerce group called the Phoenix Thunderbirds. Surprisingly, it wasn't the most popular event way back then. "I got it going again, although some of the Thunderbirds were ticked at me for doing it," Goldwater said of his "one-man meeting" with the Phoenix Chamber of Commerce. "The 'Birds said to me, 'OK, if you want this tournament so bad, put it on,' and I was the chairman for the next 15 years."

The early years of the Phoenix Open were golden, as such champs as Byron Nelson (1939 and '45), Ben Hogan (1946 and '47), and Jimmy Demaret (1949 and '50) were crowned. But for the most part, Arizona golf was defined by its amateurs.

"We had some very good amateurs in the early years," said Bob Goldwater, a three-time State Amateur champ, and just as impressive, the tournament's runner-up at age 14. "Dr. Kim Bannister was a great player, and Charlie McArthur had a beautiful swing. Milt Coggins, who started out as a tennis pro, was a good player, as was Hi Corbett from down in Tucson. The Madison family, Gray, Frank, and Les, also were pretty good.

"But the best player of all, at least from an amateur standpoint, was Dr. Ed Updegraff of Tucson, who won everything. He won a bunch of state amateurs [four], the U.S. Senior Amateur [1981], and played and captained on several Walker Cup teams. Dr. Ed was probably Arizona's greatest amateur player ever."

Updegraff's résumé was even more impressive at his home course—Tucson Country Club. It was there that Updegraff won an incredible 27 club championships, even if the biggest heartbreak of his illustrious career also came at TCC. "Oh, I remember the last match," Updegraff said of his U.S. Senior title defense, which came the year following year in Tucson, where he again managed to work his way to the final against a fellow named Alton Duhon. "I was 1-down with one [hole] to play, and he ended up winning, 2-up. Yes, it seemed the whole thing was a little ironic, me losing it on my own home course."

Still, Updegraff's place in the history of Arizona golf is well-defined. Or so says Johnny Riggle, who ran the AGA from the 1950s until the mid-1980s. "There's no question that Dr. Ed Updegraff was the finest golfer Arizona produced, and there were some good ones," noted Riggle, who doubled as a longtime rules official for the USGA. "Dr. Ed could really play. But there were others of distinction, such as Fred Siegel, Dick Hopwood, Mark Sollenberger, Joe

Dr. Ed Updegraff, receiving the Bobby Jones award in 1999.

Porter, George Boutell, Billy Mayfair, the Purtzer brothers [Tom and Paul], Bill Meyers, Jim Carter ... and more recently, Ken Kellaney has been a great player."

So who was the state's best homegrown product?

"Oh, I would say that it was either George Boutell or Billy Mayfair. Both were wonderful players beginning when they were just kids," Riggle said. "George won everything as a junior growing up on Phoenix Country Club, and could get up and down from anywhere. Billy was a good little player, too, and both he and George were two of Arizona State's best ever."

Riggle would know. The founder of the Arizona Golf Hall of Fame, he personally watched Arizona golf grow, beginning in 1932. "We always had a lot of great amateurs in this state," said Riggle, adding Vic Armstrong, Harold Tovrea, Herbert Askins, Bill Boutell Sr., Louis Curry, and Bob Warren to the list via the Hall of Fame. "The funny thing was that most of the professionals came from back East. As far as professionals, there was Red Allen, Willie Low, and Dell Urich, and a few other fellows, but they were all club pros. The first Tour player that called Arizona home, that was Johnny Bulla."

Johnny Bulla clowning around with Dean Martin and Jerry Lewis at the Arizona Biltmore.

Few, if any, characters in Arizona golf were as colorful as Bulla, who quit his job as a pilot for Eastern Airlines to move to Phoenix and pursue the game he loved. "I was one of the first to ever fly the DC-3, which was the first commercial aircraft," Bulla recalled. "But it was too damn dangerous, and golf was my real calling. I'd come out to Phoenix in '36 to play in the Open with Sam [Snead], and I told him someday I was going to come back and live here. I remember Sam snapped back: 'You're crazy! Rattlesnakes couldn't live here.'"

By 1945, at the age of 30, Bulla was splitting his years between Pittsburgh and Phoenix. Nobody ruled his roost better than Bulla, who captured 14 SWPGA Championships and 14 Arizona Opens. Even more incredible, Bulla traveled the country, winning a record 42 PGA of America section titles.

On the PGA Tour, Bulla was not quite as dynamic, as his only victory was the 1941 Los Angeles Open. But there were other highlights, such as run-ner-up finishes in the Masters and British opens, as well as making 18 consecutive cuts at the U.S. Open beginning in 1936. The consistent Bulla, who only missed seven cuts in 287 pro starts, also held the distinction of being professional golf's first player/pilot, oftentimes flying with his good friend Snead and colleague/copilot Ben Hogan. The multidimensional Bulla also tried his hand at golf course architecture, learning the craft under Donald Ross whom many consider the greatest designer ever.

"I met Donald shortly after he had been [snubbed] by Bobby Jones in the building of Augusta National [in the early 1930s]," Bulla said. "He was down in the Carolinas redoing a little course called Pinehurst No. 2, determined to make it the best course in the world, or at least better than Augusta. I ended up spending every day with him, and he shared with me his philosophy on course design. We became very good friends."

Bulla had a hand in Paradise Valley Country Club and Arizona Country Club, and did three golf courses by himself in Arizona, including Century Country Club, which later became Orange Tree. He also played a pivotal role in improving race relations in what most perceived to be a lily-white sport. "I was the first Tour pro to play with black players in a professional event—the Tam O'Shanter—way back when," Bulla noted. "And I was the first to invite black players in Phoenix to join a private club, when I got Joe Black, the baseball pitcher, and the great track star, Jesse Owens, memberships at Camelback Country Club."

In fact, Bulla added, most minorities in Arizona were not allowed access to golf courses until after Encanto came along in 1937. Women didn't fare much better, but thanks to Encanto, they were able to establish the first women's public club in 1944. Encanto also gave birth in 1946 to the Desert Mashies, the state's first golf organization for minorities.

"Those were tough times to be a black golfer," said Bill Dickey, whose pioneering efforts concerning minority involvement in the game earned him a spot in the Arizona Golf Hall of Fame. "There weren't a whole lot of courses back in those days, but there was only one where we could play. I guess you could say that Encanto has been pretty good to us over the years, which was great because it's a heck of a good layout."

Unfortunately, there wasn't a whole lot of golf course building going on in the 1940s and mid-1950s, as only about 25 courses existed within the state's borders. But Bulla got things rolling again when he built Century/Orange Tree in 1958. "That started the boom, although it was nothing back then like it is today," Bulla noted.

Other golfing entities began showing up in the

The Desert Mashies hold their first tournament at Encanto in 1948.

Karsten Solheim playing golf with astronaut Alan Shepherd.

Arizona State University and the University of Arizona. Both programs began producing All-Americans in the late '50s, even though perhaps the earliest impact player at ASU was Joanne Gunderson, who later became LPGA Hall of Famer Joanne Carner. "They didn't have a women's team back in those days, but I'd take the ASU boys, and Joanne out to Century, and she'd outdrive the boys and I'd laugh at them," Bulla recalled. "I tell you, Joanne was a great player, but she was a lot more than that. She was a great gal."

Others who helped build on ASU's storied past included such All-Americans as Boutell, Porter, the Purtzer brothers, Mayfair, John Jackson, Howard Twitty, Bob Gilder, Dan Forsman, Phil Mickelson, and Todd Demsey. For the Lady Sun Devils, there were such stars as Carner, Jane Bastanchury-Booth, Lauri Merten, the late Heather Farr, Danielle Ammaccapane, Amy Fruhwirth, Brandie Burton, Wendy Ward, Emilee Klein, Kelle Booth, and Grace Park. While the men have won two national titles, the women have won six under their legendary coach, Linda Vollstedt.

The U of A seemed just as talented. Through

Arizona State All-American Danielle Ammaccapane, 1985.

late 1950s and early '60s. Perhaps the most prominent was the Southwest Section of the PGA, which was founded in 1958, and included New Mexico and El Paso, Texas. Eventually, New Mexico and El Paso went their separate ways, and in 1980 Las Vegas was added to the SWPGA. Today, over 1,200 professionals and assistant pros form the backbone of the SWPGA.

Another significant development in Arizona golf came in the early 1960s, when the late Karsten Solheim established his PING golf club manufacturing company in Phoenix. At first, PING built putters that made a distinct pinging noise, but eventually the northwest Valley plant began producing some of the best irons in the world, called PING Eye2s. Today, PING is considered to be among the top five manufacturers in golf, and still is owned by the Solheim family.

Also making a major impact on Arizona golf was the arrival of great college golf teams at both

Arizona State All-American Billy Mayfair, 1986.

the years the Wildcats produced such stars as Dan Pohl, Larry Silveira, Robert Gamez, Jim Furyk, David Berganio, Ted Purdy, and Rory Sabatini. Women to achieve All-American status included Chris Johnson, Leta Lindley, Annika Sorenstam, Marissa Baena, and Krissie Register. The men's and women's teams at U of A have each won one national championship.

By the 1960s and '70s the state, especially the metropolitan area of Phoenix, was beginning to grow by leaps and bounds. Blame the city's popularity on air-conditioning and affordable backyard swimming pools. Also gaining in stature was the Phoenix Open, which was producing such winners as Arnold Palmer (1961–63), Gene Littler (1955, '59, and '69), Jack Nicklaus (1964), and Johnny Miller (1974 and '75).

Golf courses had been growing steadily since the late 1950s, but only about 125 were in place by 1980, when a sudden explosion rocked desert golf. That was the emergence of Desert Highlands, a "target" golf course that featured fewer acres of turf, and subsequently used less water. The revolutionary concept was the brainchild of developer Lyle

Anderson, who had hired Nicklaus to put it in place.

"I'm not sure that people really understand what a special type of golf course Lyle introduced to the game," said Nicklaus, who went on to build seven other courses in Arizona for Anderson, including five layouts at dynamic Desert Mountain, followed by a pair of courses with his sons, Jackie and Gary, at Superstition Mountain. "But without those early ideas that we formulated, desert golf never would have bloomed to the degree it has today. I know that I'm very proud of what we accomplished. We saved a lot of water and introduced the beauty of the desert to many people who never would have understood the majesty of the region had we not built it."

Other big-time architects soon followed the earlier Arizona efforts of William Bell, Red Lawrence, Jack Snyder, and Robert Trent Jones with some dazzling projects. Besides Nicklaus and Palmer, there were Tom Weiskopf and Jay Morrish, Gary Panks and David Graham, Greg Nash and Billy Casper, Tom Fazio, Scott Miller, Keith Foster, Arthur Hills, and Jones' sons, Robert Jr. and Rees.

The 1980s also introduced several new professional tournaments to the Arizona scene. The first, although it was short-lived, was the Skins Game, which featured Nicklaus, Palmer, Gary Player, and Tom Watson, and was played in 1983 and '84 at Desert Highlands before the game departed for California. The made-for-TV event was a thriller, because for the first time ever, a player could win up to $100,000 on one hole, as Palmer did during the first Skins Game.

The LPGA made its entrance in 1980, with Jan Stephenson winning the Sun City Classic at Hillcrest Golf Club. The Phoenix stop, which eventually moved to the Arizona Biltmore in '83 and then on to Moon Valley in '87, came to be known as the Standard Register PING, with Laura Davies its greatest champion, winning four consecutive titles beginning in '94. Tucson's LPGA event, which debuted in 1981 as the Arizona Copper Classic, also has a storied history beginning with its first champion, Nancy Lopez. Always played at Randolph Park North, the tournament is now called the Welch's/

Bob Goldwater, Bob Hope, and Jack Nicklaus enjoying themselves at the 1986 Phoenix Open.

Circle K Championship.

The Senior PGA Tour arrived in 1988, playing first in Phoenix at the Pointe Golf Club on Lookout Mountain before departing the following year for Desert Mountain. Called The Tradition, the tournament has been won four times by Nicklaus, and along the way achieved "major" status on the 50-and-over circuit, meaning it is one of the seniors' four championship events.

Another signifcant arrival in the 1980s was that of the Junior Golf Association of Arizona. Despite being organized in 1983, the organization was not up and running (incorporated) until 1986, when 200 youngsters joined. Today, the JGAA is 2,000 strong, with the LPGA Girls Club also under its umbrella. "The JGAA got off to a slow start, but the growth has been phenomenal lately," said the JGAA's executive director, Tom Cunningham.

Cunningham's words seem to sum up the spread of golf in Arizona in general. By the 1990s, golf in Arizona was in a supersonic state of development, well-rounded in both the professional and amateur ranks. In fact, for the past 10 years, no county in the country has built more golf courses than Maricopa County, which now includes approximately 190 of Arizona's more than 300 golf courses. With nearly 2 million visitors playing golf here each year, along with nearly 500,000 residents, the game has become

a $1 billion industry, according to a National Golf Foundation study conducted for the AGA.

Arizona also has become the home to over 20 players on the Professional Golfers Association Tour, and over 40 women on the Ladies Professional Golf Association. In addition, approximately a dozen seniors call Arizona home. Among the many notable players living in the state are PGA Tour stars Mickelson, Mayfair, Tom Lehman, Mark Calcavecchia, Andrew Magee, Jim Carter, Jonathan Kaye, Kirk Triplett, Brandel Chamblee, and Tim Herron. Those on the LPGA include the Ammaccapane sisters, Danielle and Dina; Meg Mallon; Chris Johnson; Pat Hurst; Ward; Fruhwirth; Park; and Hall of Famer Betsy King. Among the senior sensations are Hale Irwin, Gary McCord, John Jacobs, Jim Ahern, and Mike McCullough.

Some, such as Bob Goldwater, are surprised that the long legacy of golf in Arizona has become so rich. He points to the Phoenix Open, where record crowds of over 400,000 for the week have set the standard each year on the PGA Tour. "Looking back, I never would have guessed it would come to this," Goldwater said. "We've got the good weather and the great courses, so I understand how it's all come to be. At the same time, you look at the Phoenix Open since they moved the tournament to the TPC of Scottsdale [in 1987], and it's hard to believe so many people come out to watch each year."

Bulla, on the other hand, said he always knew Arizona would become an impact player in the golf world. In fact, he predicts an even brighter future for the Grand Canyon State in the twenty-first century. "I knew the first time I ever set foot in the Arizona desert that it was made for golf," Bulla explained. "We had the weather, and it was only a matter of time and technology before it all came together. It used to be everybody went to Florida or Carolina to play in the winter. Now, they all come here, and once they've experienced Arizona's fairways and greens, they always come back, because it's the prettiest place in the world to play golf." ✿

SCORECARD
A Guide to the Course Statistics

PRICE RANGE:

$10 to $30 — inexpensive
$35 to $75 — moderate
$80 to $125 — expensive
$130 and up — very expensive

Prices are approximate and subject to change

SLOPE RATING

In the USGA Handicap System Manual, USGA Slope Rating is defined as the USGA's mark that indicates the measurement of the relative difficulty of a course for players who are not scratch golfers compared to the Course Rating (*i.e.*, compared to the difficulty of a course for scratch golfers). The lowest Slope Rating is 55 and the highest is 155. A golf course of standard playing difficulty has a USGA Slope Rating of 113. If a course has a high Slope Rating, it is relatively more difficult for the average golfer than a course with a low Slope Rating. Accordingly, under the Slope System, the average golfer receives more handicap strokes playing a course with a high Slope Rating than playing a course with a low Slope Rating.

COURSE RATING

In the USGA Handicap System Manual, USGA Course Rating is defined as the USGA's mark that indicates the evaluation of the playing difficulty of a course for scratch golfers under normal course and weather conditions. It is expressed as strokes taken to one decimal place, and is based on yardage and other obstacles to the extent that may affect the scoring difficulty of the scratch golfer. A USGA Course Rating is equal to the average of the better half of a scratch golfer's scores under normal conditions.

Slope and course rating information courtesy of the Arizona Golf Association.

PUBLIC COURSES

There are over 200 golf courses in Arizona that are open to the public. Most of the 38 layouts found in this chapter would be categorized as upscale, daily-fee courses. In other words, they are the best of the best courses available to the average person.

Naturally, the vast majority of Arizona's finest public offerings are expensive to play. At the same time, where else can you enjoy courses of such quality without paying private dues? In every way, these public offerings are like being a "member for the day."

1 THE ARIZONA BILTMORE *(page 2)*
24th Street & Missouri Avenue, Phoenix, 85016
DIRECTIONS: *One-half mile north of Camelback Road off of 24th Street.*
TEE TIMES: 602-955-9655

2 DOVE VALLEY RANCH GOLF CLUB *(page 4)*
33244 N. Black Mountain Parkway, Cave Creek, 85331
DIRECTIONS: *From Phoenix, take Interstate 17 north to the Carefree Highway exit, then proceed eight miles east.*
TEE TIMES: 602-473-1444

3 ESTRELLA MOUNTAIN RANCH *(page 6)*
11800 S. Golf Club Drive, Goodyear, 85338
DIRECTIONS: *From Phoenix, take I-10 west to Estrella Mountain Ranch Parkway (exit 126), then south to course.*
TEE TIMES: 623-386-1110

4 GOLD CANYON GOLF RESORT *(page 8)*
6100 S. Kings Ranch Road, Gold Canyon, 85219
DIRECTIONS: *From Tempe, go east on U.S. Highway 60 past Apache Junction, north on Kings Ranch Road.*
TEE TIMES: 480-982-9449

5 THE GOLF CLUB AT EAGLE MOUNTAIN *(page 10)*
14915 E. Eagle Mountain Parkway, Fountain Hills, 85268
DIRECTIONS: *From Scottsdale, take Shea Boulevard east to 148th Street, turn right.*
TEE TIMES: 480-816-1234

6 GRAYHAWK GOLF CLUB *(page 12)*
8620 E. Thompson Peak Parkway, Scottsdale, 85255
DIRECTIONS: *Located between Pima and Scottsdale roads off of Thompson Peak Parkway.*
TEE TIMES: 480-502-1800

7 KIERLAND GOLF CLUB *(page 14)*
15636 Clubgate Drive, Scottsdale, 85254
DIRECTIONS: *Take Greenway west from Scottsdale Road to 66th Street.*
TEE TIMES: 480-922-9283

8 LAS SENDAS GOLF CLUB *(page 16)*
7555 E. Eagle Crest Drive, Mesa, 85207
DIRECTIONS: *From Tempe, take Highway 60 to Power Road, north to Thomas, east to golf course.*
TEE TIMES: 480-396-4000

9 THE LEGACY GOLF RESORT *(page 18)*
6806 S. 32nd Street, Phoenix, 85040
DIRECTIONS: *Just off Baseline Road between 24th and 32nd streets.*
TEE TIMES: 602-305-5550

10 LEGEND TRAIL GOLF CLUB *(page 20)*
9462 Legendary Lane, Scottsdale, 85262
DIRECTIONS: *Three miles north of Dynamite Road off of Pima Road, east on Legend Trail Parkway.*
TEE TIMES: 480-488-7434

11 LOS CABALLEROS GOLF CLUB *(page 22)*
1551 S. Vulture Mine Road, Wickenburg, 85390
DIRECTIONS: *From Phoenix, take US 60/Grand Avenue west to Wickenburg, through town, then follow signs west on Vulture Mine Road.*
TEE TIMES: 520-684-2704

12 McCORMICK RANCH GOLF CLUB *(page 24)*
7505 E. McCormick Ranch Parkway, Scottsdale, 85258
DIRECTIONS: *East of Scottsdale Road off McCormick Parkway.*
TEE TIMES: 480-948-0260

13 OCOTILLO GOLF CLUB *(page 26)*
3751 S. Clubhouse Drive, Chandler, 85248
DIRECTIONS: *From Phoenix, take I-10 south to Queen Creek Road, east to Price Road, go south and follow signs.*
TEE TIMES: 480-917-6660

14 PAPAGO GOLF COURSE *(page 28)*
5595 E. Moreland Street, Phoenix, 85008
DIRECTIONS: *Enter through the main gate at Papago Park, or take 52nd Street south past McDowell Road to Moreland Street.*
TEE TIMES: 602-275-8428

15 PHANTOM HORSE GOLF CLUB *(page 30)*
7777 S. Pointe Parkway, Phoenix, 85044
DIRECTIONS: *Take I-10 to Baseline, then west to the Pointe Hilton Resort at South Mountain and south to the golf course entrance.*
TEE TIMES: 602-431-6480

16 THE PHOENICIAN GOLF CLUB *(page 32)*
6000 E. Camelback Road, Scottsdale, 85251
DIRECTIONS: *North of Camelback Road at 60th Street.*
TEE TIMES: 480-423-2449

17 POINTE GOLF CLUB ON LOOKOUT MOUNTAIN *(page 34)*
11111 N. 7th Street, Phoenix, 85020
DIRECTIONS: *Off 7th Street south of Thunderbird Road in north-central Phoenix.*
TEE TIMES: 602-866-6356

18 RAVEN GOLF CLUB AT SABINO SPRINGS *(page 36)*
9777 E. Sabino Greens Drive, Tucson, 85749
DIRECTIONS: *Houghton Road north to Snyder Road, then west.*
TEE TIMES: 520-749-3636

19 THE RAVEN GOLF CLUB AT SOUTH MOUNTAIN *(page 38)*
3636 E. Baseline Road, Phoenix, 85040
DIRECTIONS: *Baseline Road west of 40th Street.*
TEE TIMES: 602-243-3636

20 SEDONA GOLF RESORT *(page 40)*
35 Ridge Trail Drive, Sedona, 86351
DIRECTIONS: *From Phoenix, take I-17 to Highway 179, then northwest to golf course.*
TEE TIMES: 520-284-9355

21 SUNRIDGE CANYON GOLF CLUB *(page 42)*
13100 N. SunRidge Drive, Fountain Hills, 85268
DIRECTIONS: *From Scottsdale, take Shea Boulevard east to Palisades Boulevard then north to SunRidge Canyon Drive.*
TEE TIMES: 480-837-5100

22 TALKING STICK GOLF CLUB *(page 44)*
9998 E. Indian Bend Road, Scottsdale, 85256
DIRECTIONS: *One mile east of Highway 101 at the*
Indian Bend exit.
TEE TIMES: 480-860-2221

23 TOURNAMENT PLAYERS CLUB OF SCOTTSDALE
(page 46)
17020 N. Hayden Road, Scottsdale, 85255
DIRECTIONS: *One mile north of Frank Lloyd Wright Boulevard off*
Pima Road.
TEE TIMES: 480-585-3939

24 TROON NORTH GOLF CLUB *(page 48)*
10320 E. Dynamite Road, Scottsdale, 85255
DIRECTIONS: *Take Pima Road north towards Carefree, and turn*
east on Dynamite Road.
TEE TIMES: 480-585-5300

25 TUCSON NATIONAL GOLF CLUB *(page 50)*
2727 W. Club Drive, Tucson, 85741
DIRECTIONS: *I-10 to Cortaro Road, then east 3 ½ miles before*
turning north on Shannon Drive.
TEE TIMES: 520-575-7540

26 VENTANA CANYON GOLF CLUB *(page 52)*
6200 N. Clubhouse Lane, Tucson, 85715
DIRECTIONS: *Sunrise Drive to Kolb Road, north to golf courses.*
TEE TIMES: 520-577-4015

27 GOLF CLUB AT VISTOSO *(page 54)*
955 W. Vistoso Highlands Drive, Tucson, 85737
DIRECTIONS: *I-10 south to Tangerine Road, east to Rancho Vistoso,*
north to golf course.
TEE TIMES: 520-797-9900

28 THE WIGWAM GOLF RESORT *(page 56)*
451 N. Litchfield Road, Litchfield Park, 85340
DIRECTIONS: *Take I-10 west to Litchfield Park Road and then*
north approximately one mile.
TEE TIMES: 602-272-4653

29 WILDFIRE GOLF CLUB *(page 58)*
5225 E. Pathfinder, Phoenix, 85024
DIRECTIONS: *Tatum Boulevard north to Pathfinder, then east.*
TEE TIMES: 480-473-0205

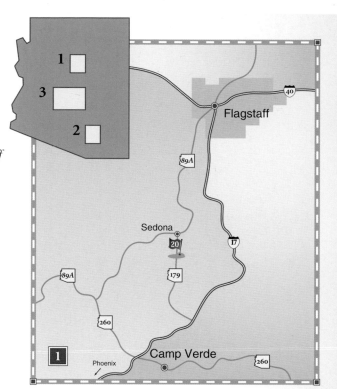

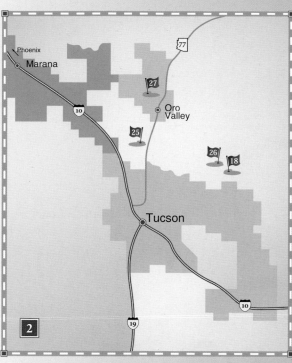

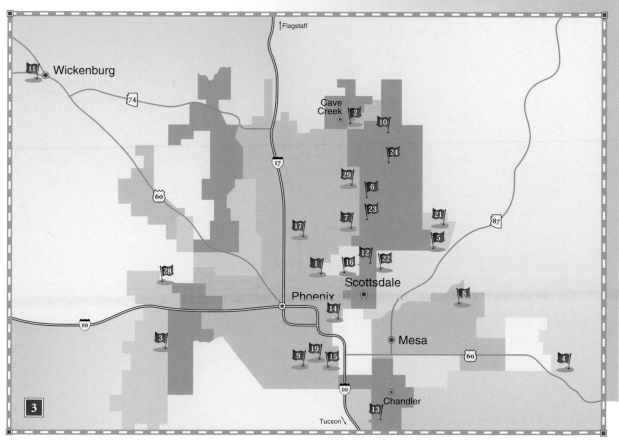

THE ARIZONA BILTMORE

ADOBE: PAR: 71 • YARDAGE: 5,763–6,449 • RATING: 68.4–77.0 • SLOPE: 115–131 • SIGNATURE HOLE: 422-YARD, PAR-4 NO 3 • GREEN FEES: MODERATE TO EXPENSIVE

LINKS: PAR: 71 • YARDAGE: 4,835–6,300 • RATING: 66.5–71.7 • SLOPE: 101–126 • SIGNATURE HOLE: 185-YARD, PAR-3 NO 15 • GREEN FEES: MODERATE TO EXPENSIVE

WHEN IT COMES TO ELEGANCE and grace, the Arizona Biltmore Resort earns its five stars with ease. The world-class retreat, which oftentimes is credited to architect supreme Frank Lloyd Wright but in fact was designed by an understudy in the mid-1920s, certainly deserves its nickname as "The Jewel of the Desert."

Through the last three-quarters of the twentieth century, the resort has hosted everybody who's anybody. In the early years, when the Wrigleys of chewing gum fame owned the place, the list of celebrities included Clark Gable, Errol Flynn, Fred Astaire, Jimmy Durante, George Burns, Randolph Scott, and composer Irving Berlin. Later on, actor-turned-president Ronald Reagan and wife Nancy honeymooned at Phoenix's most celebrated hotel. Elizabeth Taylor, Bob Hope, Gloria Vanderbilt, and the Duke and Duchess of Windsor also visited these classic corridors during that era.

Not surprisingly, several of those dignitaries enjoyed the Biltmore for more than just its opulent accommodations, the chief distraction being golf on its Adobe Course, and later on the layout known as the Links. Of the aforementioned, Gable's golf game is one of the most well-documented (it wasn't very good), while Hope might have been the best player. As Biltmore lore goes, the debonair Gable lost his wedding ring while playing 18 holes on the Adobe, and was overjoyed when later in the day an employee found the ring and returned it to him. Despite

With Squaw Peak rising up in the background, golfers are treated to a traditional, tree-lined round of golf on the Arizona Biltmore's Adobe Course.

The Arizona Biltmore was built in the mid-1920s.

the turn of events, the marriage didn't last.

The Biltmore also has the distinction of hosting every U.S. president since 1930, and several of those, most notably Dwight Eisenhower, Gerald Ford, George Bush, and Bill Clinton, brought their golf clubs. There is a tale that Ford, an infamous hacker, flushed a shot onto the clubhouse verandah while playing the par-3 ninth hole on the Adobe. Turns out, that's a fact.

Through several megamillion-dollar renovations, the resort has continued to attract Hollywood's stars and starlets. Sharon Stone, Sylvester Stallone, Michael Douglas, Alec Baldwin, and Kim Basinger have come calling. Also in the mix were late-night guys Jay Leno and David Letterman, film producer/director Steven Spielberg, basketball flash Michael Jordan, and singer Elton John. According to several members of the Biltmore staff, Douglas teed it up and took his lumps, while Jordan went to the hole with regularity (and a lot fewer strokes).

What's great about the Biltmore is that guests who love to golf have two distinct choices. And like everything else, the two courses, which were built 50 years apart, each have their strengths and weaknesses.

The Adobe was designed in 1928 by well-known architect William P. "Billy" Bell. At the time, the Adobe was considered the toast of Phoenix, one of only three courses in town, along with the San Marcos Golf Resort and the Phoenix Country Club.

Even though it was one of Bell's first projects, he later proved to be a man of vision by adding other great Arizona tracts to his résumé such as Encanto Golf Club, Mesa Country Club, Randolph Park North, Tucson Country Club, and Yuma Country Club. Bell also gets credit for such California gems as BelAir Country Club, Tamarisk, Ojai Valley Inn & Country Club, La Jolla Country Club, and the Stanford University Golf Course. His relationship with the Wrigley family also led to the Wrigley Estate Golf Club being built in Wisconsin.

Tree-lined with an oasis-like atmosphere of palm trees and water, the Adobe is golf the way it used to be. Unfortunately, its future is up in the air, as the course's current owner, Kabuto International of Japan, is threatening to turn the course into a real-estate project. At the same time, the City of Phoenix seems determined to keep the Adobe's parallel fairways and open-faced greens on the map, even if the situation tumbles into court.

Numerous holes on the Adobe border major-league mansions, one of those belonging to radio personality Paul Harvey, who lives off the 11th tee. The loss of the Biltmore's original driving range has impacted the course's layout, as a new range ate up several of its precious acres. Regardless, the best stretch on the course remains the initial three holes, all of which offer views of area landmarks like Camelback Mountain, Squaw Peak, and the stately Wrigley Mansion.

The Links Course, which was built in 1978 by Phoenix architect Billy Johnston, is much more modern in its presentation. The Links also has lots of elevations and character, compared to the Adobe, which essentially is flat and slightly mundane by today's standards. Which is a good thing, said the Biltmore's longtime director of golf, Pete Robbeloth. "In the Adobe, you have a more traditional course, and people like that, especially our winter visitors," he said. "On the other hand, the Links has more of the bells and whistles you associate with today's desert courses. So, basically, there is something for everyone."

Except that the Links is not necessarily "target"

golf. With grass from tee to green and no transition areas per se, the Links defies the stereotypical target golf course, although there is some resemblance in terms of vegetation and layout. Unlike the Adobe, the best golf on the Links comes late, as the 15th through 18th holes are stellar. The signature is the 15th, a 185-yard par 3 that is tucked below Squaw Peak. The shot drops 75 feet from tee to green, and needless to say, many a medium to long iron has been yanked onto Lincoln Drive, which runs parallel to the hole. The 17th, a medium par 4, also is a sensational tee shot straight down the pike into the Phoenix skyline.

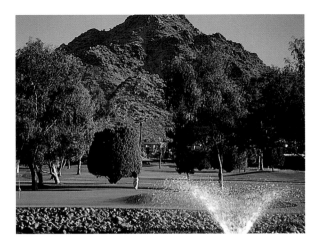

William P. Bell put his architectural stamp on the Arizona Biltmore.

Which seems appropriate because, in every way, the Arizona Biltmore is an integral part of the history of Phoenix, a royal and regal resort where the stars came out to stay and play. Sure, it has hosted such big-time golf as the Ladies Professional Golf Association from 1983 to 1986. But given its reputation, the star-studded resort seems more in the groove these days when rocker Alice Cooper brings his Celebrity Classic to these cool and classy surroundings. ✿

DOVE VALLEY RANCH GOLF CLUB

PAR: 72 • YARDAGE: 5,337–7,011 • RATING: 66.8–72.7 • SLOPE: 117–131 • SIGNATURE HOLE: 447-YARD, PAR-4 №2 • GREEN FEES: MODERATE TO EXPENSIVE

WALKING THE FAIRWAYS of Dove Valley Ranch, one might find it hard to fathom that 1,700 years ago an ancient people now known as the Hohokam made this very tract their heartland. But the artifacts enshrined in the clubhouse prove such an existence.

From A.D. 300 to 1450, the Hohokam—the first known farmers of the Southwest—cultivated the land just below Black Mountain, now known as Dove Valley Ranch. The Hohokam were "dry farmers," using cobblestones and branches to harness the monsoons into dams and terraces. Their efforts yielded corn, cactus fruits, and mesquite beans.

Artifacts that include clay pottery, primitive tools, and beads were uncovered from Hohokam trash mounds and fire pits when the course was built in 1998. The course was built by a construction crew, which was following the plans of noted architect Robert Trent Jones Jr.

The Hohokam vanished in the late fifteenth century, and whether their fate was sealed by a natural disaster, disease, or hostile intruders, no one knows for sure. Coincidentally, Jones also has not been seen around these parts since he made his initial visit to the property early in the design phase. "He actually showed up just once," recalled Gary Stapley, whose Stonebridge Development Company carried out the construction of the facility for the owner, Jack Londen of Phoenix. "Fortunately, the greens and bunkering have that traditional Jones look to them. So we got a lot for our money."

The same can be said for those who travel to this northernmost Phoenix outpost, which lies just south of the Carefree Highway, west of Cave Creek. Because green fees hover around $75 to $100, golfers get their money's worth, considering most courses in this ritzy neighborhood are considerably higher.

Brad Hansen, the director of golf at Dove Valley Ranch, says there is another reason for the course's popularity. "It's just a pleasant golf experience," Hansen observed. "You don't get your head pounded in like you do on some desert courses; there's room to navigate your ball. I must admit, I originally thought it was going to be too easy, but par has turned out to be a good score. It's tough to shoot a low number."

The par-3 16th hole is nicknamed "Coyotes' Den."

ABOVE: *Robert Trent Jones Jr. built in an abundance of bunkers at Dove Valley Ranch.*

RIGHT: *Dove Valley Ranch's water hazards nestle among green fairways and the lush Sonoran Desert.*

Obviously, Jones left his stamp even with minimal input. The oldest son of famed designer Robert Trent Jones is known for his demanding layouts, and Dove Valley fits somewhere into that scheme. Yet, and this might be a blessing of Jones' absence, the course is not too tough if a premium is placed on course management.

Like most good golf courses, a player is eased into Dove Valley Ranch, although a hint of what is to come occurs early in the round. That would be the signature, 447-yard second hole, a risk-reward tee shot over water. According to Hansen, the smart play is to take the drive directly over the left side of the water, rather than trying to carry it. "With the way the fairway is sloped, your ball almost ends up in the same spot as those who go directly over [the water]," he explained.

From that point, the front nine can be had by those who hit fairways and greens with regularity. The only other major hazard that comes into play is No. 9, another water-lined par 4 that requires accuracy off the tee and a solid approach shot. Placement continues to be a major factor on the back side, which resembles a hybrid of Terravita and Desert Forest, two of Dove Valley Ranch's elite neighbors. All three courses conclude with a similar terrain made up of arroyos and swiftly flowing fairways. The greens are good-sized (7,000 to 8,000 square feet), but not huge.

Several holes stand out coming home, including the par-4 11th, a dogleg left over transition; the par-5 15th, a workable, double dogleg to a green shrouded by mesquites; and the water-guarded 18th, a medium par 4 that features a beachside bunker that engulfs the right side of the green, making for a tense but terrific ending.

Regardless of your score, most patrons plan to add up their wins or losses in the light and airy clubhouse, where chef extraordinaire Dave Warchot always has some strange brew simmering. "I make a mean Chile Verde Borracho," Warchot quips, refer-ring to his Tequila-Drunken Green Chile that comes with a flour tortilla on the side. "Another of our specialties is German bratwurst with apples and sauerkraut braised in Murphy's Irish Stout."

In other words, Dove Valley Ranch is beginning to take on its own character. Certainly the club is reaching expectations that few thought possible when it was first announced that the course would be housed next to the Carefree–Cave Creek landfill, a fact that initially led to some trash-infested days, as well as some not-so-pleasant smells.

"The landfill has finally been filled in and capped," Hansen said, pointing to a plateau-shaped mound that overlooks the 10th hole. "It will sit there for a while and settle, then they'll sell it off. I could almost guarantee you that someday that ridge will be made up of nothing but prime lots [for housing]."

Just think, in another 1,700 years, a whole new set of artifacts will be ready for discovery. Of course, the significance of those findings might not measure up to what has come before them. Unless, that is, a Big Bertha, or possibly a PING putter, is unearthed from the rubble. ✿

ESTRELLA MOUNTAIN RANCH

PAR: 72 • YARDAGE: 5,124–6,767 • RATING: 68.2–73.8 • SLOPE: 114–138 • SIGNATURE HOLE: 194-YARD, PAR-3 № 17 • GREEN FEES: MODERATE TO EXPENSIVE

HEN MOST GOLFERS THINK of Jack Nicklaus II, they think of "Jackie," the eldest son and "the caddie" of the Golden Bear. After all, who can forget that sixth Nicklaus victory at the Masters? Jack makes the winning putt on the 18th hole at Augusta National, then turns and embraces Jackie, who is wearing a white jump suit and green cap, symbolic of the uniform worn by those who tote bags at the Masters.

These days, however, Jackie is no longer one of golf's best-known caddies. Instead, his name is rising everywhere in the ranks of golf course architects, as he has already designed 18 courses, including his last entry, Estrella Mountain Ranch Golf Club. The high-end, daily-fees layout is the first of three courses destined for this 24,000-acre project being developed by Sunchase Holdings in the West Valley.

For those who have never met the younger Nicklaus, his easygoing, friendly personality might be somewhat surprising for such a celebrated child of a superstar. He certainly has had great expectations bestowed upon him, and at one time was a championship-caliber amateur player. But it was topographical maps rather than yardage books that eventually gave Jackie his niche.

"I was a pretty good player, but never great," Jackie said of his golf career, which included a victory in the North-South Amateur. "Fortunately, my dad was also into golf course design, and with his help and guidance, I've been able to be involved and eventually begin to do courses of my own."

"We use the same supporting cast," he said of the associate designers and construction crew that also works for his father at Nicklaus Designs. "They keep me out of trouble." The same could be said at Estrella Mountain Ranch, as Nicklaus' free-flowing

design work helps rather than hinders players. For instance, slightly errant shots tend to feed back into fairways with the aid of mounding and slopes. Greens are fair but touchy, and much easier to access than the often shallow surfaces that his father employs.

Greg Ellis, the director of golf at Estrella Mountain Ranch, reports that Jackie's work is drawing rave reviews since the course opened in January 1999. "Everybody keeps saying what I've been talking about all along," said Ellis, who formerly served as head pro at the Tournament Players Club of Scottsdale. "Jackie laid it in there gently. He didn't manufacture the golf course. Without question, it is one of the most playable Nicklaus-designed golf courses that most people have ever played."

Ellis said Estrella Mountain is not as difficult as Lost Gold at Superstition Mountain, but it plays similarly. "The greens are smaller at Estrella Mountain Ranch, with less undulations, but just as fast," he added. "We've had a couple of Arizona Tour [minitour] events out here, and the best anyone has been able to shoot is [1 under] 71. At the same time, it's not overly difficult." Ellis' point is well-taken, as the Players' West Tour, a minitour for women, also made its debut at Estrella Mountain Ranch. The winner, Joellyn Erdman, fired a record 65. "Play it all the way back, it's a tough course," Ellis noted. "But play it from the right tees, and you'll enjoy it. You just can't let your ego get in the way, or you'll get eaten alive."

Estrella Mountain Ranch has a good rhythm, with outstanding stretches that roll with conviction from the fifth through the ninth, and the 14th through the 18th holes. Most visitors know they have arrived by the time they witness the sixth hole, a 424-yard par 4 that features water down the entire left side of the fairway. With the green surrounded

by the wet stuff and bunkers, it earns its nickname— "Mirage." The back nine, however, sports the signature offering, as the 194-yard 17th ("Grand Consequence") is among the most stunning par 3s in the Phoenix area. Saddled between a small hillside and a vegetated wash, and with the nearby Estrellas as a backdrop, there is purple mountain majesty written all over the hole by late afternoon.

Estrella Mountain Ranch is not the easiest place to find, as it is located about 30 minutes from downtown Phoenix on the west side of the mountain range of the same name. But most people will be surprised how much the area has already sprung up in just a short time. "It seems like we're in east L.A., but I look at us more like pioneers," Ellis quipped. "Someday . . . we'll be in the middle of the Valley."

Ellis said Estrella Mountain Ranch "already has an elementary school and everything but a grocery store, and that's on the way. Sunchase is really doing this area right," he noted. "The other two golf courses, which have been routed by Robert Trent Jones Jr. and Bob Cupp, will be strong additions, and they'll come on as we fill out with more people." But first, Ellis said, credit must go where it is deserved. "Jackie Nicklaus has given us so much. Really, he's given the West Valley a gold mine," he said. "For instance, we've already been named one of the top 10 daily-fees courses by *The Phoenix Business Journal*. I think it's great, because Jackie is such a first-class gentleman. He has made a name for himself despite growing up in the shadow of the greatest golfer of all time. The way I look at it, good for Jackie."

And good for those who tee off at Estrella Mountain Ranch! ☼

Jackie Nicklaus calls the 194-yard, par-3 17th hole "the prettiest par-3 I've ever designed."

GOLD CANYON GOLF RESORT

. . . .

DINOSAUR: PAR: 70 • YARDAGE: 4,921–6,584 • RATING: 65.5–71.5 • SLOPE: 115–140 • SIGNATURE HOLE: 467-YARD, PAR-4, №4 • GREEN FEES: MODERATE TO EXPENSIVE

SIDEWINDER: PAR: 71 • YARDAGE: 4,529–6,414 • RATING: 66.5–71.8 • SLOPE: 119–133 • SIGNATURE HOLE: 523-YARD, PAR-5, №6 • GREEN FEES: MODERATE TO EXPENSIVE

THEY SAY "there's gold in them thar hills," the ones that rise majestically into the Superstition Mountains. But the real superstition, at least the one that surrounds the legend of Lost Dutchman's Mine—the secret shaft supposedly hidden deep inside this range—is that the mother lode never will be found.

They're wrong. Actually, it's in plain sight: Gold Canyon Golf Resort glitters at the base of the Superstitions. Located just outside of Apache Junction in the booming community of Gold Canyon, its highly regarded Dinosaur Course and accompanying Sidewinder are visible golf gems.

Quite naturally, gold always has intrigued people in these parts. Supposedly, the Don Miguel Peralta family found incredible wealth from a mine in the Superstitions, but lost its claim to a prospector named Jacob Waltz, the "Old Dutchman." As the story goes, Waltz murdered to gain sole knowledge of the gold mine, and murdered again to keep it. So he went to his grave the only one who knew the exact location.

These days, more than one wannabe prospector, and perhaps an occasional hiker, search for the unfound treasure. Golfers on the other hand, know what they've got. It's there in the morning, when a hawk sails serenely over the enchanting resort. It's there in the evening, when a herd of deer crosses Gold Canyon's lush fairways and greens.

If further proof is needed to resolve this 150-year-old tale, look no further than the faces of those who tee it up at Gold Canyon, a Ken Kavanaugh–Greg Nash–Stuart Penge hybrid that

The par-5 third hole doglegs up the hill to a "saddle" green.

took more than 17 years to complete. Oh, yes, Scott Scherger knows one more reason why Gold Canyon sparkles these days. "Even though the city keeps creeping closer and closer, we're still a world away from the Valley," Scherger explained. "I guess that's why we get so many 'local' guests out here."

Gold Canyon has been one of the Valley's most rustic retreats, since 1979 when it was a dude ranch. In '81, Nash carved out the first nine holes, which is now the Sidewinder's back nine. Kavanaugh put his tender touch to the original back nine in '87, and a second nine in '96, mixing them for what is now the Dinosaur. Penge, the superintendent at Gold Canyon, built the front nine of the Sidewinder in '98, thus completing the 36-hole project. "They all came one nine at a time, but it worked out beautifully," Sherger said. "Both courses look like the nines have always been together."

Kavanaugh is especially proud of his work on the Dinosaur's second nine. "That setting is so beautiful, all I was trying to do was uncover it," he said of what now is the fifth through 13th holes. "I wanted to make big, simple, sweeping shapes that wouldn't conflict with the dramatic backdrops."

Obviously, the Dinosaur is the showcase, with no fewer than nine tee boxes offering spectacular views of three separate canyons. The list of awesome vistas, several of which are framed against regal Battleship Rock, begins at No. 2, a downhill par 3 that looks out over the Valley. It also includes Nos. 3, 4, 5, 11, 12, 13, 14, and 15.

The Sidewinder is more straightforward and down to earth—literally. The front nine can be particularly venomous, as Penge took the lower echelons of the course and snaked them through several arroyos, with the best stretch coming from Nos. 4 through 7. Nash's back nine is more scenic, but tougher and tighter mainly because of the small, turtleback-shaped greens. But there is some relief, at least financially, as the Sidewinder is about half the green fee of the Dinosaur.

For those who decide to stay and play, the resort offers large, Southwestern-styled casitas, many of which are equipped with jumbo Jacuzzis. The restaurants, which include Greenwood's sports bar and the elegant Kokopelli's, are superb. Greenwood's specializes in burgers and beer (what else?), while Chef Rob Bowser serves up such delicacies as Shrimp Cortez, Beef Tournedos, Sierra Quail, and Lamb Achiote. Save room for the Gold Canyon Delight (a white-chocolate golf bag filled with fresh strawberry mousse).

Gold Canyon's other noted amenity is Resort Golf Schools under Scott Sackett, one of *Golf Magazine*'s top 100 instructors in the country. According to Merle Makings, Gold Canyon's director, Sackett's schools complete the package. "Having one of the best golf schools in the country is so important," Makings noted. "It's helped to push us to the level of the Troon Norths and Grayhawks of Arizona. In fact, when you factor in our setting, it doesn't get much better than this—period."

Makings' point is well-taken. Everything a golfer wants is right here, right now. But for those visitors who need a diversion during their visit, an old cowboy movie set known as Apacheland lies just a mile or so down the old, dusty trail. Still open to the public (at least on the weekends), Apacheland served as the site of such legendary television westerns as *The Lone Ranger*, *Paladin*, *Bonanza*, *The Big Valley*, and *Gunsmoke*.

Of course, there always is that romantic alternative of searching for the Lost Dutchman's Mine. But, believe it or not, there are old gold mine shafts right on the golf course near the fifth, 11th, 12th, and 15th holes of the Dinosaur. But before anyone goes chasing fool's gold, just remember these words of wisdom:

All that glitters is Gold Canyon Golf Resort. ⚙

THE GOLF CLUB AT EAGLE MOUNTAIN

PAR: 72 • YARDAGE: 5,065–6,782 • RATING: 67.2–72.4 • SLOPE: 118–139 • SIGNATURE HOLE: 420-YARD, PAR-4 №18 • GREEN FEES: EXPENSIVE

MOST PEOPLE GET SWEPT AWAY with the beautiful views at the Golf Club at Eagle Mountain. The 17th and 18th holes—Eagle Mountain's one-two, finishing punch—are especially dramatic.

The Eagle Mountain story takes flight in 1995, when Miller was hired by Communities Southwest, an Arizona-based company headed by developer Dennis Knight. The property, which is draped around Eagle Mountain and includes numerous box canyons, arroyos, and cliffs, was a major challenge in terms of construction. Adding to the difficulty, there was not much topsoil, and the water in the Fountain Hills area is loaded with salt. Not good.

Given time to mature, Eagle Mountain spread its wings to full span. After all, this has always been an awesome landscape filled with equally incredible vistas. "It was a totally natural site with lots of great vegetation to add to the land features," recalled Miller, who cut his design teeth under Jack Nicklaus on such projects as Desert Highlands and Desert Mountain before setting out on his own. "My goal from the start was to try and create a golf course that was relatively easy to play, but hard to score on."

Eagle Mountain requires a lot of thought. "You need to be in the 'A' position in order to score well," said Miller, whose résumé includes Kierland and DC Ranch in Scottsdale. "At the same time, the biggest compliment we get is the fun people have playing it. It's a very friendly desert golf course, where you won't get your brains beat in."

Jay Pennypacker, the director of golf at Eagle Mountain, takes it one step further. "The way we look at it, it's the most playable desert golf course in the Valley," Pennypacker pointed out. "It's wall-to-wall grass, and you've only got one forced carry off the tee [No. 14]. Plus, the fairways are [concave] in the sense that they contain the drive and feed it back into the center of the fairway."

Eagle Mountain's greatest defense is its greens, which are loaded with undulations, slopes, and tiers.

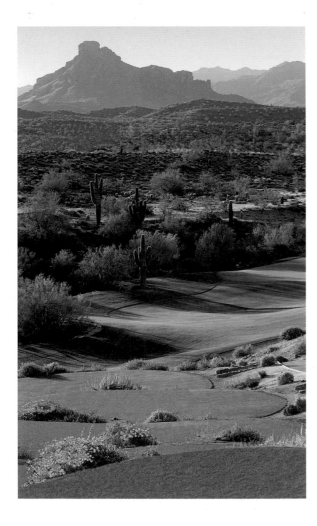

Of course, the rolling fairways and elevation changes also factor into the scoring equation. "Only Gold Canyon has more elevation changes than we do," Pennypacker added. "In fact, there is 700 feet of difference between the third green and the 18th tee."

Miller takes a player off the deep end right from the get-go, as No. 1 opens with a semiblind tee shot over a crest and down the hill. Despite the par 5 stretching out 568 yards, it's reachable in two well-struck shots. Wait, there's more, as Miller uses the same visual effect at No. 4, the other par 5 on the front side that rambles for 546 yards, but is not quite as accessible in two swings. "Actually, I don't think of them as blind shots, because you can anticipate the landing areas," Miller said. "At least there was never any attempt to create a blind shot on those two holes. I think after you've played the course a few times, you get to understand that we were just following the lay of the land there."

One of the most unique holes is No. 3, a 210-yard downhill shot to a big green that is walled off in its own canyon. No wonder it's called "Solitude."

LEFT: *The signature 420-yard, par-4 18th hole.*
ABOVE RIGHT: *The 510-yard, par-5 12th hole.*

Of the two nines, the back is the stronger. The going gets tougher beginning at the 10th hole, another demanding par 5. But this journey over 535 yards is fully in view, a good thing considering there is water down the entire left side and a green that has more waves than some oceans. The next eight holes build to a climax, with the 17th and 18th stealing the show.

"The 18th, with the water at the bottom of the hill and Red Mountain in the background, is probably the signature hole," Miller said of the 420-yard par 4 that plays much shorter because of the nearly 100-foot drop from tee to green.

But he is quick to admit that the 17th, a driveable par 4 that shoots up the hill for 345 yards, is probably the course's most photographed hole. "The 17th is awesome from the tee looking up at the green," Miller said. "It's a great risk-reward type of situation, especially at that point in your round."

According to Pennypacker, the Eagle Mountain experience does not end at the dynamic 18th green, which not only includes water but a massive beach to go with it. "Our philosophy is pretty simple," he said. "We want your day to go like you've been to Disneyland and everything went perfect—the accommodations and the conditions. But most important, we want you to remember that the service was delivered by the nicest people you will ever meet." This, of course, is why Eagle Mountain's regulars seem to double in numbers each year. No matter what they score, they come back for more. "There always are a few new surprises," Pennypacker said.

Of course, the biggest and the best comes only if you are near the 17th tee, looking up the mountain, or perhaps checking out the sky. "There is an eagle that actually nests on the mountain, and he, or she, has been here since the course first opened," Pennypacker noted. "Not that many people ever see it, but it's up there. Pretty neat, huh?"

And that, my friend, is the rest of the Eagle Mountain story. ✿

Eagle Mountain has lots of elevation changes.

GRAYHAWK GOLF CLUB

. . . .

TALON: PAR: 71 • YARDAGE: 5,143–6,985 • RATING: 67.9–73.3 • SLOPE: 116–145 • SIGNATURE HOLE: 305-YARD, PAR-4 № 13 • GREEN FEES: EXPENSIVE

RAPTOR: PAR: 72 • YARDAGE: 5,309–7,135 • RATING: 69.1–74.0 • SLOPE: 121–136 • SIGNATURE HOLE: 174-YARD, PAR-3 № 8 • GREEN FEES: EXPENSIVE

FEW GOLF COURSES in Arizona have come on as swiftly as mighty Grayhawk Golf Club, which played host to Tiger Woods' Williams World Challenge in 1999 and featured the top players on the planet.

But remember, Grayhawk does everything on a rather grand scale, which is why Tiger and Co. became the second major tournament to be played at Grayhawk since the Andersen Consulting World Championship of Golf graced these fairways from 1995 through '97.

Why would the popular Scottsdale layout, considered among the best daily-fees courses in Arizona, need such additional fanfare? Probably for the same reason Grayhawk's public relations machine,

Communication Links, wrote a book about the origin of each course before the grand openings: You can never have enough prestige. Which explains why Grayhawk also signed PGA Tour superstar Phil Mickelson to represent the club. One of Grayhawk's three restaurants is even called Phil's Grill, and features several of Lefty's favorite foods.

Then there is The Celebrity, an annual fling that brings in many of the stars from the music world, most notably those from country & western fame. John Michael Montgomery hosted several of the fund-raisers for charity along with fellow country crooner Clint Black. Even Mickelson has shown up a few times to display his talents, although not on stage.

This is the way it's always been at Grayhawk,

and for the most part, the chic Scottsdale courses have lived up to the hype. Like Troon North, which gets $200-plus for green fees during peak season, Grayhawk also tops out in the $200 range. Is it worth it? You bet, says Grayhawk's Captain of the Club Del Cochran. "It's like going to a French restaurant," Cochran says of the experience, which features perhaps the best outside service in Arizona, as well as the most awesome clubhouse and pro shop. "Sure, you don't go to it every day. But every once in a while, you treat yourself. What we've tried to create is that member-for-a-day feel. You get the works: a bag tag, your own locker, superior service, and two great golf courses to choose from."

Talon came first, bulldozing its way into existence behind the one-time architectural team of David Graham and Gary Panks. The year was 1994, and big-time desert layouts were just beginning to become the rage. Graham and Panks moved nearly 200,000 cubic yards of dirt, which explains the 50-foot-deep box canyons, island greens, and elevated tees. Even the putting surfaces, many of them made up of multiple tiers that result in roller coaster rides, required earth-moving equipment. "We gave them exactly what they wanted," Graham said in defense of the tricky greens. "Granted, they're a little outrageous, but overall, it's a darn good golf course."

Most everyone agrees, especially after they experience the course's signature holes—Nos. 11 and 13. The 11th, called "Swinging Bridge," requires golfers to cross a rope bridge to get to the tee. A medium iron from 168 yards is required over a deep chasm to access the triple-tiered green that

"Aces & Eights": The par-3 No. 8 on the Raptor Course.

boasts a beautiful McDowell Mountains backdrop. The second standout is referred to as "Heaven or Hell," a nickname that is a dead giveaway as to what can happen if your tee shot from 305 yards should end up in the deep box canyon off to the right. Go ahead, go for it!

Another great thing about Talon is its link to former Arizona State University and LPGA star Heather Farr, who succumbed to breast cancer in 1994. Farr, who also would have represented Grayhawk on the LPGA, is honored by a bronze, life-size statue on the first tee; her own hole (No. 1, called "Farr View"); her own set of tees (the Heather tees); and a banquet room that bears her name. In addition, Grayhawk is the annual site of the Heather Farr Trophy Matches that pit Arizona's top club professionals against the best amateurs.

Grayhawk's reputation continued to soar in 1995 with the arrival of the Raptor Course. Unbelievably, the Tom Fazio–designed layout was even more ballyhooed than its older sister. Tougher, too, with a rolling terrain that pinches golfers' swings, as well as their nerves. Perhaps that is why Raptor did not catch on quite as fast as Talon, although maturity has allowed it to become the dominant course.

Fazio, who is considered one of the premier course designers of his day, said Raptor was one of his most prized projects. "Del and [Grayhawk president] Gregg [Tryhus] were both just super, real golf guys, and that's important to any designer when he takes on a project," Fazio said. "Without an owner's support, a course can turn out to be a nightmare. What I really liked about Raptor was the fact I was given the property without limitations, other than those normal environmental ones that go along with desert golf courses [no more than 90 acres of turf]. That allowed me to create some contours and elevations that I feel are quite unique in desert golf."

Like Talon, Raptor has a high-tech feel because of the incredible amount of earth that was moved. Perhaps the most unique hole is No. 8, at 174 yards, dubbed "Aces & Eights." The reference is to a poker term known as a "dead man's hand," and should you come up short on this downhill par 3, a huge mound

and bunker, as well as a sweeping green, certainly can kill you. But the strength of the course is its variety, as no two holes bear a likeness.

The same could be said of the amenities. There is something for everyone at Grayhawk, provided money is no object. The experience is one-of-a-kind, from playing golf to dining in the restaurants to purchasing unusual merchandise such as baby clothes, birdhouses, luggage, leather goods, and jewelry at Grayhawk's Golf Shop and Trading Co.

"We sell a lot of guilt gifts," noted the club's director of golf, Joe Shershenovich, referring to husbands on golf junkets who are always looking for gifts to take home to their wives and kids. But, hey, when you're spending $200-plus on golf, why not another couple hundred bucks more on a Grayhawk teddy bear and purse? Like Cochran said, you're a member at Grayhawk for only a day, so live a little. ✿

TOP: *The par-5 18th hole on the Talon Course.*
BELOW: *David Graham, Gary Panks, and Tom Fazio elevated Grayhawk Golf Club to one of the most recognized names in Arizona golf.*

KIERLAND GOLF CLUB

. . . .

PAR: 72 • YARDAGE: 4,898–7,020 • RATING: 69.8–73.3 • SLOPE: 120–133 • SIGNATURE HOLE: 531-YARD, PAR-5 Nº 9 (ACACIA) • GREEN FEES: EXPENSIVE

WHAT COMES FIRST, the town or the golf course?

Well, 99 percent of the time, it's the town, with the golf course being built somewhere down the line. Not so at Kierland Commons, where the 27-hole golf facility was built in 1996, almost four years before the "Town Square" started taking shape.

Dazed and confused? Don't be. Sure, Kierland's zip code will always remain Scottsdale. But did you know that a "small-town" complex has been slowly unfolding around the golf course? Its boundaries are Scottsdale Road to the east, Paradise Lane on the north, 64th Avenue to the west, and Acoma Drive on the south.

"There's nothing like it in the Valley," noted Buzz Gosnell, the developer of the 730-acre project, which includes resort, residential, retail, and office components. It's Main Street America, the way small towns and villages used to be. The storefronts all face one centrally located street, with a town hall and a town square complete with an old-fashioned fountain as the centerpiece. "Someday we also plan to be the home of the Arizona Golf Museum and Hall of Fame," Gosnell added.

Even though it's taken time to pull it off, Kierland and its surroundings are turning out picture-perfect. Some might say it's like a Norman Rockwell painting. That the golf course was the first piece of the puzzle might be somewhat surprising. Then again, why not if it's good enough?

Scott Miller, who also designed such Valley gems as Eagle Mountain and DC Ranch, said the only debate was whether to construct 27 or 36 holes.

The Ironwood course at Kierland.

grasses. Once again, the ninth hole is the signature, a 495-yard par 5 with water running down the right side of the fairway before it pools menacingly in front of the green. A great risk-reward closer, Miller deploys graceful bunkering to frame the green.

The Acacia has a bundle of big-time offerings, including its picturesque par 3s. But, once again, the 531-yard, par-5 ninth is the most memorable, with an 80-foot drop from tee to a water-guarded fairway and green. Only three perfect shots work here, as a beach full of bunkers also defend the putting surface from easy pickings.

"I was lucky in that I had a big, open-flowing canvas at Kierland," Miller said of the masterpiece. "We moved about 1.3 million yards of dirt, which is similar to what was moved at the Raven [at South Mountain] and the TPC [of Scottsdale]. But rather than hollow out the fairways, we built up the sides and attempted to create holes that were both introverted and extroverted. Because it's a resort course, we emphasized playability. My thinking was that some courses in the Scottsdale area are more fun to look at than to play."

There are other amenities that make Kierland a joy, including the award-winning Golf Digest School headed by the husband-and-wife team of Sandy and Mike LaBauve. And, as Miller mentioned, the Westin-Kierland Resort is on its way, which brings a smile to Gosnell.

"Someday, it's all going to be there: Everything a golfer could want from a great resort to a great course to a great golf school," Gosnell noted. "Making it even better, shopping and dining will be just a short walk away, which is unique to Scottsdale." There will be such hot spots as Morton's, the Cheesecake Factory, and a new P F Chang's. Of course, not everything will be so chic, Gosnell revealed. "We're going to have an ice cream and soda fountain shop, too," he proclaimed.

Yes, Kierland's version of Small Town America is about to collide with the bright lights of the Big City. ✿

"Because of its valuable location, almost in the middle of Scottsdale, there were other considerations in order to get everything to fit. We thought about 18, 27, and 36 holes. Actually, it went back and forth more than a few times."

Finally, Miller introduced Gosnell and Co., to "core golf," and the rest, as they say, is history. Or at least it will be someday. "Basically, the concept of core golf is where you have shared corridors, parallel fairways, and traditional tees and greens," Miller explained. "Those features allow you to get more 'Class A' golf into less space. For instance, most golf courses, when you add clubhouse and maintenance facilities, need 160 to 165 acres per 18 holes. We managed to get 27 holes comfortably into 208 acres, which saved the developers about 30 to 35 acres."

Miller said the 27 holes, which include the Acacia, Ironwood, and Mesquite nines, gave Kierland flexibility as well as variety. Of the three, the Acacia generally is regarded as the flagship, although the Ironwood also is solid and serene. Ask Miller, whose résumé includes Idaho's illustrious Coeur D'Alene Golf Club, and he reluctantly agrees. "I guess, with what we did on the Acacia, it's my favorite," he said. "The elevation and movement is just a little more dramatic there, and the variety is like that old cliché: 'the spice of life.'"

The Mesquite was the first nine to unfold, and though it didn't necessarily knock anyone's golf socks off, it was functional and fair as it weaved its way through numerous housing straits. For the most part, it's traditional golf with the exception of the ninth hole, a 427-yard, downhill par 4 over a small lake to an elevated green that tilts slightly toward the rear.

That theme is taken up a notch on the Ironwood nine, which has a bit of a Midwestern flavor to it, complete with waving, wheat-colored

LAS SENDAS GOLF CLUB

PAR: 71 · YARDAGE: 5,034–6,834 · RATING: 69.6–73.8 · SLOPE: 128–149 · SIGNATURE HOLE: 510-YARD, PAR-5 № 9 · GREEN FEES: EXPENSIVE

I F LAS SENDAS means "The Pathway," then architect Robert Trent Jones Jr. took his time finding it. Thank goodness, RTJ Jr. finally saw the light. Otherwise, Las Sendas would have turned out to be the Devil instead of just devilishly difficult.

"There was over five years between the start of the project and the restart," Jones explained. "Originally, the property was sold to a group in Albuquerque. After they had some financial difficulties, Buddy Johnson and his group [Eagle Crest Limited Partnership] stepped back in and got things going again."

What began in 1988 as Falcon Ridge Country Club, an extremely demanding private golf course,

finally opened in January of 1995 as Las Sendas, a high-end, daily-fees course that still was plenty stiff in terms of difficulty. "We were influenced by the times," Jones recalled. "Back in the mid-1980s, we golf course architects were in our bold and dynamic phase, when Pete Dye and Jack Nicklaus were influencing everyone through difficulty and drama. Some of the traditional features were lost. For instance, greens became unforgiving to the point that, if you missed them, you couldn't recover. But that five- or six-year hiatus between start and finish was good for the [Las Sendas] project, because in the end we softened up the course considerably."

Gee, makes you wonder what the slope would

have been had Jones not come to his senses during the layover. As it is, Las Sendas' slope of 149 is tops in Arizona. "Yes, it's plenty tough," Jones conceded. "But the course has a complex character, like a great wine. It's funny, but some of the finest pieces of work are a long time in the making, and Las Sendas certainly fits that bill." Las Sendas' strengths are its variety of holes and awe-inspiring vistas, and the views from the signature ninth hole are among the most spectacular in Arizona. No wonder Las Sendas was chosen by *Golf Magazine* as one of the "Top 10 Places to Play in Arizona" and earned a four-star rating from *Golf Digest*.

Mark Gurnow, the club's director of golf since the beginning, said what most people fail to realize is that Las Sendas' trouble is right in front of you, like bruiser bunkers and tricky greens that can be as slick as the hood of a new Cadillac. The danger of hitting the ball into the adjacent saguaros and sagebrush is minimal. "Keeping the ball on the golf course is not a problem like it is on some desert golf courses," Gurnow observed. "The problem is avoiding the immediate trouble and scoring. It's hard to take it low here."

That is obvious from the start, as the initial three offerings at Las Sendas seem almost impossible to negotiate in par. Actually, there are some who say that pattern continues for the next 15 holes. What keeps people coming back? There never is a dull moment.

The second hole, a sharp "elevator" shot straight up Spirit Hill from 135 yards, has a semi blind element to it. The third hole, a 440-yard dogleg down and around the same hill to a tabletop green, also is

Robert Trent Jones Jr. built Las Sendas.

spectacularly scary. Then the ninth hole, a 510-yard par 5 over water—twice!—blows you away. "As beautiful as it is, it's really the weather conditions that make that hole," Gurnow noted of No. 9. "When the wind is with you, and you're heading downhill, it can be an easy birdie. But when the wind is in your face, and all that water is staring at you, par is a terrific score."

But birdie or bogey, or even double, you have to stop and smell the roses, Gurnow added. "You can see forever from that green," he said of the ninth, which was originally meant to be the 18th hole. "[The ninth] would probably play better as a closer. But the reason we made it No. 9 instead of 18 was because it's due west. I don't think it's any fun when players are finishing their rounds late in the afternoon and you can't see into the sun."

Several other holes stand out, like the 14th, a 194-yard long iron to a green saddled into the side of Spirit Mountain, and the 16th, a 120-yard pot shot that comes back down off the ridge to a small, sneaky green backed by Red Mountain. "That's a terrific trio of par 3s," Jones said. "The second and 14th holes are a very unusual pair of par 3s because of the way the greens sit into the mountain. [The 16th] is just a cute but tough little hole because the green has a false front and a tricky tier."

Despite all the living dangerously, Las Sendas is a good time and has been since the days of Tom Mix, the cowboy screen star who made the property his dude ranch in the 1930s and '40s. You just have to know your limitations. If you don't play the right set of tees, you won't have a good time.

But don't try to budge Jones too far off his position that Las Sendas was softened up just enough. After all, he said, the lay of the land had a lot to do with the way it all turned out. Sacrifices—like a golfer or two—had to be made. "Remember," Jones said, clearing his throat philosophically, "only golf courses with character are memorable."

True. You will never forget Las Sendas. ✿

Red Mountain backdrops the par-3 16th hole at Las Sendas, a 120-yard pot shot to a sweeping green.

THE LEGACY GOLF RESORT

. . . .

PAR: 71 • YARDAGE: 5,471–6,802 • RATING: 70.4–71.8 • SLOPE: 117–125 • SIGNATURE HOLE: 523-YARD, PAR-5 № 18 • GREEN FEES: MODERATE TO EXPENSIVE

CONSIDERING ITS HISTORY, perhaps a better name for The Legacy might have been The Farm, or perhaps The Ranch. Actually, at one point during the building process, the Gary Panks–designed layout was to be titled The Ranch at South Mountain.

But it didn't happen, and so the pioneer farming operation once run by the legendary Dwight B. Heard became The Legacy. Not that the farm and ranch have disappeared, mind you. Three buckboards from the turn of the century still grace the place. Two are located on the first and 10th tees, with the third ancient means of transportation sit-

ting idly in front of three grain silos that jut upward just off the 18th fairway. The silos, which were constructed in 1902, are in remarkably good shape, a reminder that back then they were the tallest buildings

---

The par-3 15th hole at the Legacy Golf Resort.

An old buckboard adds to the Legacy's ambiance.

Branding irons and horseshoes rack players' clubs.

course. You get used to it. They also flip-flopped the nines on me because they felt the last four holes were more dramatic. I still feel like what now is the front nine is stronger."

Last-minute changes aside, the $200 million project, which includes 450 home sites, 328 time-share condominiums, a health club, restaurant, and upscale clubhouse is committed to the past. Even the golf carts reek of nostalgia, complete with a buggy-type carriage and a maroon paint job that dates back to yesteryear. Thank you, In Celebration of Golf, the management team that does everything first-class.

The golf course itself is modern traditional, if there is such a style. On the "today side," the fairways are mounded and open, with 4,000 desert trees still years away from maturity. In terms of the "the past," the bunkers are large and steep with grass that rolls down into the sand. Meanwhile, greens are a nice contrast, some being large and flat while others are smaller with more undulations.

in the Phoenix area at a mere 30 feet, and built to last.

The link to Heard, who was a founding father of the region and the driving force behind the museum of the same name, is one of the key points in the marketing of the golf course. Heard's portrait graces the cover of the club's yardage book, and subsequent black-and-white photographs recall his buddy, President Teddy Roosevelt, as well as the foreman and workers who toiled on the 7,500-acre ranch.

Heard was an extraordinary man, having originally moved from Chicago to Arizona in 1897 to save his health and escape the harsh Chicago winters. He quickly caught on to life in the desert, developing a high-tech (at that time) cattle operation and buying *The Arizona Republican* (yes, *The Republic*) newspaper in order to help Roosevelt re-establish the Bull Moose Party. His former residence, the Sierra Vista House, sits to the right of the first fairway.

Eventually, he sold his farming empire with the exception of the 280-parcel that now is known as The Legacy. "Historically, this is a pretty special piece of property," noted Panks, who along with a battalion of bulldozers built the course by moving 700,000 cubic yards of dirt. "I think it's pretty neat that they've been able to tie the legacy of Dwight Heard into the golf course."

Panks, who has built 38 courses, including the neighboring Raven at South Mountain, prefers the original name: The Ranch at South Mountain. "But a lot of changes take place in the building of a golf

The clubhouse at the Legacy Golf Resort.

While The Legacy is not quite as refined or strategically demanding as The Raven, chiefly because its fairways are much wider and the penalties less severe, it does hold its own in other ways. Both courses were built on basically flat cotton fields, but The Legacy, because of its elevated tee boxes and greens, boasts more panoramic views of the downtown skyline, Squaw Peak, Camelback Mountain, and Four Peaks. The par 3s at The Legacy are especially

appealing. Two of those could easily be the signature holes, as the 136-yard seventh and the 203-yard 17th are picturesque and plenty tough. The par 5s also offer lots of variety, while the par 4s are consistent, the 442-yard ninth hole, Panks' original closer, being the best of all.

Certainly the course is an adventure, as it ranges all the way from 24th Street to 32nd Street. "It's quite a jaunt, but that was by design," Panks noted. "In order to build length into the golf course, we had to take it all the way around the perimeter. That meant that, unfortunately, two holes had to be on the street [Nos. 3 and 16]." Most golfers won't mind because The Legacy is so playable. Pretty, too, with several bodies of water and lots of wild flowers and grasses to add to the ambiance. "The vegetation is what we imagined it would be like around here at the turn of the century," Panks noted.

Of course, don't expect the prices of yesteryear to also be a novelty. That is especially true in the Trail's End Bar & Grill, an apparent reference to the fact that Heard originally was a cattle baron. For example, the half-pound hamburger known as the Round-up weighs in at $8.

No doubt Dwight B. Heard would be blown away by today's prices, especially when you consider a hamburger was just a nickel back in his heyday. At the same time, Heard would be proud that his legacy has been restored on some of Phoenix's finest fairways and greens. ✺

LEGEND TRAIL GOLF CLUB

PAR: 72 • YARDAGE: 4,912–6,810 • RATING: 68.2–72.3 • SLOPE: 122–135 • SIGNATURE HOLE: 490-YARD, PAR-5 NO 7 • GREEN FEES: EXPENSIVE

REES JONES HAS BUILT golf courses in the deserts around Scottsdale, Las Vegas, and Palm Springs. Despite the similar terrain, all are unique, he said.

Of the three deserts, Arizona's Sonoran Desert is Jones' favorite, and Legend Trail Golf Club is his shining example. "Legend Trail was my first desert-style golf course, and what I like most about it is it flows with the land," said Jones, the younger son of famed architect Robert Trent Jones and the designer of over 100 well-known layouts worldwide. "Most desert courses are so penal, but Legend Trail is not. The front nine is very gentle, and the back nine builds to a crescendo, like good courses do."

Jones actually picked up the project in northeast Scottsdale on a double rebound. The original routing was designed in the mid-1980s by Randy Heckenkamper, but the course went broke a short time later. Phoenix architect Jack Snyder redesigned the course in the early 1990s before Jones stepped in at the prodding of his good friend, Al Mengert, in 1994. "Al had been the head pro at Coral Ridge, our family's home course in Fort Lauderdale [Florida]."

Jones said he has always believed that the best golf courses on the planet are those you become totally interactive with. "That's what happened here," he said. "Al and I exchanged a lot of ideas, and through our experiences of playing golf and seeing a lot of golf courses, we came up with a very enjoyable desert golf course."

Mengert, who once played on the PGA Tour, hired Jones because he didn't want a target style of golf course. "I refer to Legend Trail as 'pure golf,' rather than desert golf," said Mengert, who is less involved in the course these days after turning it over to Troon Golf. "Ours is a much more traditional golf course that does not dictate how you must play it, but rather how you play your game."

As Jones mentioned, Legend Trail opens up with a series of holes, mostly par 4s, that are quite mellow. But the swing better be in sync by the time the 490-yard, par-5 seventh hole rolls around. A classic risk-reward situation, a birdie is possible if you can clear the small pond and waterfall that guards the entrance on your second shot. Woe be to those who come up short. "The seventh hole is the glitz offering," Jones admitted. "That one took a little bit of extra oomph. But the rest of them are quite natural."

Jones called the tee shot at the 440-yard 11th "the most demanding tee shot I've ever seen in the desert." The curling, dogleg left, which plays up, around, and down a small hillside, is the most exacting shot on the golf course. The 11th also signals perhaps the best stretch of golf, which doesn't let up until the 14th hole. Before it's over, Jones throws one more curve, with back-to-back par 5s making up the 16th and 17th holes. "The 17th [525 yards] is especially a 'go for it' [in two shots] hole," he said. "The 16th [530 yards] is a little more protected because the green sits into a hill with a big bunker left-center."

There are other features to like about Legend

Trail, which is surrounded by such landmarks as Pinnacle Peak, Troon Mountain, Goldie's Butte, and the Tonto Foothills. Chief among them is the "territorial chic" clubhouse, which is one of the most authentic and original ideas in Arizona golf. "I hand-picked everything in here," said "Big Al," who scoured the Southwest in search of paintings and photographs that fit Legend Trail's western theme.

Legend Trail also serves as a regional teaching center for the Jim McLean Golf Schools, as well as Resort Golf Schools, which are led by one of McLean's most admired instructors, Scott Sackett. In addition, Legend Trail has one of the most fascinating yet difficult putting courses in the United States. "I'm extremely proud of the way it all turned out," Mengert said. "I wanted to build a Cypress Point in the desert, because I've always thought Cypress Point was the best course in the world. I think Rees did a good job of sticking with those traditional concepts."

No doubt Jones benefited from the gene pool that is linked to his father. But he also has an impressive education that includes stints in golf course design at Yale and Harvard. "Yale and Harvard look good, but I didn't learn as much there as I've learned in the field, because golf course design is a craft you build on day by day," he said. "Legend Trail was a learning experience. What we tried to do was make the landing areas as wide as possible, and make it fun for the paying customer and challenging for the better players. We always try to exceed our client's expectations, and I think we did that at Legend Trail." ☼

LEFT: *The clubhouse at Legend Trail.*
RIGHT: *Rees Jones was the architect who sculpted Legend Trail out of the high Sonoran desert.*

LOS CABALLEROS GOLF CLUB

· ·

PAR: 71 · YARDAGE: 5,870–6,962 · RATING: 67.6–74.9 · SLOPE: 124–138 · SIGNATURE HOLE: 598-YARD, PAR-5 № 13 · GREEN FEES: MODERATE TO EXPENSIVE

Los Caballeros makes it possible for the city-bred dude to rough it in comfort . . . a nice combination of the typical western informal ranch with the luxurious appointments of the modern resort.

—DALLAS GANT, Los Caballeros founder/president
Wickenberg Sun, November 1948

ANCHO DE LOS CABALLEROS, the longstanding dude ranch that also includes the championship golf course known as "Los Cab," literally means "ranch of the gentlemen on horseback." But the Spanish translation doesn't quite fit, at least in terms of Americana. This is a retreat for wannabe wranglers and, in every way, cowboy golf.

Need to get that in-touch-with-nature feel of riding the range? You can earn your spurs at Rancho de los Caballeros, which is located in the dude ranch capital of the world. Want to tee it up among wide-open spaces surrounded by mountains and peaks? Then Los Cab, the golf course, is where you want to be. "It's a special place, not like any you'll find in Phoenix or Scottsdale," noted Carlton Blewitt, the club's director of golf.

Without question, Los Cab, lodged among the mesquites and yuccas, about 60 miles northwest of Phoenix, demands every skill in a golfer's arsenal. Constructed in the early 1970s by architects Greg Nash and Jeff Hardin, Los Cab has that rare ability of making a lasting impression after just one visit. But to truly understand the legacy of Los Caballeros, it is necessary to climb into the "Way-Back Machine." Since the resort opened its doors in 1948, it has played host to thousands of visitors, including actor Clark Gable, cowboy celebrity

Hopalong Cassidy, and former President Richard Nixon. Even back then, visitors relished the romantic yet rustic retreat, which features a mix of Spanish and Native American decor that has found its way into cowboy culture.

The complete tale of Rancho de los Caballeros actually dates to the early 1920s, when this laid-back town began catering to visitors who were seeking the cowboy experience. At that time, the trend-setter was the Remuda Ranch, where a young man named Dallas C. Gant was in charge of saddling up the

tourists. Later, after Gant had also held similar titles at Bishop's Lodge in Santa Fe and Camelback Inn in Phoenix, he teamed up with two part-time cowboys, Charles "Squire" Lorenzo and Belford "Boff" Howard—Remuda regulars—to launch Rancho de los Caballeros. The going rate back in those days was an unbelievable $14 a day per dude, about one-twentieth of what one of the 79 suites goes for today.

That's the way things stood until the late 1960s, when Gant died, leaving the leadership of this Arizona jewel to his son, Dallas Jr., known as

ABOVE: *Vulture's Peak backdrops "Los Cab."*
OPPOSITE: *Cowboy charm accents Los Caballeros.*

Rusty. Being younger and perhaps more aggressive, Rusty Gant decided that, in order to compete with the Phoenix market, Rancho de los Caballeros needed a golf course. So he turned to Nash and Hardin, who at that time were also in the early days of what would be lengthy designing careers, especially Nash, who went on to be a co-designer with former PGA Tour great Billy Casper.

Nash and Hardin had received their apprenticeship under the keen eyes of Red Lawrence, known as "the Desert Fox." Obviously, they had learned their lessons well, as Los Cab turned out to be perhaps their best-known work. All of the old master's teachings—elongated tee boxes; traditional/strategic bunkering; and elevated, sloping greens—are found on the course.

What is fascinating about Los Cab is that 14 holes have some type of upward movement. In other words, positioning shots with an eye on elevation is the biggest clue to course management. Another tip: uphill approach shots often need just one more club than you might think.

The course starts off innocently enough, as the first two holes are fairly wide open and downhill. Then the climb begins at No. 3, a 190-yard test to one of the course's many turtleback-shaped greens. If there is a stretch on the front that stands out, it's the middle holes—Nos. 5 and 7—two long par 5s (531 and 569 yards) and No. 6, a 402-yard dogleg to another classy but slippery green. The shorter of the par 5s, No. 5, is especially memorable, with palm trees starkly pinned against the horizon and the Bradshaw Mountains rising in the distance.

But the back nine is the best, mainly because the course never lets up beginning at the 13th hole, a roller coaster par 5 that takes you over three distinct hilltops, and the last being another big, hard-to-stick green backed by palm trees and the area's landmark—Vulture's Peak. Needless to say, at 598 yards, the vultures might be swirling by the time you finish this difficult test. At that point, the course plunges into a yucca forest (seriously, they're trees!), which when accompanied with the course's trademark mesquite-lined fairways make for some very unique Sonoran-style golf. The final hole, a 560-yard, dogleg par 5 that rambles downhill, concludes with a fantastic risk-reward situation. Sand be damned! Go for it (in two shots)!

You can't lose. Afterward, a big burger and a beer at Los Cab's 19th hole is the perfect ending. But don't miss out on the chef's potato salad, which is another of the secrets stowed inside the laid-back confines of Los Cab. Not necessarily cowboy food, for sure. But steaks, beans, and coffee from a tin pot still exist on the premises. Just stay at the resort, and once a week all the guests wander out into the desert evening for a fireside cookout. Next day, it's horses and golf all over again.

Yeah, it's pretty cool, dude! ☀

PALM: Par: 72 • Yardage: 5,057–7,055 • Rating: 67.5–73.7 • Slope: 114–137 • Signature hole: 422-yard, par-4 № 3 • Green fees: moderate to expensive

PINE: Par: 72 • Yardage: 5,333–7,187 • Rating: 68.2–74.4 • Slope: 117–135 • Signature hole: 470-yard, par-4 № 15 • Green fees: moderate to expensive

THERE IS A REASON that McCormick Ranch Golf Club has a reputation for being "King of the Scramble." And, no, it doesn't have anything to do with its designer, the eccentric Gordon Desmond Muirhead.

"When you do 1,200 tournaments a year, or do them back-to-back-to-back basically forever, you get things down pat," said Mike Lindsey, the director of golf at the upscale Scottsdale facility that includes the Palm and Pine courses. "Really, we've got the service for these things down to a science."

Lindsey said no matter what the tournament format (within reason) or size (36 to 500 players), it's always first-class service with a smile. That means when the J.R. McDade flooring company shows up each year for its "unique" tee party . . . hey, no problem! "They like a special contest on all 18 holes," Lindsey reported. "For instance, on one tee, you'll drive with a clubhead on the end of a hose; at another, you might use a baseball bat; and yet another requires a 2-by-4. That gets pretty wild after 18 holes."

Lindsey said McCormick Ranch has seen it all. His favorite format is the "boo-gy, birdie, bogey," which is used by a number of tournaments at the urging of his staff. "The boo-gy, birdie, bogey [format] is a typical four-person scramble, but we use all four sets of our tees," Lindsey explained. "Everybody starts on the second tee from the front, and if you make a birdie, your group moves back one set of tees; bogey a hole and you move up; par the hole and you stay where you're at. What that does is move the good players back, while your bad

Water defines the Palm Course at McCormick Ranch.

players keep moving up. It's a great way to handicap the field, because it's fun and it's fair, and really keeps things moving along."

Obviously, if you average nearly four tournaments a day, as McCormick Ranch does, you have to stay in the fast lane. "That's the biggest challenge: Doing it right almost every day, almost year-round," Lindsey conceded. "But we must be doing a lot of things really well. Since 1996, we've doubled the number of events we hold out here each year. I guess it's true. We are the 'King of the Scramble.'"

McCormick Ranch didn't start out serving up sensational hamburgers and hot dogs at tournament banquets. Originally, the golf club was the final piece, albeit the centerpiece, of a charmingly chic community by the same name developed by Kaiser Steel and Aetna Insurance in the early 1970s. It was the bizarre genius of Muirhead that put together the Palm Course in 1972, and the Pine Course the following year. True to form, Muirhead dazzled the players of the day with large bodies of water and exotic palm trees, while adding beach-like bunkers to the classically designed holes.

For nearly 20 years, McCormick Ranch ruled the resort sector specializing in golf, despite not having a hotel of its own. But time eventually caught up and passed the Pine and the Palm, especially when flashy desert layouts like Troon North and Grayhawk popped up in the early 1990s. After several years of languishing, McCormick Ranch underwent a gradual facelift in the mid-'90s, and several million dollars later was back in the thick of it. Among the improvements: 95 of the 115 bunkers were rebuilt and restored with lighter, fluffier sand; all the greens were resurfaced with tiff dwarf Bermuda; the many wooden bridges needed to traverse the water were rebuilt and accented with rock archways; some unobtrusive transition areas were added to define the course while saving water; and the clubhouse and pro shop were updated, with special attention paid to the lighting. "It's definitely back," Lindsey noted. "Remember, not everyone wants to play desert golf

courses. I think we're the perfect alternative."

Of the two courses, most prefer the Palm, which brings water into play on 10 holes. The front nine is especially fearsome for hydrophobes, with water lining Nos. 2, 3, 7, 8, and 9. The ninth hole, a 408-yard par 4, features an island fairway, and has earned numerous national honors. The best two holes on the back side—Nos. 12 and 16—also have a lot to do with the wet stuff. Adding to the ambiance, several picturesque backdrops of Camelback Mountain stand out toward the end of the round.

The Pine is more straightforward, with a myriad trees resembling small forests of the needled hazards. The fourth hole, a 536-yard par 5 that requires a 200-yard carry over water off the tee and brings water into play twice more, is set against the McDowell Mountains. The signature hole is the par-4 15th, at 470 yards. Not only is it brutal, it's also beautiful, with an island fairway and an island green. (Three bridges are required.)

The island fairway and the island green were both early trademarks popularized through Muirhead's wonderful imagination. Mixing water, palms, sand, and rocks also were Desmond's forte, and he laid a wonderful foundation of those natural elements at

McCormick Ranch. Shortly after leaving Scottsdale, he split with his architectural partner of the time, Jack Nicklaus, and went into a 10-year exile beginning in 1974. During that span, Muirhead starred as a mad scientist in the movie *The Bees*, while spending most of his time collecting and dealing artwork.

Fortunately, the Palm and the Pine were spared Muirhead's gimmicks in later years, which included a fish-shaped bunker and a "Marilyn Monroe" green, which featured two large mounds complete with nipples. "They really looked fabulous," Muirhead told *Golf Digest* of the snazzy setting at Aberdeen. "But they were removed when women objected to them."

Muirhead also once said that, "Trying to make golf fair is a waste of time. You can only give the illusion." That statement also was made after his work in Scottsdale. There is no illusion at McCormick Ranch. What you see is what you get, which is why so many tournaments call it home. The course is always in superb shape, and as Lindsey points out, the nonstop service is down to a science.

Mad science or maddening science? There's a little of both at McCormick Ranch. ⚙

OCOTILLO GOLF CLUB

PAR: 72 • YARDAGE: 5,128–6,729 • RATING: 67.7–71.4 • SLOPE: 122–131 • SIGNATURE HOLE: 332-YARD, PAR-4, №4 (WHITE) • GREEN FEES: MODERATE TO EXPENSIVE

THERE IS NO COURSE in Arizona quite like Ocotillo Golf Club. Of the 27 holes that make up the Gold, Blue, and White nines, you can get wet on 24 of them. In every way, Ocotillo is golf's version of *Waterworld*, especially when you consider it has seven miles of shoreline.

Dug out of the desert in 1986 by architect Ted Robinson, whose forte is water park–themed layouts, Ocotillo has matured into one of the Valley's finest

facilities in terms of variety and value. It's also one of the most talked about, primarily because of all that H₂0.

David Bogue, who has been the director of golf at Ocotillo since the beginning, can tell countless tales about how Ocotillo affects hydrophobes. At the same time, he said higher handicapped players have nothing to fear. "My favorite story is the one about Max Seibel, who used to cover golf for [*The Phoenix Gazette*]," said Bogue as a smile swept across his face. "I remember Max came out to the course not

long after we opened and wanted to do a little story on us. Well, he started out on the White nine, and by the fourth hole, he decided to quit. He said he'd lost two dozen balls and he was not going to lose one more ball. He wasn't mad. He said something like: 'I'll just ride the rest of the way.' It was the funniest thing, but Max was a funny guy."

Others have taken major dunks at Ocotillo, but for the most part, it's all in your head, Bogue added. "With four tee boxes on every hole, Robinson really

did take the water out of play for the higher-handi-capped players," Bogue noted. "I would say that if you play the right set of tees, there is no way you're going to lose a lot of balls." Bogue gave this exam-ple: "The Blue nine is actually the easiest of the three layouts for beginners because most of the water is taken out of play. At the same time, it's the hardest for the better players. It's all in the tee boxes—and a guy's ego."

For the most part, Bogue added, Ocotillo is a very playable golf course. "All three nines have wide fairways, generous roughs, comfortable setbacks from the housing, and more than anything, the water provides a secondary buffer zone that gives you that wide-open feeling," he noted. "Plus, there are no homes within the golf course, only around the perimeter, so you don't feel like you're playing in some housing project."

Golfers love it, too, especially the Gold nine, which combines challenge with choice green set-tings. "The Gold is probably the most popular," Bogue conceded. "At the same time, you ask three players which is their favorite, and often you'll get three different answers. The nines are that equal. I guess the Gold gets the nod because it has water on virtually every hole. At the same time, that water on the Gold is probably less of a factor than on the White or Blue nines, simply because it's right in front of you, and less intimidating unless you're a beginner."

Each nine offers numerous signature holes, although Bogue can pick out the best quickly. He likes No. 8 on the Blue, a 404-yard par 4 that demands two solid shots over water to a well bunkered green; No. 5 on the Gold, a 203-yard par 3 that requires a long iron over water to a triple-tiered green surrounded by sand; and No. 4 on the White, a 332-yard par 4, where careful club selec-tion will get you safely over the water—twice!— to a green setting that looks like it belongs in Shangri-La.

"Most people think that's our signature," Bogue said of the fourth hole on the White. "It's got those big palms, the lakes, the waterfalls, the flowers, [and] that incredible green setting on the edge of the water. But anybody who plays here often knows that the entire course is beautiful, and that's a tribute to our superintendent, Bill Todd, who has gained a national reputation [for agronomics] since we broke ground. Bill keeps the property looking like a garden oasis."

Just as impressive is Ocotillo's relatively new clubhouse, which might be referred to as South-western chic. Built out of Texas limestone and big beams of Douglas fir, and roofed with blue green, patina-coated copper, it is airy and awesome. The 27,000-square-foot building, which is built in three distinct sections (pro shop, restaurant, and cart barn), was the artistry of Scottsdale-based Nelsen Architects. "I don't know of a clubhouse in the Valley that has turned out quite as well," Bogue pro-

claimed. "We wanted an artist, not an architect. They took everything we felt was key—size, light-ing, shape, and fit—and went beyond what we had envisioned."

Bogue gives most of the credit to owner Bernie Hoogestraat, who bought the 200-acre property four years ago. "For a golf course that started out without a clubhouse, and spent its first 10 years in a temporary building, we ended up winning the lottery," Bogue said. "Bernie never spared a dime when it came time to build, which is why it turned out so right."

One of the residuals was The Ocotillo Grille, which offers some of the finest dining in the East Valley, with Wolfgang Puck disciple Michael Schook serving up wonderful dinners built around certified Angus beef. Of course, it should come as no surprise that his specialty is fish. What else would you expect to eat after a round of golf in "the Land of Lakes?" ❖

PAPAGO GOLF COURSE

Par: 72 • Yardage: 5,781–7,068 • Rating: 71.5–76.9 • Slope: 121–130 • Signature hole: 443-yard, par-4 № 18 • Green fees: inexpensive

MOST BIG CITIES have one, a popular municipal golf course where tee times are often tough to secure. But when it comes to Papago Golf Course—Phoenix's crown jewel—odds of getting on the golf course are taken to new heights.

"They just love it so much, I guess they don't mind getting in line," said Joe Huber, the longtime head pro at Papago. "I can't blame them, because this is one golf course that's worth getting in line for."

Huber's point is well-taken. Papago is such a solid golf experience that it's no surprise when 25 to 30 cars are lined up outside the front gate at dawn, all seeking nirvana in the form of a tee time. Heck, some mornings as many as 50 cars might be stretched down East Moreland Street. Would you believe those up front have been idling there since midnight? "They look at it like winning the lottery," Huber said, chuckling at the course's reputation of giving golfers a lot for their money. "The first 10 or 12 guys all get tee times [depending on the time of year], and the next 10 or 12 battle it out for standby slots. I've seen a lot of them sit around all morning before they finally get a chance to tee it up."

Fortunately, there is a silver lining for the diligent "lottery losers." They get to secure an additional tee time two days out, which means that the pressure to play Papago will subside—at least for a day or so. "It is one of the most amazing phenomenons in the Valley," Huber noted. "I know that we've been accused of being a 'country club' in the past, because the same group of guys show up daily to secure tee times. But I can't blame them one bit.

The Papago Buttes rise above the third hole.

100 courses, including famed Torrey Pines.

All of Bell's signature elements are present at Papago—traditional tee boxes and bunkers; lots of gently rolling fairways; and large, subtle greens. Bell made all of the par 3s long and interesting, with his par 4s and 5s a classic mix of movement. There is not a bad hole at Papago, a statement most other courses only wish they could make. It's also hard to choose the best nine, which is another veiled reference to Papago's overall strength.

Both the front and back nines open with reachable par 5s, and both are loaded with demanding yet delightful dogleg par 4s, which pop up at Nos. 2, 6, 7, 13, 16, and 18. Just to tie it all together, each nine closes with a bang that is backed by the surreal, redrock buttes.

Afterward, most patrons seek out the Double Eagle Restaurant, where breakfast is the main meal and lunch is dinner. For a "muni," the fare is typically straightforward, although the Papago Roll (turkey, ham, bacon, and lettuce wrapped in a jalapeños-and-cheddar tortilla) draws rave reviews. The Double Eagle also remains true to its legions, with a burger and beer that can be purchased for under $5. "We pack 'em in, and the restaurant packs 'em in," Huber said. "And everybody is happy, which is the beauty of the operation."

Mike Terek, one of the small army of assistants who helps tend to the masses, said that for the most part, everybody tows the line, literally. "Not long ago, we had a guy who came and got in line, then left his car parked while he slipped off to a nearby hotel with his girlfriend," Terek said, shaking his head at the thought. "When he came back, they wouldn't let him back in line, and it almost led to fisticuffs. But that's the way it goes out there in 'the Line.' They make up their own rules, and we have nothing to do with it until they pass through the gate. By that time, everybody is happy."

Being first off the tee at Papago Golf Course will do that to you. ✿

They are dedicated to this golf course, because it's the best value in the Phoenix area. I know that we could easily charge $40 or $50 [per green fee], instead of half that much, and still be the best course for the money. But I'm note too worried about a couple hundred guys getting all the early tee times, because a lot of other people are getting to play, too."

Huber, who took over for the legendary Arch Watkins in 1981, points to the fact that Papago usually averages 100,000 rounds a year. "Obviously, not everybody is waiting in that line," he quipped.

No, maybe they secured a tee time via the telephone. Then again, maybe not. Beginning as early as 5 A.M. each morning, the phones ring off the hook. "During peak season, we get over 500 calls each morning in rapid-fire succession," Huber added. "That means that, for about three hours each day, we have two assistants that do nothing but field phone calls. After that, it's just a steady stream all day."

What is it that makes golfers go bonkers for Papago?

"I'm prejudiced," Huber admitted, "but I think we've got it all: beauty, great design, and playability. The course keeps you in the game. It doesn't take a dozen balls like it does at Desert Mountain. Heck, some of Papago's regulars only use one ball for the whole season. Seriously."

William F. Bell, who carved Papago out of the desert landscape below the buttes of the same name in 1963, probably never knew that his efforts would be so well received. All Bell realized back then was that he was on a roll, having already designed 10 other Arizona layouts, including such beauties as Tucson Country Club and Mesa Country Club, along with Tucson's most popular municipal—Randolph Park North. Papago turned out be Bell's last work in Arizona, as he pulled up stakes shortly after and headed for California, where he constructed over

PHANTOM HORSE GOLF CLUB

PAR: 70 • YARDAGE: 4,550–5,992 • RATING: 64.6–68.2 • SLOPE: 110–124 • SIGNATURE HOLE: 244-YARD, PAR-3 №. 18 • GREEN FEES: MODERATE TO EXPENSIVE

ROM THE 18TH TEE BOX at Phantom Horse Golf Club, a player can see the entire Valley of the Sun. At that moment, you sit high atop South Mountain, with downtown Phoenix to the left, Sun Devil Stadium and Camelback Mountain straight ahead, and the landmark Four Peaks and Superstition Mountains rising off to the right. Suddenly, your score doesn't matter anymore.

"It's an awesome sight," said Bruce McNee, the director of golf at Phantom Horse. "I've probably arrived at that tee several hundred times now, and it's still special every single time." Evidently, others agree—and just not the golfers who venture out on this course designed by Phoenix architects Forrest Richardson and Jack Snyder in 1988. Apparently the Hohokam once treasured the site, as petroglyphs dating back 750 years still exist. Also taking a fancy to the spectacular view were gold miners from the early 1900s, as three abandoned mine shafts are within 100 yards of the 17th green and 18th tees.

Actually, the trip into yesteryear starts at the bag drop. Golfers who enter the course's circular driveway are immediately attracted to the 10-foot-tall bronze centerpiece designed to be the Phantom Horse. But a closer look at the rock outcropping that the statue is built on reveals the first glimpse of the rockart credited to the Hohokam.

The Phantom Horse theme was the idea of the resort's general manager, Brad Jenks, who felt the course was over-shadowed by being named after the resort. So in 1998, Jenks sacked the Pointe Hilton Golf Club at South Mountain for the catchier Phantom Horse name. There is precedent, as Phantom Horse Trail Ridge is a hikers' path that picks up near the 18th tee box and runs throughout

South Mountain Park—at 16,000 acres the largest municipal park in the world. The old trail dates back to cowboy days, when the area was known as the Heard-Bartlett Cattle Ranch.

Not surprisingly, there was a lot of commotion when environmentalists learned of the plan to drape a golf course over the eastern part of the park. After a two-and-a-half-year court battle, developer Bob Gosnell was allowed to build a scaled-back version of the course. "In the end it made for some interesting holes," Richardson said. "The [course] ended up under 70 acres. In reality, we could have used another five or six acres on those holes in question."

Even though Phantom Horse has had its critics, particularly over the tight quarters on the "holes in question"—Nos. 15, 16, and 17—no one disagrees that it's an interesting golf course. Several expansion projects in the late 1990s have improved the course's playability.

According to McNee, Phantom Horse is two courses in one. "I think that really adds to the fun factor," he said. "The first nine holes are fairly traditional, with grass tee to green, and palm trees and water thrown in to give it just a little bit of that exotic feel. The last nine holes are pure desert golf, where you need to emphasize course management if you're going to post a good score."

Phantom Horse, which features over 250 varieties of plants and over 150 species of animal life, opens with a blind tee shot to a short, dogleg par 4. Then you arrive at Nos. 2–4, a stretch that twists and turns its way around a babbling brook and series of lakes, which are accented by palms and weeping willows. The fourth hole, a medium-ranged par 4 to a partial island green is the signature. But the most challenging hole to make par on the front side is the

eighth, a lengthy par 3 that is bordered by a gold-fish-filled pond that encircles most of the green.

The variety continues on the back nine, with the 13th hole, dubbed "Jailhouse Steps" for a series of bunkers that runs up a cliff fronting the green. Go for the green in two shots and come up short, and not even a "Get Out of Jail Free" card can release you from these nasty bunkers. From the 15th hole on, it's time to club down, as tee shots into tight quarters on those three par 4s take the driver out of most players' hands. Then you arrive at the wonderment of the 18th, which at 244 yards and a drop of nearly 100 feet, makes for a most intriguing conclusion.

What's cool is that, unlike most public facilities in Arizona, Phantom Horse offers its players the luxury of a shower and massage in the resort's new Phantom Horse Sports Club, perhaps the Valley's most state-of-the-art training facility. With a whirlpool and steam room also available for aching muscles, no wonder so many players leave the course feeling as if they've just struck it rich, much like those who came before them.

Which brings up one last tale of the Phantom Horse. As legend has it, a herd of wild mustangs once roamed South Mountain Park, led by a white stallion with a dark mask. Yes, the Phantom Horse! As Phoenix eventually grew from a small settlement to a city, the herd was captured and tamed—all except the Phantom Horse, whose wild heart and spirit kept him faster than any wrangler's rope. Sure, it's a bit of a reach. At the same time, there is some lore that a golfer just wants to believe. ☼

The signature par-5 13th hole at Phantom Horse is called "Jailhouse Steps."

THE PHOENICIAN GOLF CLUB

Par: 71 • Yardage: 4,852–6,327 • Rating: 67.8–70.3 • Slope: 112–131 • Signature hole: 379-yard, par-4 № 9 (Oasis) • Green fees: expensive

IKE THE RESORT of the same name, The Phoenician Golf Club is elegant and exotic. From its par 3s high on the cliffs of Camelback Mountain, the views are simply out of this world. Adding to the ambiance are exquisite par 4s and 5s that weave their way through the ubiquitous palms, as well as a myriad lakes and waterfalls.

This could be the French Riviera or Hawaii. Actually, there's a little of both, which was purely by design. It all fits together in a bizarre tale of riches gone wrong. At the same time, what was left in the wake has become the Valley's monument to fun in the sun.

John Jackson, director of golf since 1989, remembers the fall of former Phoenician owner, Charles Keating who was convicted for his role in one of the largest savings and loan scams of all time. "I'll never forget it—Nov. 16, 1989," recalled Jackson. "That was the night when the hotel's management received termination notices from the Resolution Trust Corporation (RTC), which had taken over Keating's savings and loan empire. Jackson also has witnessed the resort's rise from the ashes, to a splendor that seems to unfold daily.

To its credit, The Phoenician continues to set standards for being the "best of the best." The resort is annually rated as a five-star retreat, and the golf course is getting better by the moment, with variety and views, as well as excellent service, paving the way.

It wasn't always so. Once upon a time, way back in the 1960s and '70s, this very ground was the site of Valley Country Club. But a group of Canadians bought the old golf course and razed it. In its place Phoenix architect Jack Snyder built The Phoenician Golf Club, which opened with the resort in 1978. "Jack really did a good job on the first course," said

Jackson, one of the best players in the Southwest Section of the PGA, and the owner of the course record at The Phoenician with a fabulous 58. "But after Keating bought the resort in the mid-1980s, he brought in Homer Flint, who totally redesigned it. I think Keating spent something like $10 million and told Homer to give it the Hawaiian look. That was one of Keating's things: He loved Hawaii and Europe, and the golf course ended up accordingly, while the resort has a European look."

Keating's Phoenician opened in the fall of 1988, with the original 18 holes boasting 10,000 palm trees. Jackson laughs at the memory. "He had a palm tree nursery in Florida, and he brought in a back -hoe and just kept planting them. But over time, we've taken out a couple of thousand trees, mainly because they were blocking out the irrigation system and creating brown spots on the fairways."

There have been other changes of note. For instance, architect Ted Robinson added nine more holes in the mid-1990s and redesigned several of Flint's originals. Robinson, who is known for his creative use of water, proved to be the perfect answer. That gave The Phoenician 27 holes: the Oasis, Desert, and Canyon nines, the latter being the majority of the work done by Robinson.

"Two things you need to remember when you play here," Jackson advised. "Don't try to overpower the course, because length is not the key; it's accuracy. Second, everything breaks away from Camelback Mountain more than you think it does."

Most golfers regard the Canyon, which climbs to the highest points allowed on Camelback Mountain (1,500 feet), to be the most solid stretch of holes. Robinson did the first seven, and closed it out by bringing the layout back to the old 17th and 18th holes. The Desert, which rambles around

Camelback Mountain, includes numerous redesigns and two new holes. The Oasis, where most of the water and palms are found, is the original front nine.

What's great about The Phoenician is that each nine sports numerous signature holes and distinct features. Among the highlights: the Canyon has back-to-back par 3s at Nos. 7 and 8 that require a shot over water to picturesque greens; the Desert's par-3 diamonds are the sixth and eighth holes, which are built on the cliffs of Camelback with vistas that are to die for, even if a rattlesnake warning greets golfers near the sixth green; and the Oasis not only offers marble-lined bathrooms complete with ceiling fans in the on-course restrooms, it also is where you'll find the awesome ninth hole, a dynamic dog-leg par 4 to a green fronted by water and backed by a palm forest.

The resort is even more magnifico. Keating scoured Europe for paintings, rugs, and other artsy things. The hallways are palatial, the rooms regal. There has been no expense spared, as pricey rates keep the property in a state of richness reserved for royalty. A prime example is Mary Elaine's, the restaurant christened in the name of Keating's wife. There might not be a better place to dine in the Phoenix-Scottsdale area, especially with revered chef Jim Boyce in the kitchen. "Without question, it's the best restaurant in the Southwest," noted Jackson, who is backed up by Mary Elaine's 5-diamond rating.

The Phoenician has always been the top of the line, even in its darkest moment. "Funny thing about those RTC guys," Jackson said, smiling at the thought. "I never saw them again after that night. They just disappeared." ⚙

The Phoenician boasts three nines.

POINTE GOLF CLUB ON LOOKOUT MOUNTAIN

· ·

PAR: 72 · YARDAGE: 4,326–6,535 · RATING: 65.3–71.2 · SLOPE: 113–135 · SIGNATURE HOLE: 510-YARD, PAR-5 № 18 · GREEN FEES: EXPENSIVE

FEW GOLFERS who journey to the Pointe Golf Club on Lookout Mountain know how close the Bill Johnston–designed course came to being the host site of the Phoenix Open. Or realize that the Pointe would have been the first-ever Tournament Players Club in PGA Tour history. But in golfing parlance, "the TPC on Lookout Mountain" turned out to be a "lipout" for the prestigious Hilton resort known as the Pointe at Tapatio Cliffs.

The scenario unfolded in the mid-1980s, when PGA Tour officials led by then-Commissioner Deane Beman toured the canyons and hillsides of the

Phoenix Mountain Preserve, which is nestled just to the north and east of Tapatio Cliffs. They liked what they saw, but, then-Phoenix Mayor Margaret Hance and a group of area environmentalists had other ideas, and a TPC golf course was not one of them.

"I remember it well," said Bob Brooks, the general manager of the Pointe at Tapatio Cliffs. "[Designer] Pete Dye came out with Beman, and they met with Mayor Hance and Eddie Lynch of the [Phoenix] Thunderbirds. We were excited, because it looked like we might become the host of the Phoenix Open, and in the process become the first-ever TPC course on the PGA Tour. But then everything got politically sideways with the Phoenix

Mountain Preserve people, and to make a long story short, it didn't happen. In retrospect, had things been different, we would have kept the Phoenix Open in Phoenix, rather than have it move to the TPC of Scottsdale. But it just wasn't meant to be."

Instead, Johnston was hired to erect the Pointe Golf Club on Lookout Mountain into a hilly terrain that was limited by the boundaries of the 11,000-acre preserve. To his credit, the Phoenix architect did a wonderful job, incorporating several different design techniques into the 6,535-yard layout that opened in 1989.

"Billy built the course into three distinct stretches," Brooks added. "The first six holes are relatively flat, and traditionally grass from tee to green. Beginning at No. 7, the course really takes off, with lots of elevation and views, and a more target style of golf. The last six holes are a combination of both traditional and desert [golf], with lots of mountains and water hazards along the way."

If there is a hole that embodies all of Lookout Mountain's traits, it is the relatively short, par-5 18th. At 510 yards, a big drive can set you up for a classic risk-reward situation on your second shot, but beware the island green. The only entrance point is a narrow, 10-yard alley on the left side, and because the green is relatively shallow, second shots tend to take a couple of hops and bound off the back side into a watery grave.

No wonder NBC's made-for-TV Skills Challenge chose the palm-laden 18th at Lookout Mountain for its setting from 1994 to '96. The event probably would have remained at the Pointe had NBC not quadrupled the site fee in '97, sending

Namesake Lookout Mountain rises up in the background.

the Skills Challenge scurrying to California. "They loved us, but we couldn't afford them," Brooks sighed. "But along the way we made some incredible friendships with participants like Arnold Palmer, Chi Chi Rodriguez, John Daly, Hale Irwin, and a kid named David Duval."

Duval was another interesting story, Brooks added. "[International Management Group] made us a package deal with Palmer and Duval, who at that time was a virtual unknown," Brooks recalled. "I remember the guys at NBC saying to me, 'David Duval? Why do we have to take him?'"

The Skills Challenge was not the Pointe on Lookout Mountain's only brush with professional golf. It also hosted the Arizona Classic on the Senior PGA Tour. "The very first day we opened the course we put on the Classic," Brooks said. "The plan was for us to host that tournament for two years, but a guy named [Jack] Nicklaus got involved shortly after that, and the next year The Tradition at Desert Mountain came along and we were gone."

But not forgotten.

"Over the past 10 years we've tweaked the course a few times, rebuilt six greens and five tee boxes, and widened four fairways by taking out some of the transition areas," Brooks explained. "But for the most part, it's the same course we started out with—one of the great amenities at a world-class resort."

There are other things you will enjoy about the golf experience at Lookout Mountain. First of all, everything—lodging, restaurants, shopping, and other forms of recreation—can be found without leaving the 172-acre site. And hiking and horseback riding are basically just out the back door. But best of all, there is the Pointe in Tyme Bar and Grill, which serves as the course's illustrious 19th hole. With nearly every type of exotic wood in the world molded into the massive bar area, and an equally expansive array of beers on tap [including root beer], it's a terrific way to top off a long day of golf.

No doubt fans of the Phoenix Open would have loved the place, if only . . . ⚙

THE RAVEN GOLF CLUB AT SABINO SPRINGS

· ·

PAR: 71 · YARDAGE: 4,752–6,926 · RATING: 66.6–73.2 · SLOPE: 112–144 · SIGNATURE HOLE: 513-YARD, PAR-5 № 18 · GREEN FEES: EXPENSIVE

FEW GOLF COURSES in Arizona move like the Raven at Sabino Springs. From a low point of 2,500 feet, it soars up the side of the Catalina Mountains some 400 to 500 feet. Twisting and turning, sliding and gliding, it's hard to stay on your feet.

Of course, architect Robert Trent Jones Jr. planned it that way. "Great elevation changes give the course a third dimension," says Jones, who carved the Raven at Sabino Springs out of these foothills in 1996. "They keep you on your toes in every way." For the most part, the Raven is a difficult but fair layout. It would have been more tenacious had Jones not softened his original design, but 86 bunkers are still a lot for a course that hops up and down the slope as quickly as the Raven. However, had the changes not been made, the Raven would be so severe that there would be no time to appreciate its beauty—and it is gorgeous! The view from the tee box at the signature 18th hole is so incredible that on a clear day a player can see all the way to Mexico, almost 100 miles to the south.

One thing must be said about Robert Trent Jones Jr., the oldest son of the legendary designer of

A sea of saguaros define the Raven at Sabino Springs.

the same name: He has vision. And fortitude, as he stuck with the project for several years before it finally got off the ground. "The Raven at Sabino Springs was a long and arduous story," Jones recalled. "The environmental concerns were so huge that it ended up going all the way to the Arizona Supreme Court before they finally said we could build a golf course on that mountain. Then when it finally [was approved], they had some concerns about the difficulty."

Sabino Springs, which gets its name from the nearby canyon as well as the nine natural springs found on the property, specializes in variety, views, and wildlife. The environment remains pure and sacred. Over 2,500 saguaros were revegetated during the construction, along with 60,000 desert plants.

Kirk Kokoska, the original head pro at the Raven at Sabino Springs and the current vice president of golf operations for Intrawest, which purchased the course from Larry Lippon in 1998, remembers the extremely sensitive nature of the building process. "There was a horticulturist moving out in front of the bulldozer when they scraped the fairways, and she was looking for ruins, watching out for plants, and trying to scare all of the animals away," Kokoska recalled. "That was the kind of stuff that was going on back then."

Nature rewarded the Raven's gentle approach with a knockout golf course. The first hole is straightforward; then these fabulous fairways and greens take flight. By the time a player reaches the 321-yard, par-4 third hole, an amazing 75-foot climb to a green saddlebacked into the Catalinas, the "oohs" and "aahs" are everywhere. The fourth hole, a 184-yard tee shot back down the mountain, is one of the state's most stunning—and scary— par 3s. Below you lies all of Tucson and a green that appears to be the size of a backyard swimming pool.

About the only controversial section of the Raven is the ninth, 10th, and 11th holes, a 223-yard par 3 followed by a 433-yard par 4 that seem to backpack their way upward to the Raven's highest

point before a blind tee shot at the 625-yard 11th starts your descent. "People take potshots at blind shots these days," Jones said in defense. "Back in the old days, blind shots were the quirky strengths of the greatest courses in the world, and they were applauded. Today, people call them 'invisible' and 'hard to read.' Personally, I think the tee shot [at the 11th] is a wonderful diversion. I think it adds character. You can feel that shot off the tee even if you can't see it."

Any pileups are forgiven by the home stretch, as the 16th through 18th holes—a par 4, 3, and 5— offer a wonderful mixed bag. The best shot comes at the 513-yard No. 18, and it will be taken with your camera. Of course, the drive is just as good, as it falls approximately 75 feet to a well-bunkered fairway lined all the way down the left side with water.

There are other things to like about Sabino Springs. The course has assumed a major role in the Tucson golf community, and serves as the home course for the University of Arizona and neighboring Sabino High School. Among its brief history, the

1998 Arizona Amateur was played here, as was the 1997 Women's Pac-10 Championship. "It's just been the philosophy of the Raven since the beginning," Kokoska noted. "If Arizona State didn't already have a home course, we'd probably have them at the Raven at South Mountain (in Phoenix)."

Kokoska said every effort is made by Intrawest to run both Ravens in similar fashion, with an emphasis on service, course maintenance, and dramatic designs. "I love both, but the Raven at Sabino Springs is the more spectacular," he said. "There are so many great holes there that, really, it's hard to decide which one is the signature, although most people lean toward the 18th."

Jones, whose younger brother Rees also is a well-known architect, said that was in his original plans, too. "The reason there are so many signature-type holes," he said with a wink, "is because we Jones boys like to write our names all over our golf courses."

Yes, this one came out pure Robert Trent Jones Jr. ☼

THE RAVEN GOLF CLUB AT SOUTH MOUNTAIN

PAR: 72 • YARDAGE: 5,544–7,056 • RATING: 68.8–73.9 • SLOPE: 124–133 • SIGNATURE HOLE: 221-YARD, PAR-4 №7 • GREEN FEES: EXPENSIVE

Once upon a midnight dreary, while I pondered,
weak and weary,
Over many a quaint and curious volume of
forgotten lore—
While I nodded nearly napping, suddenly there
came a tapping,
As of some one gently rapping, rapping at my
chamber door.

—EDGAR ALLEN POE
The Raven

HERE IS SOMETHING poetic in his stance, this jet-black Raven that stands like a butler—complete with tux and tails—outside the restaurant's door. Or perhaps this overstuffed character immortalized by Edgar Allen Poe is actually a bow-tied waiter, an assumption that stems from the silver platter that is offered from his wing tips. Nay, you say! This is merely the 5-foot-tall mascot that stands like a sentry overlooking the entrance to perhaps the most service-oriented golf club in Arizona, not to mention one of the finest.

Welcome to the Raven at South Mountain, good sir!, where this "Big Bird" gets spirits soaring daily. "Everybody thinks he's cool," said Dwight Wintringer, a burly Chicagoan who has transformed the Raven's restaurant into one of Phoenix's most sought-after lunch spots. There is a great deal of symbolism in the Raven's feathered friend, who seems so set on satisfaction. It's the same at the golf course, where no amenity is spared in treating everyone like "a houseguest."

Whether it's a special message flashed to the clubhouse and quickly responded to via the Global Positioning System that serves as radar for each cart, or the misters that can be summoned in seconds for instant heat relief, or the iced, mango-scented towels—a Raven original—your wish is their command. "Our people make it special," said John Gunby, the club's director of golf. "You can have the greatest golf course in the world, but if the people that work there aren't really into it, it won't go."

Few, however, go as hard and as far as the Raven when it comes to meeting a golfer's every need. Marshals are called "player assistants," a far less threatening term, and even the golf carts are allowed to travel off the cart paths in 90-degree fashion, almost unheard of at most of the top daily-fees courses in Arizona. "Everyone is family," Gunby reiterated. "Especially our guests." And to the club's credit, even though it was sold in 1998 to corporate giant Intrawest, the down-home feel remains rock-solid.

Yep, nothing much has changed since the former team of Gary Panks and David Graham created the Raven out of a cotton field. In every way, it is regarded as one of their most impressive works, along with Grayhawk Talon, Tonto Verde, and

A lake divides No. 1 and No. 18 at the Raven.

hockey tough guy Jeremy Roenick, and many of the Arizona Diamondbacks. "We're the host course for the Diamondbacks, which is why Diamondback Chicken is one of our more popular entrées," Wintringer noted, citing a barbecue shrimp BLT complete with melted brie as the course's favorite concoction.

Of course, it helps when everything comes with a big smile, especially the golf. There is no mystery to unravel here, like some poem from the dark but dynamic Edgar Allen Poe: "This I sat engaged in guessing, but no syllable expressing/To the fowl whose fiery eyes now burned into my bosom's core..../Quoth the Raven, 'Nevermore.'" ✸

Chaparral Pines. If moving nearly 800,000 cubic yards of dirt wasn't enough to make it unique, then 7,100 pine trees certainly set it apart. Maturity has made it the "Shadow Creek of Arizona." "Some of those trees were just 6 feet high when we opened," Gunby recalled. "I know, because I planted quite a few of them. Today, some of them are 30 to 40 feet tall. You can hardly tell you're in the middle of Phoenix."

Those mini-pine forests make each fairway and green like a private drive, separate and serene. With houses only on the perimeter of the course, many hidden behind branches, golf doesn't get much better. Playable or plenty tough, take your pick, as Gunby points to the fact that the Raven has hosted the Arizona State Stroke Play Championship three times, the U.S. Open qualifying for both men and women, a Southwest Section Championship, and numerous major tournaments for the Junior Golf Association of Arizona. "The course always holds its own," he said with a certain sense of pride.

The initial six holes are a wonderful warm-up for No. 7, the signature par 3 that requires a 220-yard shot over water to a green guarded by an enormous bunker on the left. But, hey, the beach is better than the wet stuff, right? The back nine is good throughout, especially the stretch beginning at the short, par-4 15th, a superb dogleg that backdrops against South Mountain. Many mistakenly think the 18th, a penalty-laden par 4 that hangs precariously close to a small lake and waterfall, is the signature hole. Perhaps that is because the European archway that dissects the water looks so elegant? "Actually, what makes the course so neat is that it has all the shots," Gunby explained. "Short and long par 5s, long and short par 4s, all kinds of par 3s. Take your pick."

The Raven also has one of the top instructional studios in the Valley in the Raven Learning and Performance Center headed by Zach Padgett. PGA Tour veteran Andrew Magee represents the course, which explains why more than one golf commercial has been shot on this location. The course also is a frequent gathering spot for such notable hackers as ex-NBA stars Michael Jordan and Charles Barkley,

SEDONA GOLF RESORT

PAR: 71 • YARDAGE: 5,069–6,642 • RATING: 67.0–70.6 • SLOPE: 114–129 • SIGNATURE HOLE: 210-YARD, PAR-3 № 10 • GREEN FEES: MODERATE

STARING OUT at the surreal red rocks that surround Sedona Golf Resort, a visitor suddenly realizes the major obstacle of teeing it up here. Yes, the chief challenge is simply keeping focused on the game at hand.

Panoramic vistas, sweeping mountain backdrops, and contrasting tones of red and green are boundless. "The golf course was an immediate success from Day One," noted John Benzel, who was among a group of 35 investors who hired Gary Panks to design Sedona Golf Resort, which opened in 1988. "It was amazing. Anybody that played here always wanted to come back. You look around . . . it's pretty easy to see why."

Benzel, who served as the head pro at Sedona Golf Resort until his retirement in December 1999, probably knows more about this gorgeous golf course than any man alive. He loves it, even though it's taken a toll in blood, sweat, and tears. As hard as it is to imagine, Sedona Golf Resort went bust in late 1989 before it became a raging success in the '90s under Phoenix-based SunCor Development. "We got caught in a down draft of the real estate market," Benzel recalled of the humbling experience. "We used the golf course as collateral for a $4 million loan, and when the economy went down, they took the golf course."

A Swiss company claimed Sedona Golf Resort out of bankruptcy, and decided to stick with "the

Silver Fox of the Red Rocks," as Benzel is affectionately known. "I'd like to think it was because I was a good guy," Benzel said, smirking. "But the reality was, I knew every nook and cranny on the golf course, and they needed someone to pick up the pieces. So I hung on with the Swiss, and caught on later with SunCor."

The 306-acre parcel, which has been the setting for approximately 40 television and movie westerns, was sold to SunCor for the modest price of $13 million in 1995. Even though SunCor has developed the property extensively, there still is no better place in the Sedona area to play golf while having that "Kodak moment."

"Obviously, this is one of the most beautiful places on Earth," Benzel noted. "But even more than that, it's a great golf course, one that requires some thinking. It's also quite consistent. Usually, you'll find a hole or two on each course that's a dog. Here, there are no dogs."

Panks eases a player into the playing ground, but from No. 4 on there is no letup as you climb the ridge to the 10th tee box, the highest point. Not surprisingly, this awesome outpost, an incredible, 210-yard par 3 that points directly at Cathedral Rock, is the signature offering.

"We didn't necessarily plan the course that way [for the front nine to play up the hill and the back nine back down]. It just turned out like that," noted Benzel, who worked side by side with Panks during the construction. "I call Gary's design 'geographic dictation,' meaning the holes roll, or fit together, with the definition of the land. The whole package

LEFT: *The par-4 8th hole shares a green with No. 5.*

OPPOSITE: *The 210-yard, par 3 10th hole is the signature.*

just works very well, because by the time you get to No. 9 [a steep par 5], you're starting to wear down a little. But you've also made the turn, and now you're heading for the barn."

The 10th hole is not the only par 3 that is a knockout. The 17th, a 155-yard shot over water to a green framed by those rusty-colored rocks, also is worthy of signature status. Another terrific test is the fifth hole, a legitimate, 3-shot par 5 that plays 623 yards uphill to a huge double green it shares with No. 8, one of the many terrific par 4s along with Nos. 4, 6, 11, 13 ,15, 16, and 18. "Actually, there are those who claim every hole on the course is their favorite," Benzel chuckled.

Despite going years without a permanent club-house, Sedona Golf Resort also struck it rich in that category in 1996, with a smashing version of cowboy chic. Perhaps the most incredible feature of the 17,000-square-foot building is its huge picture window that faces due north, framing mystical Bell Rock like a painting. The 19th hole is the perfect place to enjoy the local brew—Oak Creek Amber Ale.

For those who seek culinary adventures, Sedona offers a smorgasbord, from the relaxed atmosphere of the Wild Toucan (near the course) to the exquisite fare of Heartline Cafe, Rene, Joey Bistro, and L'Auberge de Sedona. And for the pure and simple palate, there is the old roadside grocery store at Fudian Gardens, a throwback that boasts some of the best deli sandwiches in America. (Yes, the bread is homemade and all the fixin's are organic!)

Of course, there are so many other must-see sights in Sedona, which is known for its New Age philosophy, vortex activity, and Pink Jeep tours. Other inspirations include the Chapel of the Holy Cross, a Frank Lloyd Wright–inspired cathedral, and the world famous art galleries found at Los Abrigados and Tlaquepaque Village.

Naturally, most golfers realize that the real masterpiece of the red rocks is Sedona Golf Resort. Benzel, who still teaches at the course and does consulting work for SunCor, knows the secret of the course's success. "For most people, once is not enough," Benzel said. "Sure, it's spectacular, but it's also pretty darn good."

The statement seems slightly contradictory, but given the laid-back nature of the Silver Fox of the Red Rocks, most people get the message. ☼

SUNRIDGE CANYON GOLF CLUB

PAR: 72 • YARDAGE: 5,122–6,787 • RATING: 66.9–73.4 • SLOPE: 117–140 • SIGNATURE HOLE: 142–209 YARD, PAR-3 № 17 • GREEN FEES: EXPENSIVE

IMAGINATION on the golf course is considered to be a wonderful attribute. But get too creative when it comes to *building* a golf course, and you can get yourself in trouble with today's rating teams, which seem to prefer the traditional styles of yesteryear.

Give architect Keith Foster and SunCor Development credit. They dared to be different when it came to SunRidge Canyon Golf Club. In fact, the initial burst of creative thinking came right from the get-go, as Foster decided that a links style of layout, or one that featured nonreturning nines (to the clubhouse) was the best route for constructing this course in a tricky canyon that drops 600 feet down the side of the McDowell Mountains.

Foster had two choices in routing the course. He could put the clubhouse at the top of the canyon and let it flow down the hill and back, creating two nonreturning nines. Or, he could put the clubhouse in the middle of the course with returning nines. "There were other considerations, like housing," Foster said. "But eventually we settled on putting the clubhouse at the top of the golf course. I guess the big drop could be considered a negative, but nonreturning nines didn't bother me at all. All the great golf courses in the world, from Pine Valley to Pebble Beach to St. Andrews, have nonreturning nines. I knew we could make a great golf course if we just concentrated hard on the golf."

What Foster didn't know was that SunRidge Canyon would be a little bit more complicated than even he suspected. Originally, he was told that the clubhouse would go up on the ridge that overlooks the property. But because of housing considerations,

SunRidge Canyon is Keith Foster's masterpiece.

out for Tom [Patrick]," Foster recalled. "He said to me, 'What are you thinking,' and I told him about this punch bowl green I'd played in Ireland. I said, 'It's kind of different . . .' and before I could finish the sentence, he said, 'Let's do it.' I was so impressed, because a lesser guy never would have gone for such a radical idea. As it turned out, we all fell in love with the hole. I'm not sure everyone agrees, but a lot of golfers finish it and say, 'Gee, I'd like to have another crack at it.'"

Actually the same could be said for most of SunRidge Canyon, especially the last six holes, which form one of the most demanding stretches of golf in Arizona. And true to the management's nature, they have fun with it. For example, Jeff Lessig, the director of golf, said brainstorming sessions have gone long into the night trying to capitalize on the reputation of those last six holes. "The typical reaction we get is: 'That last six holes really kicked my but,'" Lessig said, laughing mischievously. "We thought maybe we should dub it 'The Wicked Six,' and put 'I Survived the Wicked Six' on the back of our SunRidge Canyon caps."

Foster laughs at such a notion. But there is no such thing as a bad idea, he said. "If a golf course has certain holes that really stand out, and there are so many of them at SunRidge Canyon, my opinion is that's what really makes a great golf course," he said. "And it's true, playing at SunRidge Canyon is an adventure, and it's a fun one."

It is an amazing trip. Obviously, others agree because SunRidge Canyon already has hosted one national championship, the 1998 USGA's National State Team Tournament for men.

Yep, SunRidge Canyon deserves a tip of the golf cap. They dared to be different and *still* earned their national ranking [No. 42] from *Golf Magazine* as one of the "Top 100 Courses You Can Play." ✿

---

it was pushed below, cutting about 100 yards off the first hole. "The first hole was supposed to go back up the hillside, but then that became the clubhouse and a parking lot," Foster noted. "Thank goodness, I was working with [SunCor Vice President] Tom Patrick, and every time we ran into a problem, he was right there to help fix it."

The positive was that a lot of the golf course didn't have houses on it, Foster explained. The negative was that some of the greens, because of the sharper drop, were not as receptive as he had hoped. "Yeah, those first few greens are kind of tough on approach shots, especially the one at the third hole, because from tee to green, that hole drops 75 feet, so the green naturally falls away," Foster conceded. "But SunRidge Canyon just forced us into some very unique settings, and what I'm most proud of is that the course fits beautifully into the land that

it was built on. We took what God gave us, and moved only 150,000 [square] yards of dirt, which is minimal by today's standards."

Foster said a lot of the course's success reflects directly on SunCor, "because they allowed me to do a lot of different things, which in turn provided the course with a lot of different looks." That variety Foster spoke of starts at No. 1, a driveable par 4. Along the way a player also experiences a unique dogleg with a double carry-over transition at No. 7; a blind approach at No. 9; cross bunkers at No 10; a partial island green at No. 14; and a double tee box at No. 17 that allows a player two distinct angles to the green, one from 150 yards and the other from 210.

But the most unusual hole at SunRidge Canyon is the par-5 16th, which features a blind shot to a punch bowl green. "I had just gotten back from playing golf in Ireland, and I was sketching the hole

TALKING STICK GOLF CLUB

. . . .

NORTH: PAR: 70 • YARDAGE: 5,530–7,133 • RATING: 70.0–73.8 • SLOPE: 116–125 • SIGNATURE HOLE: 261-YARD, PAR-3 N⁰ 11 • GREEN FEES: MODERATE TO EXPENSIVE

SOUTH: PAR: 71 • YARDAGE: 5,248–6,818 • RATING: 69.1–72.7 • SLOPE: 101–126 • 323-YARD, PAR-4 N⁰ 18 • GREEN FEES: MODERATE TO EXPENSIVE

TALKING STICK GOLF CLUB takes its name from the traditional Pima calendar stick, an ornately carved wooden branch that the Salt River Pima–Maricopa Indian Community uses to mark significant events in the tribe's history. Appropriately, 1997 holds a special place on the talking stick.

That was the year the architectural team of Ben Crenshaw and Bill Coore carved the North and South courses out of the desert landscape now known as Talking Stick Golf Club. That the 36-hole facility turned out so superbly is a tribute to Crenshaw and Coore, as well as Troon Golf management and the Indians who own the land.

"Bill and I were given a lot of latitude, and I think that was the key," said Crenshaw, the PGA Tour star who has built 16 golf courses across the country with the help of Coore. "I don't know if we've ever had a project that went so well. There was not one problem at all. Perhaps that's why the courses turned out so beautifully. Not only that, but they really do exude enough variety that they complement each other perfectly."

So if latitude, and not attitude, are what a golfer seeks, Talking Stick is a solid fit. With a green fee that hovers around $100 during peak season, the courses are a bargain in the Phoenix-Scottsdale market, which explains why the supermarket-sized parking lot is always full. "Mostly, our customers talk about playability, the fantastic bunkering and the top-notch conditioning of the golf courses, which is as good as you'll find in the Valley," noted Scott Heideman, the director of golf at Talking Stick since its inception. "The views of Camelback Mountain, Pinnacle Peak, Four Peaks, and Red Mountain also are incredible. Plus, it's very pure: No houses in sight, nor will there ever be."

The only real neighbor, so to speak, is Casino Arizona, which rises up at the end of the driving range, a symbol of the wealth that helped the Salt River Pima–Maricopas build the golf courses in the first place. That Talking Stick turned out to be such a wise investment is a credit to the skills of Crenshaw and Coore, and to the vision of Troon Golf, which manicured the project to the point of perfection. The presence of the Golf Digest Schools, which are headed by noted instructor Tim Mahoney, also adds to Talking Stick's presence.

Of the two, the North is the front-runner, having opened in the fall of '97. Long, wide, and playing to a rugged par of 70, it's a hitter's ball park in every way. With eight of the 12 par 4s stretching out for more than 430 yards, as well as a par 3 of 261 and a par 5 that goes 582, this is one tremendous test of golf at 7,133 yards. No wonder the PGA Tour holds its first-stage qualifying school at Talking Stick each year.

The truth of the matter is, when played all the

The South Course features tree-lined fairways.

way back, most amateurs have bitten off more than they can chew. Especially when the Scottish-styled bunkers, which feature lips that rival Mick Jagger's, are added into the equation. But when the North is shortened to 6,500 yards (5,500 for the ladies), it can be very player friendly. Numerous holes stand out, such as Nos. 3, 5, 6, 8, 11, 12, 13, 17, and 18. Of that bunch, the par-3 11th, called "Brassie," can be more like a driver when played at 261 yards. It's a simply spectacular hole, with wild grasses sprouting from the crater-like, greenside bunker and mountains in the background. Others agree that the North is a superior tract, as *Golfweek* magazine selected it No. 82 on its top 100 list of "America's Best Modern Courses."

The South's niche is tree-lined fairways and lots of mounds that break up the desert look with more of a traditional feel. In all, 4,500 cottonwoods,

sycamores, eucalyptuses, and acacias were planted. In the next five years or so, the South might actually become the preferred golf course. At the moment, the par 3s are super strong, ranging from 125 to 228 yards, meaning every club in the bag can be used. The closing stretch—the par-5 16th, par-3 17th, and par-4 18th—all bring water into play. The final exam, the 323-yard 18th called "Judgment," earns the signature status, with lots of bunkers on the left and the wet stuff doglegging its way down the right side.

"They're just two totally different courses," Heideman observed. "But both offer a wonderful golf experience, and just as important, a source of pride for the Salt River Pima–Maricopa Indian Community." This is especially true of the unique, Native American–themed clubhouse at Talking Stick. The $3-million facility, which was created by tying together a series of indoor and outdoor rooms, was made of straw-and-mud adobe bricks similar to those used by the tribe's forefathers. Stick roofs, rough-sawn timbers, and trellises with a rusted patina finish add to the architectural flair of yesteryear, as does an open fireplace and rock-lined firepit. Just as

interesting are the artifacts on display throughout the pro shop and restaurant, which include pottery, baskets, and artwork that date back to the early 1900s. And, yes, they sell talking sticks, along with other Native American–inspired gifts. The menu also includes such delicacies as a fry bread taco, a tribe favorite.

Ironically, the restaurant, which is open for dinner on the weekends under the guidance of Chef Roy Pfund, is called the Wildhorse Grille. Yes, there actually is a herd of wild mustangs that roam just outside the fences of Talking Stick, and mountain lions occasionally frolic in the bunkers. (Relax, they're mostly nocturnal!) But that's the beauty of Talking Stick. It's a slightly different golf experience that offers a lot of options while subtly exposing its guests to the Salt River Pima–Maricopa legacy.

"I'm happy for [the tribe], and proud that Bill and I did the golf courses," Crenshaw said in his nasal, Texas twang. "I like the North Course just a tad better, which might surprise some people after they play the South. But I guess the best thing is, there's just a little bit of something for everyone out there." ⚙

TOURNAMENT PLAYERS CLUB OF SCOTTSDALE

PAR: 71 • YARDAGE: 5,567–6,992 • RATING: 68.7–74.4 • SLOPE: 122–133 • SIGNATURE HOLE: 501-YARD, PAR-5 № 15 • GREEN FEES: EXPENSIVE

F THE 28 GOLF COURSES that make up the Tournament Players Club chain managed by the PGA Tour, none can do what the TPC of Scottsdale can: Give more than 100,000 spectators an unobstructed view of the action—all at once.

No wonder over 400,000 fans jam through the turnstiles of the Phoenix Open every year. What better tournament to watch the game's biggest stars? With spectator mounds virtually everywhere, watching a professional golf tournament never has been quite this easy. But what about all of those hills and dales—don't they make for a rather surreal landscape for the golfers?

"That's the amazing thing," said Paul Azinger, who captured the very first Phoenix Open held at the TPC of Scottsdale in 1987. "The course was set up to handle all of those fans, and it still turned out to be an excellent track." The tour wanted Tom Weiskopf and Jay Morrish to build a "golf arena" in Scottsdale that could handle the largest crowds in professional golf. Only the pride of one of the greatest architectural teams of all time made it the great test it is today.

"Truthfully, I'm surprised it turned out that good," admitted Weiskopf, who said that they had so many things working against them. The site was as "flat as a pancake," the contractor specialized in roads and had never built a golf course, the duo's already small budget was cut by $1 million halfway through the work, and even though they had babysat the project since Day One, the course still fell four months behind schedule. "Every decision had to be made 'right now,'" Weiskopf said. "It was awful. I hated the fact that we had to fast-track it."

But somehow, Weiskopf added, the finished product came out pretty well. "The front nine [is]

the more difficult of the nines, and that's something not everyone picks up on," he said. "The back side, however, is a great test, lots of risk-reward situations, especially those last four holes, where so much can happen. The funny thing is, of all those TPCs, it's probably had the least amount of change since it opened, even though we have gone back on numerous occasions to refine the product."

Weiskopf has been the "tinkerer," with touch-ups coming at eight of the 18 holes. In addition, the greens have been redone numerous times, the most recent renovation coming in 1998, when the surfaces were switched from bentgrass to a tiff dwarf overseed, which made them faster and firmer. "The course is playing now like it was meant to play in the beginning," Weiskopf said. "The championship feel has been restored [and] the TPC's one-of-a-kind nature has allowed the [Phoenix Open] to flourish like few could have imagined."

Technically, the TPC of Scottsdale is a municipal golf course owned by the city and leased to the PGA Tour. But the reality is that, with a $150-plus green fee in peak season, few "muni-type" golfers ever get to play it. That oversight is corrected somewhat by the neighboring TPC Desert Course, which lies just to the east of the Stadium Course.

But, obviously, lots of golfers like to play where the pros play because the course does over 45,000 rounds each year. No doubt the memories of past Phoenix Opens are fictitiously replayed in the minds of the everyday player, and the majority come at the very end on that well-known stretch mentioned by Weiskopf.

For instance:

- The 501-yard, par-5 15th turned out to be the linchpin to Mark Calcavecchia's victory in 1989. A great risk-reward hole that allows a player a

chance to go for the island green in 2 shots, Calc made two eagles and two birdies to finish 6 under on it for the week.

- The par-3 16th is the TPC's holy grail, being the site of Tiger Woods' well-documented hole-in-one during the 1997 Open. The 7-iron from 159 yards was dubbed the modern-day version of the "Shot Heard Round the World." It still makes the tour's highlight reel each year.

- The 332-yard 17th is a drivable par 4 with water to the left and behind the green. It's an easy birdie, as Phil Mickelson proved in 1996 when he made a 10-foot putt for a 3 to prevail in a four-hole playoff with Justin Leonard.

- The 438-yard, par 4 18th is a rugged test over a lengthy lake on the left with a huge fairway bunker on the right, which forces a player to hit a perfect tee shot. The green, which features a false front on the left side, also is tricky with a deep bunker on the right. Fred Couples was perhaps the 18th hole's biggest casualty, hitting back-to-back 3-woods into the drink to lose the 1988 Open to Sandy Lyle.

"That's probably the thing that Jay and I are most proud of: It's produced some marvelous champions," Weiskopf said of past battles on the Stadium Course. "And it affords the regular guy a chance to play where the pros play. I think that's important, too."

Well, how about the crowds?

"Yeah, it defines its purpose," Weiskopf said. "Better than we ever dreamed." ✿

Designed by Tom Weiskopf and Jay Morrish, the TPC of Scottsdale has hosted the Phoenix Open since 1987.

TROON NORTH GOLF CLUB

MONUMENT: PAR: 72 • YARDAGE: 5,901–7,029 • RATING: 68.3–75.4 • SLOPE: 117–147 • SIGNATURE HOLE: 392-YARD, PAR-4 № 10 • GREEN FEES: EXPENSIVE

PINNACLE: PAR: 72 • YARDAGE: 4,980–7,044 • RATING: 67.5–76.6 • SLOPE: 123–150 • SIGNATURE HOLE: 407-YARD, PAR-4 № 18 • GREEN FEES: EXPENSIVE

DANA GARMANY and his Troon Golf management company realized they were going where no one had gone before when they decided to build an upscale, public golf course in Arizona with green fees that were nearly 10 times that of the competition.

"Risky but rewarding," Garmany said of the Monument Course at Troon North, generally regarded as the most outstanding public tract in the state since it was built by Tom Weiskopf and Jay Morrish in 1989. "Basically, we spent a lot of money, and were very fortunate to be able to hire the right people who could build in the same quality, as well as maintain the same conditioning, of a private golf course. Then we turned around and offered it to the public at a daily fee. We also gave the public an incredible clubhouse facility, one that would again rival the best private courses, and we put an emphasis on service that also was generally reserved for the private sector. In retrospect, everything turned out even better than we expected."

So good, in fact, that Weiskopf was called back in 1995 to add the Pinnacle Course. Many publications rank the two layouts as the top two courses in Arizona, with the only disagreement being which of the two is Numero Uno. "I like both for different reasons," Weiskopf explained. "The Monument Course has so many special holes on it, and it's very playable. The Pinnacle Course is tougher, with some mystery, illusion, and subtleness."

Weiskopf said he remembers the original gamble to apply private standards to a public golf course only too well. "What's funny was that back then there were people who thought a daily fee of 80 or 90

Troon North features the Monument and Pinnacle Courses.

bucks would never fly," he said, chuckling at the thought. "Now, they're charging over $200, and people are standing in line to play the golf courses."

The toughest thing about Troon North for Weiskopf was trying not to screw it up. "That's such a beautiful piece of property that anybody could have done those courses and had them turn out pretty good," he noted. "So you try not to get overwhelmed."

According to Weiskopf, the idea to name the facility Troon North came from a partner of Jerry Nelson's. It was Nelson who developed Troon Golf & Country Club. "Doug Simonson was the guy who actually came up with the name Troon North," he said. "Jerry had wanted to spin off the popularity of Troon, which was the top-rated course in Arizona at the time."

Morrish, who along with Weiskopf, made Troon their first award-winning course, also recalls the comparison. "Personally, I think Troon is the better course, a few shots tougher than Troon North," he said of the Monument. "But Troon North is more fun and attractive even if they have built it up to the point of being overdeveloped."

Yes, multimillion-dollar homes and condomini-

The picturesque, par-3 13th hole on the Monument Course.

ums have smothered some of the beauty of the Monument Course, and to a lesser degree the Pinnacle. And, yes, the fabulous Four Seasons Resort has arrived on property, adding elegant accommodations while sucking up yet more space and tee times.

In 1993, Troon Golf hired Vernon Swaback Associates, a Scottsdale architectural firm, to create an unheard-of-at-the-time, 37,000-square-foot clubhouse for the public sector. The $6.5 million structure remains state of the art, blending into the desert like a chameleon, with panoramic views of the course as well as the high Sonoran Desert. As one might expect, its menu rivals some of the finest restaurants in Phoenix, with its 19th hole prominently overlooking the 18th green of the Monument Course.

As good as the amenities can be, the golf courses still take center stage. The great debate continues to rage about which is better, as signature holes abound on both. The best of the Monument includes Nos. 3, 6, 9, 10, 11, 13, 14, 15, 16, AND 18. The Pinnacle Course's standouts are Nos. 2, 3, 6, 7, 8, 9, 12, 16, and 18. Whew!

"My favorite hole is the 10th [on the Monument], although I don't like it quite as well now with all those [expletive] condominiums out there," Weiskopf said of the medium-ranged par 4 that doglegs left over a wash to an elevated green that features a false front [a la Alister Mackenzie] and a massive boulder pile for a backdrop. "But I think the thing I'm most proud about, in terms of the Monument, is that there is not one hole that I would change. Jay and I always tried to get it right the first time, and not worry about someone else liking it. That's the Augusta [National] syndrome, and as an architect, you don't want to get caught up in that trap. Once you start changing everything, you can't stop."

Morrish also likes No. 10, except . . .

"They reversed the nines on us after we built the course. That was supposed to be No. 1," he noted. "But No. 10, or the old No. 1 as I call it, is a truly fantastic golf hole. Tom always loved Mackenzie's work, so I can understand why we both agree on that one."

The clubhouse at Troon North is state-of-the-art.

Weiskopf said it was Garmany's decision to make the Pinnacle more challenging. "I agreed with Dana totally," Weiskopf said. "So I built in some semiblind shots, more deception, and a different style of bunkers that were bigger and deeper. I also tightened it up slightly. You really have to play the Pinnacle five or six times to fully understand it, and that's why I think it's the preferred course among the better players."

While the Monument basically flows through the center of the facility, the Pinnacle is slightly disjointed with the front nine on the south side of Dynamite Road and the back nine on the north side. A lengthy cart ride is required to get players from the ninth green to the 10th tee.

"What most people don't know is that Troon Golf spent over $50,000 an acre to put those two parcels together—the ones that became the Pinnacle," Weiskopf revealed. "Let me tell you, that took a lot of balls. But when you think about it, that's pretty much the concept behind the entire Troon North project. There were a lot of copycats that followed them, but the original idea, the real deal to give a private-type golf course to the public, that was the genius behind Troon North." ☼

TUCSON NATIONAL GOLF CLUB

. . . .

PAR: 73 (GOLD AND ORANGE NINES) • YARDAGE: 5,679–7,197 • RATING: 71.6–74.6 • SLOPE: 127–136 • SIGNATURE HOLE: 440-YARD, PAR-4 N₂ 9 (GOLD) • GREEN FEES: EXPENSIVE

IT SEEMS FITTING that the Tucson Open is played each year at Tucson National, and not just because of the name. The more obvious comparison comes in terms of change, as both the tournament and the course have gone through a constant barrage of new looks—some willingly, some forced.

But let's start with the tournament, which has undergone 12 name changes since it was first played in 1945. That means that every four or five years, the tournament gained another sponsor or celebrity. Two of the more well-known stars to shine on the "Old Pueblo" (Tucson) were Dean Martin and Joe Garagiola, whose names graced the tournament title. Currently called the Touchstone Energy Tucson Open, six other corporation names have been used in its title, the most notable being Seiko and Northern Telecom, although NBC actually sponsored the tournament for one year (1976). If that's not enough, three local organizations have served as sponsors, the most prevalent being the Tucson Conquistadores, while the host course has changed five times. The kicker to all this is that in 1999, the tournament was dealt a severe blow by the PGA Tour, which reduced it to satellite status on the schedule up against the World Match Play Championship. Fortunately, actor Kevin Costner

Tucson National annually hosts the PGA Tour.

tournament. In more recent times, Steve Jones led the tournament nearly all the way [in 1997], then lost it on the very last hole to [Jeff] Sluman with a bogey."

The Green nine is a sharper contrast, and is more dramatic in terms of elevation. Its signature hole is the fifth, a wonderful par 3 over water to a green framed by railroad ties. Ironically, it was one of the original holes on the Orange.

Several other amenities make Tucson National a unique experience, chiefly the Omni Tucson National Resort & Spa. Unlike its competition, most notably Ventana Canyon, the Westin LaPaloma, and the Sheraton El Conquistador, the Omni's resort is relatively small at 167 suites, which makes for a more intimate stay. There also is a world-class spa that features such exotic offerings as Turkish mineral scrubs and reflexology.

Golfers, however, will be more interested in the Omni's sports bar, a Scottish-themed pub called Legends. The burgers are dynamite, even if they do cost $7, and several hearty brews are pulled on tap. Of the three restaurants, which also include the Fiesta Room and Catalina Grille, Legends is the champ, especially after 18 holes.

There's also a lot of nostalgia to be uncovered in the links between the Tucson Open and the course. For instance, Johnny Miller captured four Tucson Opens, including three in a row at Tucson National from 1974 to '76, which earned him the nickname "the Desert Fox." And Phil Mickelson was a three-time Open winner, including two times at the National after winning his first at Starr Pass as a 19-year-old amateur.

But the most sacred piece of trivia, or at least the tidbit few people know about, is that Jack Nicklaus initially represented Tucson National on the PGA Tour, designating it as his first home course as a professional. The deal was spawned by Nanini, who met the Golden Bear in 1963. Ironically, Nicklaus never did count Tucson among his 70 tour titles. ❀

showed up to save the marque.

Which brings us to Tucson National, a traditional tract built in 1960 by noted architect Robert Bruce Harris. "The National," as the locals refer to it, has hosted the tournament 24 times, which makes it the clear-cut winner of the Tucson Open sweepstakes. What many people don't know, however, is that the course began as a private facility in the 1960s and early '70s, the dream of Chicago roadbuilder William Nanini. Also, there was a miscommunication between Harris and the contractor on the original routing, which resulted in the bunkers and mounds being situated a great distance away from the greens. The correction was finally made 10 years later, when Robert von Hagge and Bruce Devlin were called in to redesign the original 18, called the Orange and Gold nines, and add nine more holes that are referred to as the Green nine.

"The tournament and the course do have a colorful history," noted Rick Price, the easygoing director of golf at the National. "But mostly, Tucson National is known for being traditional golf in Tucson, and the host course of the Tucson Open." The wall-to-wall grass and big native trees spread out over several hundred acres are a throwback. Desert golf this is not, although it certainly is in the desert. The National is not an easy course, either, especially when it stretches all the way back to Tucson Open standards of 7,197 yards.

Of the three nines, the Orange and the Gold are the most challenging, which is why the tournament is played on them. Both signature holes happen to be No. 9, and both are doglegs to the right that have water off the tee with giant bunkers planted in front of big, elevated greens. The distinction comes into play when the Gold's No. 9 becomes the 18th hole for the tournament, a 440-yard brute that requires a tee shot to a peninsula-like fairway. Annually the hole finishes among the five most difficult on the PGA Tour each year. "There's a lot of great history behind that hole," Price said. "Back in the '60s, Arnold [Palmer] made a 7 there to lose the

VENTANA CANYON GOLF CLUB

. . . .

CANYON: PAR: 72 • YARDAGE: 4,709–6,818 • RATING: 67.6–72.6 • SLOPE: 114–140 • SIGNATURE HOLE: 503-YARD, PAR-5 N̊ 18 • GREEN FEES: EXPENSIVE

MOUNTAIN: PAR: 72 • YARDAGE: 4,709–6,948 • RATING: 66.9–73.0 • SLOPE: 112–147 • SIGNATURE HOLE: 107-YARD, PAR-3 N̊ 3 • GREEN FEES: EXPENSIVE

I F JESSE JAMES and Billy the Kid had ever played golf, their favorite hole would have been a secret little hideout located on the Mountain Course at Ventana Canyon. Nicknamed "Hole in the Wall" by its creator, Tom Fazio, the 107-yard shot through a small canyon is perhaps the most intriguing par 3 in the wild, wild West.

"Its remote setting is unreal," noted Fazio, who has done more than his share of outstanding par 3s throughout the world. "It's one of the shortest holes I've ever designed, as well as being one of the most expensive at $400,000."

Actually, Fazio's estimate is about half right. Yes, his construction costs on Hole in the Wall were accurate, but that was before a state-of-the-art heating and cooling system was devised underneath the green. After five miles of Biotherm tubing were added to keep the putting surface at an always-comfortable 72 degrees, the price jumped to $1 million.

"It's our most perfect green," noted Chris Lamberti, the director of golf at Ventana Canyon. "But a heck of a lot of work went into it. First of all, it was constructed entirely by hand, with only pulleys, buckets, and a lot of scraped knees going into the effort. But it was worth it, because there is not a more talked-about golf hole on this course, and we've got a lot of great holes."

Lamberti is right-on, as the Mountain and adjacent Canyon courses combine for a host of designs that easily could be signature holes at other courses. Two of the most memorable combine both layouts. That would be No. 10 on the Canyon, a short par 4 up the hill, and No. 15 on the Mountain, a long par 4

The signature par-3 No. 3 on the Mountain Course.

that also travels skyward. The two holes share a common green with a backdrop of Whale-back Rock, an ancient piece of sandstone that is reminiscent of Moby Dick.

According to Fazio, the landmark is just one of the many reasons this place is so special. "Ventana Canyon has incredible character," Fazio explained. "It's alive and growing, and offers a tremendous variety of desert vegetation and massive boulder outcroppings. The whole setting is so spectacular, and that's what makes both courses such a great environment for golf."

Century-old saguaros take on forest-like proportions as they dot the adjacent Catalina Mountains, which top out at 6,000 feet. Natural springs also are to be found among the many oco-tillos, blue yuccas, and prickly pear cacti.

"I've done hundreds of golf courses, and Ventana Canyon is still among my top 10," Fazio added. "I think that's because it was designed with classic principles rather than those associated with 'target golf.' That was a trend and I've never been into trends."

Ventana Canyon is mostly wall-to-wall grass, with lots of mounding and elevation changes that keep golfers on the edge of their game. While the fairways and greens are quite accessible for the most part, errant shots are punished severely by washes, ravines, and all of those cacti. (Perhaps a few rattle-snakes, too!) Still, the surroundings, which include panoramic views of Sabino Canyon and the Tucson skyline, are so spectacular that scorecard watching takes on a secondary nature. No matter which nine you're negotiating, the "oh, mys!" just keep coming.

Of the two courses, the Mountain is considered the more dramatic. Besides No. 3, there is an almost equally impressive par 3. That would be No. 6, a scary, 230-yard shot down the hill to a green that is partially hidden. On the back nine, the closing stretch is stunning, especially No. 17, a par 4 that rolls uphill over a split fairway to a green tucked into the mountain, and the 589-yard 18th, a dynamic par 5 that begins high on a tee box overlooking the 17th green. The length of the 18th is not nearly as difficult as the descent, which filters its way between a large wash on the left and a grove of Chilean mesquites on the right. A bunker that stretches nearly 100 yards defines the final path to the green.

The Canyon Course is the gentler offering, and those with higher handicaps should take note. Its closing stretch also is outstanding, especially the signature hole, a short par 5 that doglegs right up the hill for 502 yards to an island green encircled by water. Just beyond the flagstick, a cascading waterfall caps your round.

Also gracing this 2,000-acre property are two of the finest retreats in Tucson: the Loews Ventana Canyon Resort, which features 398 rooms and suites, and the Lodge at Ventana Canyon, which offers 50 villas. The ownership situation is complicated, with Ventana Canyon Golf & Racquet Club owning the two courses. Fortunately, guests at both resorts are given top priority for tee times. "We have 528 golfing members, and a lot of guests, so both courses get quite a bit of play," Lamberti noted. "Plus, our members, while not year-round guests, are beginning to realize what the rest of us have known awhile. Except for [July and August], you can live here very comfortably for 10 months of the year. That makes for a very busy situation."

But a good one. Everything about the Ventana Canyon experience is first-class. The service and accommodations are perhaps the best in Tucson, and there is no question that the setting also is right at the top, with only the Raven at Sabino Springs sharing the honor for raw beauty. Of course, prices are expensive at Ventana Canyon, with green fees topping out at $185, and rooms going for $250 and up. "Expensive, but worth it," is the way Lamberti summed up the situation.

Plus, there is that golden opportunity to play Hole in the Wall. "There are a lot of wonderful stories that surround that hole," Lamberti said, "like the one about Tom Watson, who 4-putted the green during the Merrill-Lynch Shootout [in the early 1990s]. Of course, that was before we took out the second tier to make the hole more playable. The redesign might have made it less tough, but it's still a terror—all or nothing!—for such a short shot."

Yeah, the James Gang and "the Kid" would have loved it. ✺

GOLF CLUB AT VISTOSO

PAR: 72 • YARDAGE: 5,165–6,905 • RATING: 68.0–72.1 • SLOPE: 124–145 • SIGNATURE HOLE: 323-YARD, PAR-4 №̲ 14 • GREEN FEES: EXPENSIVE

GOLF COURSES of superior quality tend to congregate. Certainly that was the case when Arizona's "Rodeo Drive of Golf" came together in the northeast corridor of Scottsdale. With Troon North and Grayhawk laying claim to the neighborhood in the early 1990s, others clamored to be next on the block. The same could be said of other great golf enclaves, such as Pinehurst, North Carolina; Myrtle Beach, South Carolina; and the Monterey Peninsula of northern California.

Another notable golfing fortress is forming in Tucson. Sure, it took a few more years than in Scottsdale to get things going. But once again, it was a northern exposure situated near the awesome Catalina Mountains that drew the attention of golf course architects and developers.

First on the scene was the Golf Club at Vistoso, a solo design by Tom Weiskopf that the Scottsdale architect did shortly after splitting with longtime partner Jay Morrish. Weiskopf's work, which featured a desert look with a more traditional approach than courses he had done with Morrish, received immediate acclaim, as it was nominated by *Golf Digest* for "Best New Public Golf Course" in 1997.

"Vistoso has a pure look, and even though it has mostly forced carries off the tee like desert golf, there are a lot of basic design concepts used there that date back to the early work of some of the masters, like [A. W.] Tillinghast, [Alister] Mackenzie, and [Donald] Ross," Weiskopf noted. "I think the bunkering, with the Winged Foot-type fingering, is especially old school."

Also unique to this Weiskopf design, as well as

Arizona courses in general, were the use of square tee boxes. "In the past, we had used circular or oval shapes," Weiskopf said. "So going to square tee boxes was different yet very traditional."

For the most part, Vistoso was an easy sell because it is an excellent piece of property. "That's always the key to great golf courses—the setting," Weiskopf added. "You look at every great golf course in the world, and all of them have a piece of land that is special."

Vistoso fits that category. Not only are the Catalinas in full view, but much of the surrounding area is as well, with sensational backdrops that include the Tortolita and Tucson Mountains. Adding to the ambiance, the course is always in superior shape with a rainbow of desert flowers. Of course, Vistoso translates from Spanish into "colorful views," so it was a natural.

Slowly but surely Vistoso has risen on the Tucson golf horizon. *Golf Digest*, for one, thought so much of the course that it made Vistoso the No. 1 public layout in Tucson, and No. 3 in Arizona behind the Monument and Pinnacle courses at Troon North. "It's just a very playable desert golf course, and people notice things like that, especially after they play the competition," said Mark Oswald, the director of golf at Vistoso. "Plus, the thing we hear over and over is how well our course is conditioned. It really is amazingly perfect."

Oswald said the agronomical credit goes to Terry Todd, the superintendent at Vistoso, who has been grooming the club since its infancy. "Terry even worked in the construction of the course," Oswald said. "And I think by being here since the

The Golf Club at Vistoso has a "pure look."

Tom Weiskopf built traditional, square tee boxes.

beginning, it helped him to learn everything he possibly can—every nook, every cranny.

The course, which is owned by Tempe-based Vistoso Partners (Conley Wolfswinkel and John Beerling), also has an abundance of signature-type offerings. Two stretches stand out: the seventh through ninth holes, and the 16th through 18th. Of that bunch, the eighth, a 388-yard par 4 that requires an approach over water to a green backed by a waterfall, might be the most beautiful. As far as challenge, the 16th and 18th, both par 5s, will wear a player down.

The irony is that the course's true "signatures"—

No. 3 and No. 14—are not found in either of those wonderful runs. "The [323-yard, par-4] 14th, because of its split fairway and the fact you can drive the green if you really smoke it, is probably the most memorable," Oswald said of "Risky," as the hole is dubbed. "But the one that gets photographed the most is No. 3, a little [166-yard] shot to a well-bunkered green that is backed by the Catalina Mountains. It's a classic golf hole, which is why it's called 'Tillinghast.'"

Enjoying Vistoso doesn't necessarily mean you have to tee it up. Most mornings or evenings, the air is clear, clean, and crisp, easily enjoyed while you sip a beverage on the patio known as the Tortolita Terrace. While there is no immediate lodging on property at the moment, a Ritz-Carlton will soon

open at Stone Canyon, and a Marriott is targeted down the line for Vistoso. In the meantime, those in the know retreat to the Golf Villas at Oro Valley, which is just down the road a mile or two from the clubhouse. There are numerous restaurants, like Buster's, Keagan's, and Suite 101, in the area. Or for those who like local "health conscious" Mexican fare, try El Saurito.

"This area is just beginning to boom," Oswald noted. "We've got some strong competition in the area . . . but it's not threatening because I really do believe we're the best public course you can play in Tucson. We're definitely in the right area of town, and our reputation grows every year."

Yes, golf is a lot like real estate: location, location, location. ✿

THE WIGWAM GOLF RESORT

. . . .

GOLD: PAR: 72 • YARDAGE: 5,673–7,093 • RATING: 64.0–74.2 • SLOPE: 113–138 • SIGNATURE HOLE: 370-YARD, PAR-4 №18 • GREEN FEES: MODERATE TO EXPENSIVE

BLUE: PAR: 72 • YARDAGE: 5,235–6,030 • RATING: 64.0–74.2 • SLOPE: 102–122 • SIGNATURE HOLE: 149-YARD, PAR-3 №18 • GREEN FEES: MODERATE TO EXPENSIVE

RED: PAR: 70 • YARDAGE: 5,821–6,894 • RATING: 66.5–75.1 • SLOPE: 104–128 • SIGNATURE HOLE: 551-YARD, PAR-5 №18 • GREEN FEES: MODERATE TO EXPENSIVE

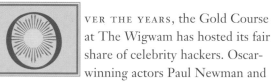

OVER THE YEARS, the Gold Course at The Wigwam has hosted its fair share of celebrity hackers. Oscar-winning actors Paul Newman and Robert Mitchum cruised these lush fairways only to struggle on the elevated greens built by the legendary Robert Trent Jones Sr. Big hitters like Jackie Robinson, Mickey Mantle, Joe DiMaggio, Yogi Berra, Hank Aaron, and Reggie Jackson also took a crack, and Jones gave them all they could handle on this lengthy layout that stretches for 7,100 yards. Even former football great Joe Namath and ex-hoops star Magic Johnson had trouble when they passed through these tree-lined fairways.

But the guy who really met his match was Gerald Ford, the former president who stayed here with members of his cabinet during the 1970s. As the story goes, and there are several versions that have been enhanced over the years, Ford's penchant for errant drives scared the daylights out of Henry Kissinger, his former Secretary of State. Known as one of the Oval Office's more out-of-control players, Ford somehow managed to fan a drive through the window of Kissinger's wickiup, as the casitas were known back then. What's even harder to believe, the errant shot was Ford's mulligan, as his first drive had bounded off the roof of the nearby cart barn.

As the story goes, Kissinger's bodyguard, alarmed at the sound of shattering glass, thought a bullet had blown out the window. Gun drawn, the bodyguard came flying out of the room, looked around only to find Ford's foursome making its

Robert Trent Jones Sr. created the Gold Course.

way toward the green. "Oh, it's only you, Mr. President!" the bodyguard said as he holstered his weapon.

Funny thing about great golf courses: Over the years, the lore seems to grow in proportion to the play. And the Gold Course at The Wigwam has some wonderful stories to tell. The first starts with Jones, the legendary architect whose résumé includes nearly 600 golf courses. The Gold Course was built by Jones in 1964 as part of a 36-hole complex known as Goodyear Golf & Country Club, a reference to Goodyear Tires, the rubber maker who had founded the resort in 1918. What few people know, however, is that the original nine holes had been constructed in 1930 by an unknown maintenance man with only a tractor. In 1941, a construction crew added another nine holes, and the inaugural 18 holes were christened by longtime Director of Golf Red Allen and former Masters champ Horton Smith. Then Jones came along to mint the "real" Gold, and added his second 18 holes, known as the Blue Course, a year later. In 1974, Red Lawrence, "the Desert Fox," completed the project with yet a third 18, dubbed the Red (what else?) Course.

All three layouts, which actually were named for Goodyear's three dominant colors in its advertising, are throwbacks. But it's the Gold that remains the crowning jewel to this 54-hole complex, the only one of its kind among Arizona's thirtysomething resorts. And like all monuments to the past, the Gold has since been passed over by today's desert supercourses. Fortunately, there remains a lot of glitter in the Gold, thanks to a major renovation done by Jones in the early 1990s.

A classic golf course, players must think their way around the Gold, as powerful swings just won't get it done. All of Jones' trademarks are evident: elongated tee boxes, strategic placement of sand and water, those elegant but elevated greens that feature subtle putting surfaces, and variety that requires every shot in the bag.

With nearly 150 acres of turf, about 60 more than designers are limited to these days, Jones essentially constructed a parklike playing field. This is one walk that is definitely not spoiled, as folksy author Mark Twain once asserted. The experience is made even more pleasant by an abundance of mature trees that run the gamut from palms to pines, and from eucalyptuses to weeping willows. In other words, when the sizzling Arizona sun beats down during the summer months, few courses offer the respite and the shady lanes of those you'll find on The Wigwam Gold.

Still, don't get too swept away. As Jones once said: "Every hole must be a hard par and an easy bogey." The first thing to remember about the Gold is to stay out of the trees. When a player gets going crosswise, even "an easy bogey" is tough to card. Avoiding the big, well-designed bunkers also is paramount, as some of these lips can kill you. The best advice: it's better to be short than long when approaching the greens, and always be below the cup. The par 3s and par 5s are wonderful tests, but it's the intricate par 4s that form the backbone of the course. Nine holes stand out—Nos. 1, 3, 5, 6, 10, 12, 13, 14, 16, and 18. Of the lot, the last one combines all of Jones' requirements for good golf.

The best way to experience the Gold is to stay at this quiet but cool resort, which lies on the edge of the West Valley. As you exit Interstate 10, palm-lined Litchfield Park Road sends signals that a player is in for something exotic. All three courses, however, offer their own niche, as the Gold is the championship tract, the Blue is short but demanding, and the Red is more wide-open and friendly. The resort has something for everyone, ranging from water slides to horseback riding to skeet shooting. The restaurants also are unique, but it's the award-winning Arizona Kitchen that serves up some of the finest cuisine in the Southwest.

Which brings up one last tale from The Wigwam's fabled past. Not every famous face who has stayed here was charmed by the Gold. Actress Debbie Reynolds and singer Connie Stevens often visited the resort just to get away from it all. And Jaclyn Smith, one of the original Charlie's Angels, filmed the movie *The Kill* on property. Nope, the flick had nothing to do with The Wigwam Gold. That's not the way that Robert Trent Jones Sr. intended the game to be played. He's too much of a gentleman to commit such a dastardly deed.

Former President Ford, on the other hand . . . ⚙

WILDFIRE GOLF CLUB

· ·

Par: 72 · Yardage: 4,876–7,077 · Rating: 67.2–73.3 · Slope: 112–135 · Signature hole: 530-yard, par-5 No. 5 · Green fees: moderate to expensive

THEY HAVE ALWAYS referred to Arnold Palmer as "The King." Of course, Arnie deserves such recognition, having won over 100 tournaments worldwide while popularizing the game for the masses.

What few people realize, however, is that during Palmer's prolific reign he also found time to build over 250 courses worldwide. Two hundred fifty and counting, actually, as Arnie and partner Edwin Seay have worked nonstop since founding the Palmer Course Design Co. in 1975. Among their accomplishments: the first golf course in China.

Along the way, Palmer and Co. designed five courses in Arizona, the most noted being Wildfire Golf Club, a desert dandy located in northeast Phoenix on a 5,800-acre development known as Desert Ridge. Despite a rather low-key debut in March of 1997, the course has gone on to draw some strong accolades.

Perhaps the biggest came when *Golf & Travel* magazine selected Wildfire as one of "10 Arnold Palmer Standouts." The list, which also included The Legend at Shanty Creek, Myrtle Beach National, the Bay Hill Club, Oasis Golf Club, Semiahmoo Resort, Aviara, Teton Pines, Hapuna at Mauna Kea, and Cherokee Run Golf Club, was an impressive one. That Wildfire was held in such high esteem is a testament to its playability and overall beauty. "That article put us in some really good company," noted Doc Belitz, the general manager at Wildfire. "Most of those other courses have been around. But we're still in our infancy, so it was a bigger deal for us."

Belitz brings up an interesting point, because Wildfire is the first piece of a giant puzzle that will follow. In fact, it's the first of two golf courses that are targeted for Desert Ridge, a massive project spearheaded by Northeast Phoenix Partners. In addition to the golf courses, the project includes a 600- to 900-room hotel, a one-million-square-foot mall, restaurants, movie theaters, and a second downtown area (for Phoenix) that "will revolve around a business core and office complex complete with eight-story-high buildings." All of which will make Wildfire just that much more popular.

Wildfire's reputation took another significant step forward in November 1999, when the course played host to the EMC2 Skills Challenge. The event, which featured PGA Tour stars Ben Crenshaw, Tom Kite, Nick Price, Peter Jacobsen, Craig Stadler, Jeff Sluman, Brad Faxon, and Billy Andrade, who was the eventual winner, received major coverage on NBC.

"We spent a lot [of money] to get [the Skills Challenge], and the residuals are still trickling in," Belitz reported. "Mostly, people told us how good the course looked on television. But just as important, the PGA Tour guys all played it the day after the event, and they were very complimentary."

If there has been a rap against Palmer-designed golf courses over the years, it's that Arnie doesn't spend enough time at each project during the construction. But considering his schedule as one of the game's great ambassadors, who can blame him? The reality is that most player/golf course architects are little more than figureheads for those who actually build the fairways and greens.

But Rob Kohlhaas, the original GM at Wildfire who continues to work for the company, said that Palmer made numerous site inspections before finally playing the course during its grand opening. "Arnie did a lot of hands-on work here," Kohlhaas said. "In fact, he was on-site at least six times during the construction. He also stayed in contact with us constantly."

Palmer was quite taken with the project during the grand opening, dispensing such words of praise as "outstanding" and "spectacular" to describe the generous landing areas, solid bunkering work, and manageable bentgrass greens. "Wildfire uses the desert very well," The King proclaimed. "And, environmentally, I think we did a fantastic job."

With arroyos and mountain backdrops of the McDowells seemingly everywhere, as well as views of Camelback Mountain and Squaw Peak, Palmer and Co. take the player for a gentle, natural ride. The strength of the golf course begins at No. 5, a 530-yard par 5 that features a split fairway en route to a well-guarded green boasting eight bunkers. Not that the first four holes are duds, but the character of the golf course is more apparent over the last 14 holes, with the best stretch being the 15th through 18th. The preferred time to play the course is in the spring, when the many wild flowers are in full bloom.

"Mostly people like Wildfire because the course is pretty forgiving," Belitz noted. "We used the maximum of 90 acres, which keeps you out of the desert. And the greens are fast and true. Plus, our conditioning is always great."

At the moment, there is not much else on the Wildfire scene in terms of dining or entertainment. A temporary clubhouse with a snack bar offering up some tasty hot dogs will have to suffice. But as Belitz predicted: "Someday, we'll be surrounded by city."

The timetable, of course, will give Wildfire more years to mature. At this point, it's too early to say that it will become a course fit for a king—even if it was built by one. ✿

Arnold Palmer was "the King" when it came to Wildfire.

PRIVATE COURSES

ONCE UPON A TIME, being a member at a private course meant being a member at a country club. But times have changed quickly in Arizona, and today there are nearly 100 of these elite clubs throughout the state, the vast majority being upscale tracts driven by housing. Being a member of a club seems less important than the lifestyle that goes with such elite offerings, of which there are 38 in this chapter.

Arizona's private golf courses have become the model for today's developers, with such clubs as Desert Highlands, Desert Mountain, and Forest Highlands leading the way. But this chapter also has a heavy emphasis on the past, as the roles of Phoenix Country Club, Arizona Country Club, and Tucson Country Club should not be forgotten.

1 ANTHEM GOLF & COUNTRY CLUB *(page 62)*
2708 W. Anthem Club Drive, New River, 85086
Directions: Take I-17 north from Phoenix to Anthem exit, head east.
Information: 623-742-6262

2 ARIZONA COUNTRY CLUB *(page 64)*
5668 E. Orange Blossom Lane, Phoenix, 85018
Directions: One block south of Thomas Road off 56th Street.
Information: 602-946-4565

3 THE BOULDERS CLUB *(page 66)*
34831 N. Tom Darlington Drive, Carefree, 85377
Directions: Just north of Carefree Highway off Scottsdale Road.
Information: 480-488-9028

4 GOLF CLUB AT CHAPARRAL PINES *(page 68)*
504 N. Club Drive, Payson, 85541
Directions: From Payson, take U.S. Highway 240 two miles east.
Information: 520-472-8330

5 COUNTRY CLUB AT DC RANCH *(page 70)*
9290 E. Thompson Peak Parkway, Scottsdale, 85256
Directions: Pima Road to Thompson Peak, east to gated entrance.
Information: 480-342-7200

6 DESERT FOREST GOLF CLUB *(page 72)*
37207 N. Muletrain Road, Carefree, 85377
Directions: North on Pima, west on Cave Creek Road, north on Mule Train.
Information: 480-488-3527

7 DESERT HIGHLANDS GOLF CLUB *(page 74)*
10040 E. Happy Valley Road, Scottsdale, 85255
Directions: North on Pima Road, east on Happy Valley to entrance.
Information: 480-585-8521

8 GOLF CLUB AT DESERT MOUNTAIN *(page 76)*
10333 Rockaway Hills, Scottsdale, 85262
Directions: Take Pima Road north to Cave Creek Highway, then east to course entrance.
Information: 480-488-1362

9 ESTANCIA CLUB *(page 82)*
27998 N. 99th Place, Scottsdale, 85262
Directions: North on Pima Road, east on Dynamite to entrance.
Information: 480-473-4415

10 FOREST HIGHLANDS GOLF CLUB *(page 84)*
675 Forest Highlands Drive, Flagstaff, 86001
Directions: Two miles south of Flagstaff Airport on Highway 89A.
Information: 520-525-9000

11 GAINEY RANCH GOLF CLUB *(page 86)*
7600 E. Gainey Ranch Drive, Scottsdale, 85258
Directions: Just east of Scottsdale Road off Doubletree Ranch Road.
Information: 480-483-2582

12 THE GALLERY AT DOVE MOUNTAIN *(page 88)*
14000 N. Dove Mountain Boulevard, Marana, 85653
Directions: I-10 to Tangerine Exit, east eight miles to entrance.
Information: 520-744-2555

13 HASSAYAMPA GOLF CLUB *(page 90)*
2060 Golf Club Lane, Prescott, 86303
Directions: From downtown Prescott, take Gurley Street southwest to Hassayampa Village Lane to Golf Club Lane, then right.
Information: 800-835-4966

14 LA PALOMA COUNTRY CLUB *(page 92)*
3660 E. Sunrise Drive, Tucson, 85718
Directions: Between Campbell and Swan off E. Sunrise.
Information: 520-299-1500

15 MESA COUNTRY CLUB *(page 94)*
660 W. Fairway Drive, Mesa, 85201
Directions: One block north of Brown on Country Club.
Information: 480-964-351

16 MOON VALLEY COUNTRY CLUB *(page 96)*
151 W. Moon Valley Drive, Phoenix, 85023
Directions: Thunderbird Road east to Coral Gables Drive, north to Moon Valley Drive, east to golf course.
Information: 602-942-0000

17 ORO VALLEY COUNTRY CLUB *(page 98)*
200 W. Valle Del Oro Drive, Oro Valley, 85737
Directions: 15 miles north of Tucson on Oracle Road.
Information: 520-297-3322

18 PARADISE VALLEY COUNTRY CLUB *(page 100)*
7101 N. Tatum Boulevard, Paradise Valley, 85253
Directions: One-half mile morth of Lincoln Drive on Tatum Blvd.
Information: 602-840-8100

19 PHOENIX COUNTRY CLUB *(page 102)*
2901 N. Seventh Avenue, Phoenix, 85014
Directions: Corner of Seventh Street & Thomas
Information: 602-263-5208

20 PINETOP COUNTRY CLUB *(page 104)*
6734 Country Club Drive, Pinetop, 85935
Directions: Arizona Highway 260 north from Show Low to Buck Springs Road, then left 1 1/2 miles.
Information: 520-369-2461

21 PINNACLE PEAK COUNTRY CLUB *(page 106)*
8701 E. Pinnacle Peak Road, Scottsdale, 85255
Directions: Pima Road to Pinnacle Peak Road, west to golf course.
Information: 480-585-0385

22 THE RIM CLUB *(page 108)*
300 S. Clubhouse Road, Payson, 85541
Directions: From Payson, take Highway 260 two miles east,
    entrance on right.
Information: 520-472-6840

23 STONE CANYON CLUB *(page 110)*
945 W. Vistoso Highlands Drive, Oro Valley, 85737
Directions: From Tucson, take I-10 north to Tangerine, east twelve
    miles to Rancho Visto Blvd., then two miles north.
Information: 520-631-6884

24 SUPERSTITION MOUNTAIN GOLF AND COUNTRY
    CLUB *(page 112)*
8000 E. Club Village Drive, Superstition Mountain, 85219
Directions: Highway 60 to mile marker 201, left on Superstition
    Mountain Drive.
Information: 480-983-3200

26 TERRAVITA GOLF AND COUNTRY CLUB *(page 114)*
34034 N. 69th Way, Scottsdale, 85262
Directions: On Scottsdale Road, three miles south of Carefree.
Information: 480-488-1333

27 TONTO VERDE GOLF CLUB *(page 116)*
18401 El Circulo Drive, Rio Verde, 85263
Directions: North on Pima Road, then east 10 miles on Dynamite
    Road, south 1 mile to entrance.
Information: 480-471-2710

28 TORREON *(page 118)*
3800 W. Sugar Pine Way, Show Low, 85901
Directions: Located just west of the intersection of highways 60 and
    260 as you enter Show Low.
Information: 520-532-GOLF

29 TROON GOLF AND COUNTRY CLUB *(page 120)*
25000 N. Windy Walk Drive, Scottsdale, 85255
Directions: Go north on Pima Road towards Carefree to Happy
    Valley Road, then east to Windy Walk.
Information: 480-585-0540

30 TUCSON COUNTRY CLUB *(page 122)*
2950 N Camino Principal, Tucson, 85715
Directions: East of Wilmot Road off of Tanque Verde Road, north
    on Camino Principal.
Information: 520-298-2381

31 WHITE MOUNTAIN COUNTRY CLUB *(page 124)*
P.O. Box 1489, Pinetop, 85935
Directions: East on Highway 260, a mile out of Pinetop
Information: 520-367-4913

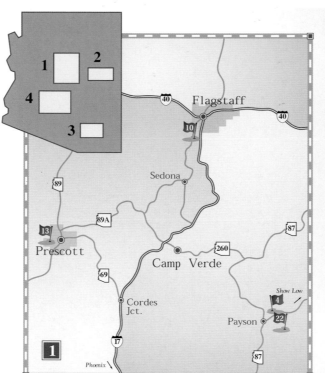

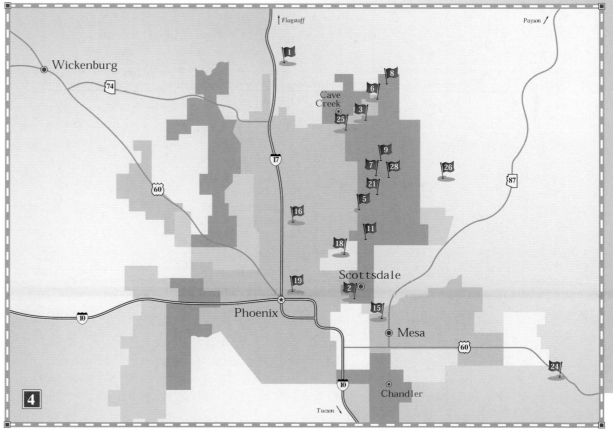

ANTHEM GOLF AND COUNTRY CLUB

PAR: 72 · YARDAGE: 5,326–7,219 · RATING: 68.2–74.5 · SLOPE: 120–139 · SIGNATURE HOLE: 581-YARD, PAR-5 № 16

HAVING SPENT a good deal of his career building retirement-type golf courses for megadeveloper Del Webb, most notably in the Sun City area, Greg Nash jumped for joy when he was unleashed to create Anthem Golf and Country Club.

"Del Webb is changing," Nash explained while pointing to Anthem, an upscale community for all ages that debuted in 1999 on the outskirts of New River. "I give them a lot of credit, because they're seeking a higher-end course that is well-maintained and a lot more demanding."

In that regard, mission accomplished. Nash, who has built over 30 golf courses in Arizona, was thinking red, white, and blue when he carved Anthem out of the slopes that roll discretely off Daisy Mountain. "It's a desert golf course, but not like a lot of desert courses in the sense that there are no real forced carries off the tees," Nash said. "I call it a 'new desert course.' . . . It's natural and flows with the lay of the land."

Actually, the whole package at Anthem is quite impressive. The golf course, which is the first of two courses planned for the 5,800-acre project, is smashing. In terms of playability, variety, conditioning, and setting, move over north Scottsdale. But the same could be said about Anthem's community center, waterpark, fitness centers, parks, and trails.

So it wasn't so surprising, really, when 23,000 people visited Anthem within two weeks of its grand opening. Already, 1,000 homes have been built, with another 11,000 on the way. The place has everything from a rock-climbing wall to a four-acre lake.

Naturally, the golf course is, by far, the biggest perk. It cost over $10 million to build and, with a $30,000 initiation fee, is quite reasonable. What's even better is that, for a limited time, the course is open to the public. Call it a teaser.

The terrain tumbles 300 feet from top to bottom, as awesome sunrises and sunsets burst over the zigzagging arroyos and saguaro-studded canyons. "The golf course does have terrific flow," Nash agreed. "Because of that, you'll get just about every shot imaginable. I also tried a few new things, relying on a more Scottish or Irish influence in the bunkering and greens. That brought back the bump-and-run, and numerous other types of shots that require imagination."

The strength of the course is the par 3s, which are all unique and can be played from four to seven different sets of saucer-shaped tee boxes. Adding to the variety, most of the tees are spread out horizontally, offering several different views of the hole.

"Somebody asked me, 'Why all the tees?'" Nash said with chuckle. "I said, 'To . . . open up or pinch the golf course, making it play easier or more difficult. The only problem with so many choices, as I see it, is getting people to play from the ones that fit them best."

Yes, there is a vast difference in 5,326 yards and 7,219, the extremes at Anthem. Add the massive bunker complexes and large greens into the equation, and the tee boxes can make or break a round.

Anthem unfurls with three fairly straightforward offerings accented by water. But from that point on, the course explodes with a barrage of different looks. The first postcard comes at No. 7, a 168-yard shot into a small valley backed by mountains. Five bunkers surround the green, adding to the magnitude. "This is my kind of golf hole, because nothing is going to go behind that green—ever," Nash noted. "It's the kind of hole where you can say, 'This is what it is today, and this is what it will be tomorrow.'"

The rest of the course might not remain as

pure, what with all the housing on the way. But the ninth and 18th holes, demanding par 4s that share a common, 28,000-square-foot green, will always be in that category. The best stretch is probably Nos. 11–14, which all play up the mountain. But Nash likes the 16th, a par 5 that rambles its way up and over 581 yards of wide fairway to a well-bunkered, intricately divided green. All of Anthem's magic comes into play. "There's some mystery to that hole, because you can't see the green until your third shot," Nash said. "If you take the high route, you can perhaps get the ball to roll onto the green in two [shots]. If you go low, it's three shots. But that first shot is special because you have no idea what you're getting into."

Nash added that Anthem is among the top three courses he has ever designed. That's saying a lot, considering Terravita and Los Caballeros also are on his résumé.

Anthem's clubhouse also is major league. Of course, the exquisite Persimmon Bar and Grille is where you'll eventually want to end up. Who knows who you'll run into? Perhaps you'll sit down next to Nash! "This is a golf course that you can play time and time again and never tire of it," he said, pausing for effect. "Which is why I bought a home here on the third hole."

Is Arizona's most prolific architect heading for retirement?

"No, I wouldn't say that," Nash countered. "But I just turned 50, and I said to myself: 'Damn it, it's time to play some golf again rather than just build courses and raise kids.'"

Ask any member at Anthem and they'll tell you, Greg Nash picked the right place to do just that. ⚙

The par-4 15th is among Anthem's best stretch.

D² Productions, Inc. Murphy/Scully

ARIZONA COUNTRY CLUB

· ·

PAR: 72 · YARDAGE: 5,558–6,73 · RATING: 70.2–72.3 · SLOPE: 122–133 · SIGNATURE HOLE: 189-YARD, PAR-3 №11

WHEN IT COMES to the elite country clubs of metropolitan Phoenix, Arizona Country Club has its own niche. Brett Upper, the relatively new head pro at ACC, had it figured out almost immediately. "They're hard-core golf addicts," said Upper with a smile. "The game is a large priority in their lives. In a lot of ways, Arizona Country Club is like a club in Scotland in that golf is almost like a religion."

Their temple is all-natural, made up of lush fairways and greens, as well as vegetation that was planted way back when Ernest Suggs and Willie Wansa constructed the original 18 holes in 1946. Actually, some of ACC's ancient cedars, pines, eucalyptuses, oaks, cottonwoods, and palms date back to 1909, when little Ingelside Golf Resort was bustling on this very ground.

Ingelside, which earned the distinction of being Phoenix's first winter resort, entertained well-heeled visitors from the East Coast, reaching its zenith during the Roaring Twenties. Many were investor friends of Ingelside owner W. J. Murphy, a Phoenix pioneer who built the Arizona Canal. But Ingelside went belly-up during the Great Depression, and it lay there as unclaimed property until Suggs and Wansa ventured onto the scene, using several of the old holes in their routing of ACC.

Since then, the course has been renovated four times, the latest coming in 1999, when Gary Stevenson added some slippery slopes to the green complexes; extended, added, and squared up the tee boxes; lengthened and shortened bunkers; and changed the putting surfaces from bentgrass to tiff

The 189-yard 11th is Arizona Country Club's signature hole.

dwarf. "All the changes were initiated to look like they belonged with the original design," Upper noted. "But mostly it was strategic work made to enhance the course's championship quality without changing its difficulty."

Upper said that of all the face-lifts, the most drastic, as well as dynamic, came in the 1960s, when Phoenix legend Johnny Bulla rerouted much of the work done by Suggs and Wansa. "Johnny really revitalized this course and made it what it is today," Upper said of the many conversations he has had with the older members of ACC. "Johnny played on the [PGA] Tour, and you can see that this course was built with a player's eye."

Upper would know. He, too, played on the PGA Tour from 1983 to '89, "but never reached the winner's circle." He arrived at ACC in 1998. "I was working as the head pro at Bent Creek Country Club in Lancaster, Pennsylvania, and looking to move out West," Upper said of his path to ACC. "I was contacted by a friend at this club, Del Cochran. I was really lucky to get this job because, just like the members, I love the old style of golf course."

Standing on the first tee at ACC, looking straight down the fairway through bunkers and big trees to a sunlit green that beckons 515 yards away, it is like yesteryear. And that feeling of nostalgia never lets up as a player winds his way through five fantastic par 3s, four reachable and one unthinkable par 5s, and some wonderful dogleg par 4s. Along the way, limbs, bunkers, and water keep toying with a player's mind. "A good golf course should take you near the trouble in order to set up your ideal spot for your next shot," Upper noted. "This course certainly does that. It requires lots of thought."

With so many good to great holes to select from, it's difficult to point to ACC's best stretch of golf. But the ninth through 12th holes certainly would come to mind. Often called "ACC's Amen Corner," the stretch starts with a scenic 177-yard par 3 that is surrounded by tall palms and backed by

the Papago Buttes. Next up is the "unthinkable" 605-yard par 5 that winds its way to a big green that doubles as a waterfall. The 189-yard 11th hole is the signature, a brilliant par 3 where a player must avoid a tall cottonwood off the tee as well as a lake that fronts the green. The 435-yard 12th is a narrow, tree-lined dogleg left.

Of course, it's hard to leave out the third, fourth, and fifth holes, which also work their way around a large body of water and offer up Camelback Mountain in the distance. And the 18th is a pure 519-yard par 5 that is especially spectacular from the tee box looking down the fairway. That's one of the neat things about ACC, it starts and ends on a "birdieable" par 5.

"Really, there are so many things to like about this golf course," Upper added. "I guess the par 3s are what everybody talks about, and that's with good reason. You take those five holes, and for a good player, they'll make you use a 5-iron, 8-iron, 3-iron, 7-iron, and a 6-iron. That goes through the bag pretty good. You don't see that very much these days with the modern architects. Sure, we don't have a 235-yard par 3, but we really don't care."

Instead, the members just want to tee it up and occasionally revel in the tradition and history of the golf course. The clubhouse is 44,000 square feet and includes a men's grill and a mixed grill, along with one of the club's most prized monuments— The Phoenix Open Wall of Fame. The collection of photographs date from 1955 to 1973, the nearly 20 years when ACC shared the tournament with Phoenix Country Club on an every-other-year rotation. Among the champs at ACC were multiple winners Gene Littler (1955, '59, and '69) and Arnold Palmer (1961 and '63). "Everything about this golf course is just classic," Upper noted. "That's why it's so fun to work here."

One characteristic of ACC particularly excites Upper, whose game remains solid, the proof lying in his runner-up finish at the 1999 PGA National Club Pro Championship. "You can always get a game here, whether it's a gentleman's bet, or a bet for pride," he said with a smile. "That's part of golf, and it's a mark of a good club."

Sort of like Scotland, eh laddie? ✿

THE BOULDERS CLUB

· ·

NORTH: PAR: 72 · YARDAGE: 5,380–6,98 · RATING: 65.7–76.5 · SLOPE: 118–144 · SIGNATURE HOLE: 183-YARD, PAR-3 NO. 14

SOUTH: PAR: 71 · YARDAGE: 4,715–6,926 · RATING: 66.6–76.6 · SLOPE: 121–145 · SIGNATURE HOLE: 545-YARD, PAR-5 NO. 5

THE MESSAGE didn't come in a bottle. But there was no surprise when the Arts and Entertainment Cable Network selected The Boulders Resort as one of the top 10 romantic getaways in the world for 1999. The latest honor follows a similar theme, as *Andrew Harper's Hideaway Report*, known as the connoisseur's guide to "peaceful and unspoiled places," has picked The Boulders as the top resort in the United States for 12 straight years.

Yes, you're going to love this place. As it is, The Boulders' semiprivate golf courses—the North and the South—are just a bonus. But as a rule, most visitors treasure these fairways and greens as much or more than the opulent accommodations. "The golf is great, the service is the best, and there is no better place to be in the world than The Boulders," said Tom McCahan, the resort's director of golf. "In every way, it's an Arizona treasure."

How the North and the South courses came to be sisters is a twisting tale of fortitude and imagination. Noted architect Red Lawrence actually built the first nine holes in 1969, and Phoenix's Jack Snyder completed the original 18 a few years later. In 1984, Jay Morrish returned to add 10 new holes, and at that point the course was played in three distinct nines until 1992, when Morrish returned to add yet another new nine. When Morrish finally finished, everything was scrambled into the North and the South.

"The Boulders was my first real job by myself," recalled Morrish, who had worked for several architects, most notably Jack Nicklaus. "What I did [in 1984] was, basically, blow up the course with 10 new holes and remodel the existing 18. Then I came back, added nine more, and tried to put together two, coherent golf courses.

"As it turned out, I really like the South Course much more than the North. I did those opening five holes, and the majority of the 18 on the South. Unfortunately, it's kind of strung out and doesn't tie together all that well. But if you look at each hole individually, they're pretty darn good."

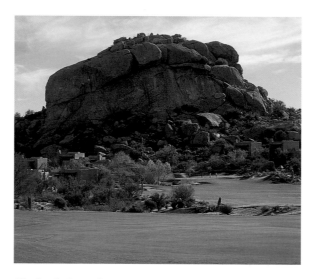

The South Course features huge boulder outcroppings.

Morrish's assessment seems to be shared by the resort's management, as most of the publicity surrounding the golf courses is centered on the South. The No. 1 hole, a short, downhill par 4 to a boulder-backed green, is postcard material. There might not be a better par 5 in the state than No. 5, which zigs and zags its way uphill to a green backed by a mountain of billion-year-old granite balls. Nothing, however, prepares you for the six-story-high boulder that sits all by itself next to the seventh tee. Surreal, to say the least, as the South keeps your interest throughout.

The North is more traditional and tight, with white stakes seemingly everywhere along the house-lined fairways. The heart of the North starts at No. 10, where it reels off three demanding doglegs in a row. If there is a signature hole, it comes at the end of that run, as the par-3 14th is a scary long iron over water to a well-guarded green. The course closes out with another good dogleg par 4 at No. 18, where water and sand once again come into play. Unlike the public and resort guests, the members of The Boulders enjoy both courses equally, perhaps because they have the local knowledge to do so.

But like the A&E people and Andrew Harper have proclaimed, The Boulders is so much more than golf. It's the total experience, especially when you are sitting atop one of those many boulder piles and the sun is setting amid orange, purple, and peach colors. Actually, the activities are endless, ranging from massages at the resort's world-class spa to stargazing at night.

It's easy to take it easy at The Boulders, where the charming rock bungalows are so posh that it's difficult for most couples to leave the luxury behind. But exiling yourself to the splendor of your surroundings would be a huge mistake. Restaurants like the Palo Verde, an oval-shaped cathedral complete with blue sky and stars, are calling.

Afterward, a valet-driven cart waits to return guests back to those cozy/cushy suites snuggled deep in the boulder piles. Just say no. Walking down these nature-filled paths filled with shadows can be much more exhilarating. Especially when the Man in the Moon is smiling down, lighting the way to play. ☼

The sweeping beauty of The Boulders is unbridled.

GOLF CLUB AT CHAPARRAL PINES

PAR: 71 · YARDAGE: 5,543–7010 · RATING: 69.3–73.4 · SLOPE: 122–147 · SIGNATURE HOLE: 624-YARD, PAR-5 Nº 7

ABOVE: *Gary Parks and David Graham blended nature and golf to perfection at Chaparral Pines.*

RIGHT: *At 228-yards, the 13th hole is a stunning par-3.*

NCE UPON A TIME, golf and nature were perceived as rivals, incapable of coexisting harmoniously. But through the years, the opposite has proven true, and nowhere is the story more compelling than at the Golf Club at Chaparral Pines.

Located among the largest stand of Ponderosa pines in the country, the stories that involve people and nature and this golf course are many. In fact, they happen every day on these fairways and greens. Even in the bunkers, where more than one elk calf has been born on top of a natural blanket of soft sand.

Craig Swartwood, the director of sales at Chaparral Pines and the former mayor of Payson, came across one of those special moments not long ago. "Several of us saw the calf, which was still wobbly, probably less than a couple hours old," Swartwood said of the celebrated birth that took place on the fifth hole. "It was so cute, and had no imprint of the fear that sometimes is developed toward humans. The members just watched, and left it alone. I suppose it spent the first 24 hours of its life on the golf course."

Swartwood said Chaparral Pines, which was created by Gary Panks and David Graham in 1997, constantly reverts back to its natural self. "The elk have always lived here, and there is not a day that goes by that they're not on the course," he said. "I've watched a whitetail (deer) raise three different sets of twins on the eighth hole, and we've got every other conceivable species, from javelina and bobcats to mountain lions and bears.

"It's a uniquely located golf course. Gary left the terrain so natural that it didn't displace the wildlife at all. If anything, it just gave them another source of food."

Members also feast here daily, devouring the blend of nature and golf that came out so well, thanks to the last act performed by Panks and Graham. Yes, despite building such noted Arizona layouts as the Talon Course at Grayhawk and the Raven at South Mountain, this one ended up being the coup de grace for the talented tandem, as Graham pursued the Senior PGA Tour and Panks tired of the work.

"It's not important," Panks said of the split. "What matters is that this golf course came out so good. You can never get it 100 percent right, but this one makes me awfully proud. I really believe it's the best course in Arizona."

Panks, who has won the club championship twice, started the ball rolling by simply draping these somewhat narrow tree-lined fairways and massive greens on top of the terrain dealt him. Along the way, the golfer is given a bit of everything—long and short, left and right, wide and tight.

According to Mark Aulerich, the director of golf at Chaparral Pines since the beginning, nature interacts with the course in other ways, too.

The signature 624-yard, par-5 seventh resembles famed Augusta National.

"The course plays dramatically different throughout the seasons," said Aulerich, noting that the club, despite being at an elevation of 4,000 feet, is open year-round. "In the winter, it gets dormant and hard, so it's fast and you get some advantageous kicks. In summer, the grass gets so lush, it's like Velcro and the ball won't even roll off the slopes."

Chaparral Pines, which offers memberships from $15,000 to $50,000, brings on one adventure after another. The front nine is loaded with unique holes and incredible vistas, like the 341-yard third hole. The rambling par 4 starts from on high, takes a big dip, then quickly scrambles up the hill to a green with a backdrop of Diamond Point Mountain

and the Mogollon Rim. The 624-yard seventh hole, which is reminiscent of No. 13 at Augusta National, and the 234-yard eighth hole, a marvelous par 3, also are memorable.

The back nine is a constant blitz of changing beauty and elevations. The 13th, a stunning, 228-yard par 3 to a big, well-bunkered green below, starts a run that never lets up. The 14th, which plays 500 yards straight downhill, was supposed to be a par 4, but the members talked Panks into making it a par 5. Grab your birdie there, as the 15th through 18th holes offer few opportunities, with the possible exception of the 551-yard, par-5 17th that brings the two babbling brooks into play.

"That's the beauty of Chaparral Pines," Aulerich noted. "Gary and David created a course that didn't destroy the environment; it only enhanced it."

Aulerich himself has experienced a rare black mountain lion, although the encounter he'll never forget was the old whiskey still he discovered on the 14th hole. Yes, it was in working condition, still producing moonshine.

"About two weeks before the golf course opened, we were down on the 14th fairway, and there was this cowboy on a horse snooping around," Aulerich explained. "No doubt he was looking for the still, but it was gone. I informed him where it was and he said, 'I didn't even know there was a golf course here.'"

No, at Chaparral Pines, everything remains pretty much the same as its always been. Call it a "natural state" of existence. ✿

COUNTRY CLUB AT DC RANCH

PAR: 72 · YARDAGE: 4,926–6,872 · RATING: 67.1–73.4 · SLOPE: 118–130 · SIGNATURE HOLE: 143-YARD, PAR-3 № 13

Tom Lehman, the best-known member of the Country Club at DC Ranch, understands the finer points of this elite layout. "The greens have a lot of movement and character to them that help you become a better player," said the PGA Tour star whose home is located along the 10th fairway. "They make you visualize the shot and really think about what you're doing.

"For me, the course is a wonderful place to work on my game, rather than having to go to the range all the time. Plus, unlike a lot of desert courses, DC Ranch is fun to play. That might be the biggest deal of all, because some of the desert courses they're building aren't fun to play. I especially enjoy the par 3s, which are about as good as they get, as a group, in the Valley."

Those words represent high praise from Lehman, who has built a few golf courses of his own, including the spectacular Gallery at Dove Mountain near Tucson. Great minds must think alike, as Lehman's endorsement of DC Ranch is exactly what Scott Miller was shooting for when he created the course in 1997. "I think what really surprised me was how good a piece of land this was to build a golf course on," said Miller, whose other efforts in the Valley include Eagle Mountain and Kierland. "I know that the developer [DMB] kind of underplayed the project to me, but when I finally saw it I told them: 'You've got a real gem here.'"

Miller kept it pure by convincing DMB to put 400-foot corridors between the homes and fairways. The 8,300-acre project, which soon will include a public golf course designed by Tom Weiskopf, also added space when DMB sold back 4,000 acres of the McDowell Mountain preserve to the city and scaled back on the number of homes it planned to build.

Naturally, such generosity did not come without expense. DC Ranch's memberships are stiff at $125,000, especially for a family-oriented club, which someday will be 400 members strong.

At the same time, everything was done right, beginning with the course. Unlike some desert tracts, DC Ranch has lots of grass on its wide-open fairways. With only a few exceptions, intimidation is kept to a minimum. "Over the years, I had watched as the housing really impacted the golf at such courses as Desert Highlands, Troon, and The Boulders," Miller said. "That's why I'm so proud of the way DC Ranch turned out. We used about 200 acres for the golf course, which is about 40 acres more than is normally required for a desert layout. You can see and feel the difference when you play it."

Like Lehman, Miller loves the five par 3s, which range from 143 to 224 yards. Perhaps the best of the bunch is No. 7, which provides an awesome backdrop of Wingate Pass, a natural "W" in the nearby McDowells. The hole, which has a big feel to it, stretches from 127 to 224 yards to a green that covers 10,000 square feet. "They're the best collection of par 3s I've ever done," said Miller, whose

DC Ranch offers panoramic views of the Valley.

short holes at Kierland and Eagle Mountain also are exceptional.

There is no debate about the most memorable stretch at DC Ranch. That would be the 12th through the 14th holes, which climb high on the mountain. The 12th is a straight-up-the-hill, 285-yard, go-for-it par 4 with trouble (bunkers and desert) encompassing the green. Not nearly as threatening is the 13th, a glamour shot of 143 yards across a small canyon to a green sandwiched between a man-made rock wall and a natural version in the rear. Yes, the 13th is the signature, although the 14th, a 443-yard par 4 that drops 150 feet to the green below, might be good enough to stir up a small argument.

As good as the course is, and all 18 holes are playable *and* pretty, the hacienda-style clubhouse is very cool. Designed like a ranch house in Mexico, with a big courtyard filled with buckboards, wagon wheels, and old-fashioned pumps used to water the horses, it exudes originality. With lots of wood, leather, and tile, the 31,000-square-foot structure comes off as cowboy chic. Perhaps it is a reminder of the past, as the area was once a cattle operation known as Desert Camp Ranch. Yep, "DC" for short.

Like all of the more respected private clubs in Arizona, DC Ranch already has hosted a major event in the 1998 Goldwater Cup Matches. Members of the Southwest PGA and the Arizona Golf Association loved it, praising Miller's work for its playability, fairness, and character. They also thought highly of the service, which came with a smile.

According to Jerry Collins, the head pro at DC Ranch, those are the same attributes that the members hold so dear. And, no, Collins emphasized, you don't have to be a prestigious member of the PGA Tour to enjoy them.

"Tom's a super guy. The best," Collins said of Lehman. "But, seriously, we treat him just like all of our other members, which means first-class." ✿

DESERT FOREST GOLF CLUB

PAR: 72 • YARDAGE: 5,699–7,011 • RATING: 67.0–75.4 • SLOPE: 130–149 • SIGNATURE HOLES: 440-YARD, PAR-3 № 13; 523-YARD, PAR-5 № 16

EW GOLF CLUBS or courses can be described in one word. But when the club and the course are among the best of the best, thoughts become more precise. Such is the case of Desert Forest Golf Club, where a single syllable gets it done: Pure.

Not only does it apply to the free-flowing golf course that Red Lawrence built on the edge of Carefree in 1962, but also to the club's philosophy.

Desert Forest is a golf club, not a country club, and therein lies the difference. The business is golf, not swimming or tennis or bridge. Just golf, and Desert Forest is the office.

The attitude behind Desert Forest starts with the club's mission statement: " . . . welcoming those who share our core values of a challenging, high-quality course with uncrowded playing conditions and modest facilities." How refreshing.

Desert Forest is one of only 31 courses in the country that have made *Golf Digest's* list of "America's 100 Greatest Golf Courses" every year since 1966, when the game's oldest rankings were established.

The club was founded by K. T. Palmer and Tom Darlington, developers whose strong ties to

The 18th hole at Desert Forest is dazzling and demanding.

Arizona golf started with Paradise Valley Country Club, another upper-crust membership they helped put together a decade earlier. This time, the emphasis was on Desert Forest being the catalyst to attract residents and visitors to Carefree, a remote area north of Scottsdale that Palmer and Darlington (Carefree Development Company) were ramrodding. As a result, not all play at Desert Forest was private in the beginning, as 50 tee times a day were available to guests of the next-door Carefree Inn.

Slowly, issues like a clubhouse and water were resolved, and Desert Forest became totally private to its 250 members. Yet this pristine piece of property was shared with the golf community by hosting such events in the early years as the Dunlop Masters, Arizona Open, and Arizona Amateur. In 1973, Desert Forest was the site for the prestigious Pacific Coast Amateur, and in 1990 hosted the U.S. Senior Amateur Championship.

As a result, Desert Forest's reputation, somewhat to its chagrin, grew by leaps and bounds. Yet the same clubhouse stayed in place, as did the members, who simply savored the experience even more. Considering memberships in this neighborhood go for as much as $175,000 at Desert Mountain, the $70,000 that Desert Forest charges looks mighty good, even if there is a two- to three-year wait. "We're a golf club and nothing else," said club president Jay Christensen. "We have no criteria for membership other than you love the game of golf and respect it."

Especially when it's played at Desert Forest, which boasts Arizona's only bentgrass fairways and some of the slickest yet subtle putting surfaces around. Like top-ranked Pine Valley, to which it often has been compared, Desert Forest is loaded with hopscotch fairways, alternate routes, tight doglegs, semiblind shots, smallish greens, and traditional bunkering. In fact, while most regard nearby Desert Highlands as the forerunner of target golf in the early 1980s, many of Desert Highland's traits are present at Desert Forest. "They tend to forget about us, but we were here 40 years ago with that exact [target] concept," Christensen noted. "At the same time, that's OK. We're not worried about [publicity]."

Yes, life is good at Desert Forest, which has been tweaked a few times by Tom Weiskopf, but mostly runs true to Lawrence's original routing. Nature is given paramount attention, as deer, javelina, quail, and coyotes are recognized as the area's original residents. Lawrence also did his best to keep things natural, literally draping the course over this rolling terrain of arroyos and sand hills. Each fairway seems to be its own space, with constant movement adding to the vast variety. The surrounding desert is like a cactus garden, full of staghorn, agave, prickly pear, yuccas, ocotillos, and saguaros.

The first six holes are tight and testy, with the fun beginning at No. 7, a 557-yard dogleg over the mesquites and palo verdes to a well-bunkered green high on the hill. Birdies are commonplace, but so are bogeys, as the green slides significantly. Two holes on the back nine—the 440-yard, par-4 13th and the 523-yard, par-5 16th—were named to *Golf Magazine's* "Top 500 Holes in the United States" list. The 13th is a slight dogleg left with a 16-yard wide landing area in the fairway, and an uphill green deemed the club's most difficult. The 16th, a rambling par 5 that incorporates a 100-year-old mesquite into the middle of the fairway, might be the most unique hole on the course.

According to Doug MacDonald, the head pro since 1991, there are several dos and don'ts at Desert Forest. "You've got to drive it straight, and you can't be above the hole [on the green]," MacDonald noted. "The course is consistently good throughout, but you can't overpower it. And, yes, it's tight, but it's a fair tight. Best of all, every time you play it, it's different. That's why no one ever tires of it."

Located down the sleepy little side street called Mule Train Road, it might be obvious why the membership keeps this desert gem under wraps: Course preservation. Not long ago, the U.S. Golf Association approached Desert Forest about hosting the 2004 Walker Cup Matches. There was no interest. "They wanted to make some changes to the course, which is pretty much a normal procedure for those courses," Christensen noted. "We said, 'No, thanks.' We like this golf course just like it is."

The late Red Lawrence, a common fellow who had a strong sense of humor, would have loved such a gesture. He always coveted this course among his 15 layouts in Arizona. After all, Desert Forest was his Mona Lisa, the one that helped him earn his legendary nickname—"The Desert Fox." ✿

DESERT HIGHLANDS GOLF CLUB

PAR: 72 • YARDAGE: 5,025–7,062 • RATING: 67.9–74.1 • SLOPE: 122–151 • SIGNATURE HOLE: 417-YARD, PAR-4 № 14

At the time, Jack Nicklaus and Lyle Anderson were just trying to build a new and different style of golf course on one of the more pristine pieces of property in Arizona. That the end result, Desert Highlands, took desert golf into a whole new world was as much innocence as it was ingenuity.

Architect Nicklaus and developer Anderson were linked by another designer, Jay Morrish, who was an associate with Nicklaus in 1980, the year Anderson started the ball known as "target golf" rolling. Sent by the Golden Bear to check out this awesome site on the south slope of Pinnacle Peak, Morrish reported to Nicklaus that all systems were go. "Jay took one look at Pinnacle Peak and said Jack would love to do it," Anderson recalled. "That Jay went on to become one of the best [designers] in the business, was really no surprise to me."

Nicklaus, who was playing in the Byron Nelson Classic in Dallas at the time of Morrish's visit, jumped on his jet and flew to Scottsdale the next day. "We met in Jack's hotel room that night, and worked out the concept for what became desert golf," Anderson added. "They called it 'target golf,' but to me the name was not as important as what we accomplished, which was the idea of building great golf courses without using too much water or grass."

The new environmentally aware design technique kept the grass and desert in separate sections. They were linked by transition or waste areas of dirt and sand. Most important, the concept worked, as desert golf exploded like wild flowers. Naturally,

Pinnacle Peak pops up behind the signature 14th hole.

Desert Highlands was the setting for the original Skins Game, which featured Jack Nicklaus, Arnold Palmer, Gary Player, and Tom Watson.

clubhouse facilities. The horizon was expanded to include a new state-of-the-art tennis facility. But the past is preserved, too. Scorecards from the original Skins Game in 1983 adorn the locker room walls, telling all that Gary Player was the winner in the match that also featured Nicklaus, Arnold Palmer, and Tom Watson. The following year, Nicklaus was the Skins champ, and then the original "Silly Season" event departed for California. Over the years, Desert Highlands also hosted the Spalding Invitational, as well as several state championships.

Good players have always cherished this course. The front side is the more difficult of the two nines, especially the stretch from No. 5 through No. 8, where Nicklaus weaved together a tenacious test of split fairways, multiple-tiered greens, and massive moguls. A fine example is No. 8, a 438-yard par 4 that offers two different routes to the green. The best of the back side begins at No. 13 and concludes with back-to-back par 3s followed by back-to-back par 5s. The signature hole is No. 14, a 417-yard climb straight into Pinnacle Peak, although there are some who argue that the shorter tee shots at the 145-yard 15th and the 245-yard 16th are what a player remembers most.

"Actually, the greens have always been Desert Highlands' calling card," said Steve Satterstrom, the director of golf. "When they get them rolling, they have as much speed and undulations as any in the Valley. If you changed them, you wouldn't have Desert Highlands."

Toning down the greens has always been bantered about. Even Nicklaus has attempted to make several functional changes. "But Lyle has always said: 'Don't touch them,'" Nicklaus added. "He feels that was the way [my] design philosophy was back in the early '80s, and it should be preserved."

Yes, never mess with a classic, especially one done by golf's Golden Bear. ⚙

such success did not come without critics. Some felt Desert Highlands, at least the original version, which included some tough recovery areas around the greens, was too extreme and possibly unfair. Nicklaus had a different view.

"Looking back, I was actually pretty mellow in those days," said the Golden Bear, whose design style has often reflected the times. "Some people felt the greens were too tough, but others found them easy. I spent my next five years making them bumpier. But over the years, I think that my best work was where the design was dictated by the demands and enhanced by variety. In that sense, I'm proud of Desert Highlands."

Even though some elements of the course have been revved down, others remain as Nicklaus, Morrish, and Bob Cupp, the other associate designer on the project, left them. And make no mistake, this

talented architectural trio had a lot to do with the success of Desert Highlands, which took four years to complete from the dream state to the grand opening in 1984. "There was a lot of talent on that job, and it shows," said Cupp, who like Morrish set out on his own shortly after Desert Highlands was completed. "But I have to give a lot of the credit to Jack, who spent so much time there. Trust me, he knows every square inch of that golf course."

Cupp said the real rap on Desert Highlands was not the greens, but how to get from tee to green. "Jack won't compromise length, and that's why his courses are for the better players," Cupp noted. "Desert Highlands is a wonderful course that fits that bill. But more than that, it's the one that changed Arizona golf."

Desert Highlands still is evolving. Recently its 650 members spent $7 million to renovate its

GOLF CLUB AT DESERT MOUNTAIN

APACHE: Par: 72 • Yardage: 5,650–7,191 • Rating: 68.5–73.9 • Slope: 125–137 • Signature hole: 551-yard, par-5 №18

CHIRICAHUA: Par: 72 • Yardage: 5,034–7,418 • Rating: 69.0–76.1 • Slope: 127–154 • Signature hole: 159-yard, par-3 №8

COCHISE: Par: 72 • Yardage: 5,058–7,002 • Rating: 68.2–74.3 • Slope: 122–142 • Signature hole: 548-yard, par-5 №15

GERONIMO: Par: 72 • Yardage: 5,565–7,414 • Rating: 68.8–77.7 • Slope: 132–153 • Signature hole: 197-yard, par-3 №18

RENEGADE: Par: 72 • Yardage: 5,136–7,008 • Rating: 67.8–75.1 • Slope: 120–139 • Signature hole: 230-yard, par-3 №4

MOST PEOPLE would have passed on the opportunity to hike a mountain on that fateful day back in 1984. Oh, sure, the morning was balmy, and spring had definitely sprung. But still, weaving your way up the side of a steep slope through cactus and sagebrush and rattlesnakes—oh, my!—wouldn't have that much appeal, especially if you were alone. Would it?

Most people don't know Lyle Anderson, and if the truth be known, the golf course mogul likes it that way. If they did, they would realize that nothing much gets in the way of Scottsdale's most dynamic developer of mansions, fairways, and greens. Vision has always been his calling card, and there was no turning back as he ground his car to a halt on the eastern outskirts of Carefree, then laced up his tennis shoes for an eight-hour trip to who knows where.

"For months, I had tried to get someone to take me out to look at that piece of land, but with no success," recalled Anderson in reference to the 8,000-acre parcel that soon would become known as the Golf Club at Desert Mountain. "Finally, I just parked the car one day and hiked from the road all the way to the top of the highest peak. As it turned out, it took all day, and I had to go it alone every step of the way, but that was when I really became enthused."

What Anderson saw that day, only he knows for sure. But the revelation must have been a clear one, because five golf courses and nearly 2,300 members later, Desert Mountain continues to be the toast of the Great Southwest. With memberships now selling for $175,000 per pop, and two more layouts designed by his buddy Jack Nicklaus yet on the way, even Anderson is somewhat blown away by the secret of his success. "Amazing," said Anderson, who purchased "the Mountain" for $45 million, or about the total sum these days for one month's worth of

OPPOSITE: *The Apache's boulder-strewn 18th is its signature hole.*
RIGHT: *The seventh and 15th holes at Cochise form a double green.*

sales. "I knew we had stumbled onto something big even back then, but I never knew it would be this enormous."

Despite some growing pains in the mid- to late 1980s, Desert Mountain continues to bloom like the many stately saguaros that stand watch over this special piece of ground. With acre lots selling for $450,000 and up, the place could easily be referred to as the Gold Club at Desert Mountain.

"I'm not sure that people really understand what a special type of golf course Lyle introduced to the game," said Nicklaus. He and Anderson had formulated the concept of desert or target golf in a Scottsdale hotel room back in 1980, just prior to building Desert Highlands, their first venture. "But

without those early ideas that we formulated, desert golf never would have blossomed to the degree it has today. I know that I'm very proud of what we've accomplished. We saved a lot of water, and introduced the beauty of the desert to many people who never would have understood the majesty of the region had we not built it."

Anderson and Nicklaus christened the Renegade Course in 1987. It was followed a year later by Cochise Course, the annual site of The Countrywide Tradition, one of the major championships on the Senior PGA Tour. In 1989, Geronimo was opened near the apex of the mountain, followed in 1996 by Apache, a links-style endeavor designed to add variety to the foursome.

Most people thought Desert Mountain was complete at that point, but Anderson's vision went onward, and in 1999 the newest member of golf's Mount Rushmore, Chiricahua, was added to the mix. "I really thought Chiricahua might be our last course at Desert Mountain," Anderson conceded. "And if it had been, then I would have been very satisfied, because Chiricahua is such a wonderful golf course."

As it turns out, Anderson and Nicklaus are still scaling "the Mountain," even though they are planning something big on the Gold Coast of Kona in the Hawaiian Islands. But then, what would you expect from the Bill Gates of golf course development? "Yes, Jack and I have got the plans for a sixth course ready to go, and we'll break ground soon," Anderson said, not divulging the name of the new course, though existing courses all have honored the history and traditions of Native Americans, the original owners of this sacred setting. "I'm also exploring the possibility of an executive nine or 18 holes on the western corner of the property. I think it would be great for kids, and for people who don't want to spend four or five hours on the golf course."

Will so many courses dilute the posh pool? Anderson doesn't think so. "To have such a variety of great golf courses, it just makes me immensely proud," he said. "Each one is special in its own right."

And here's why:

Apache

SEEKING DIVERSITY, Nicklaus added a wee bit of Scottish flair to this links-style layout that stretches 7,200 yards through the undulating desert. As a result, Apache is more traditional in the sense that it's less target golf than the other four courses. It's also more player friendly, as grassy approaches to the relatively large greens seem to tie together with the fairway.

The front nine plays down the hill and then back up. Along the way is No. 3, a 150-yard par 3 that offers an outstanding view of the entire Valley. The back nine is more rambling, with lots of elevation that comes at the golfer in spurts. The variety also is wonderful, as there are three par 3s, three par 4s, and three par 5s. Among the memorable ones are the 17th, a 226-yard blind par 3 that plays uphill, and the 18th, a 551-yard par 5 that features two separate greens tucked behind a large rock outcropping.

Although Apache is presently the least favorite of the five courses among the members, that view might change in the near future with the addition of a rustic Southwestern clubhouse. With lots of fireplaces throughout, the new addition will feature a large patio facing its namesake, Apache Peak.

Chiricahua

NICKLAUS WOULD NEVER SAY SO, but his enthusiasm was obvious when he carved the Chiricahua Course out of the top of "the Mountain." Perhaps that's obvious when Nicklaus says that he wants his fifth course here to be the "Pine Valley of the desert."

Certainly, Chiricahua has a chance to live up to its creator's wish. With an elevation that drops 600 feet from top to bottom, and with some spectacular views of the Valley, the word "awesome" comes into play often. The red-sand bunkering and a variety of big, gently sloping greens, further distinguish the layout.

Is Chiricahua the best Desert Mountain has to offer? Many think so, including the majority of the membership, which refers to it as the "jewel in the crown." Of the five courses, it clearly has the most playable greens and widest fairways. There are very few forced carries, adding to the playability.

Seven holes play down the hill, six up, and the remaining five are a mix. According to Nicklaus, the course really doesn't take off until the seventh hole. Perhaps the best test on the front side, or maybe it's just the prettiest, is No. 8, a 159-yard shot slightly uphill and across a big wash to a green nestled into a small hill. A stately saguaro off the tee adds to the look. The back nine is just one great hole after another. The closing stretch starts at the 15th hole, and is a steady climb until you reach No. 18, a picturesque par 4 saddled into the mountain.

If the golf course isn't enough to knock your golf socks off, then the future clubhouse will be. Located at the highest point of Desert Mountain, it looks out on the Valley near the point where Anderson once discovered the site. The view is to die for.

Nicklaus, who considers the work he did at Desert Mountain among the best of his nearly 200 courses worldwide, gives all the credit to Anderson. "You're the one who thought of all this," the Bear tells Anderson.

Anderson, a modest man, smiles at the comment and winks. "But remember, we're not done yet," Anderson says of the ongoing hike up "the Mountain."

Cochise

WHAT MOST PEOPLE DON'T KNOW about the course that hosts The Countrywide Tradition is that it wasn't originally intended to do so. Nope, the Senior PGA Tour event actually was supposed to be played on the more difficult Geronimo layout. "Cochise was going to be the members' course—softer and prettier," Nicklaus recalled. "But the tournament came along in 1988, and Geronimo wasn't finished. But it all worked out, probably for the better."

The members of the senior tour certainly think so. In fact, they regard it so highly that every year it's voted as the best-conditioned course on the senior tour. There are several reasons for this.

- Cochise contains tee shots better than Geronimo—even errant shots like the one struck by Terry Dill into a member's pool during the 1997 Tradition, a miscue he ended up getting a free drop on. Seriously!

- Botched approach shots are not quite as penal as the ones chunked at Geronimo.

- The course features five par 3s and five par 5s, the variety going a long way. It also helps to have six signature holes, which include Nos. 5, 7, 13, 15, 17, and 18.

- Cochise is shorter than Geronimo, which means the forced carries are not quite as gargantuan, and the "Over the Hill Gang" likes that a lot.

There might be some debate over its reputation as the most popular course on "the Mountain," but considering the vast majority of the members here also are growing older, it would make sense. Plus, they see Cochise year after year on network TV, and that also makes a lasting impression.

If the Cochise course is not enough, there is always the opulent, 52,000-square-foot clubhouse, which also serves as the chief retreat for those playing the Geronimo course. The views are so spectacular, and the confines so exquisite, that the senior players also have dubbed it best on the tour.

Geronimo

Once upon a time, Geronimo struck fear into the hearts of pioneers. The notorious Apache leader was ruthless in battle, laying many ambushes during his days of glory. The same can be said of the namesake golf course, although several improvements since the course's conception have mellowed it slightly.

From the pro tees, Geronimo plays a staggering, 7,437 yards. Its 77.1 slope is one of the steepest in Arizona. Considering the sharp inclines and rugged elevations, this can be one tenacious golf course.

But it also can be beautiful, with an abundance of great views and picturesque tee and green settings. When the sun begins to settle, the shadows simply dance across its sweeping fairways, hiding behind the many mounds that cloak this course in mystery. In that sense, Geronimo stands out from its four brethren.

Despite its toughness, there is hope if you select the right tees. A clear mind also is key, as course management is paramount on Geronimo. Of the two nines, the front is much easier, which is the way it should be. But woe to those players who are not in a groove by the time they reach the 13th hole, as the closing stretch's tightness and shallow greens can be very mean.

Fortunately, the extremely difficult 14th, which originally featured a blind approach shot into a bowl-like green, has been redesigned. When the the 40-foot flagstick was replaced with an 8-foot rendition, it was a move that drew a standing ovation.

The signature hole remains the 197-yard 18th, the only time Nicklaus has ever finished off one of his nearly 200 courses with a par 3. It's perfect, really: An intimidating medium-to-long iron to a two-tiered green that is surrounded by rocks and a steep cavern.

"The lay of the land dictated the finish," Nicklaus explained. "It certainly leaves a lasting impression." Geronimo would have loved it.

Renegade

Renegade has a split personality, primarily because each hole has five or six tee boxes, and each green has two sets of flags. High handicappers take the white route, while scratch players go gold to gold. "It's a great golf course, because it appeals to golfers of every level, as they can mix and match," said Dick Hyland, the longtime general manager at Desert Mountain. "You can bite off as much as you want to bite off. What other course can offer that?"

Located at a lower elevation on the property, Renegade is quite playable, with fairly wide landing areas. The greens are gigantic, but lack big tiers or shelves, so they are not too imposing. The best stretch is the ninth through 12th holes, which begin with back-to-back par 5s followed by a short par 4 and a long par 3 to an hourglass green. The final shot is fairly typical of Renegade, as most greens offer several distinct sections to separate the pins. The signature hole, however, comes early, as the 230-yard, par-3 fourth is framed by water and a stone wall featuring a mountain backdrop.

Depending on how you choose to play it, Renegade can be a lion or a lamb. ☼

ABOVE: *The par-3 fourth hole on the Renegade Course.*

OPPOSITE: *The Renegade's two greens and numerous tee boxes gives golfers of all skill levels a great outing.*

PAR: 72 • YARDAGE: 6,108–7,146 • RATING: 68.9–75.1.4 • SLOPE: 126–140 • SIGNATURE HOLE: 137-YARD, PAR-3 Nº 11

NO GOLF COURSE architect in recent memory has built more award-winning courses than Tom Fazio. One of the reasons for his success is that no one holds Fazio to higher standards than he does himself. "It's nice when someone considers me to be the best, even though I've still got a lot to learn," said the 54-year-old Carolinan, whose résumé is fast approaching 200 golf courses, many of them among the elite of the world.

"You know, I rest my reputation on a course every time I do one. I always look back at it, put myself in the box, and say: 'What would you have done differently if you could do it all over again?' because the reality is, you always can. You can always play things back and find a better way. I do that constantly, and I have my staff take the same approach."

One of the perks of being such a highly regarded designer is that the opportunities are often greater, and the variety of spectacular parcels often secures your standing in the golf community forever. Such was the case with Estancia, which blew even Fazio away.

"What separates Arizona's courses from [other parts of the country] is that desert courses can be so dramatic," Fazio explained. "But the first time I saw the property that became Estancia, I was in shock. I knew almost immediately I'd never been offered a greater place to design a golf course."

Nestled on the northern slope of Pinnacle Peak, with an abundance of nooks and crannies, as well as some awesome rock outcroppings, this was a "gimme" when it came to golden opportunities. To his credit, Fazio delivered with the 1996 New Private Course of the Year award, from *Golf Digest*.

Even today, the magazine's opinion of Estancia remains quite lofty, as it was the highest-rated course in Arizona—No. 65—when *Golf Digest* released its list of "Top 100 Courses in America for 1999." An amazing feat, considering no outside golf association has ever played the course due to the club's restricted charter.

What's odd, however, is that the original Estancia project went bust in the mid-1980s shortly after Tom Weiskopf and Jay Morrish had laid out the course. For almost five years, Estancia remained in limbo until the developers eventually recovered

Pinnacle Peak is the sentry at the Estancia Club.

the project and turned it over to Fazio. "When it came out of bankruptcy, it was the original piece plus more acreage," said Fazio, who also built the Raptor Course at Grayhawk and both courses at Ventana Canyon. "Everything just fell into place."

Estancia takes off immediately, as the first four holes weave their way through the westernmost section of the property, then climb Pinnacle Peak for some fun. "Some of my favorite holes come right out of the chute," Fazio added. "For instance, the first hole has awesome green settings in those rocks, the same place where you'll find the tee box for No. 2. Those rock outcroppings simply made that golf course."

The same could be said of the sixth and seventh holes, which work their way into the course's southern corner. The sixth, a 365-yard dogleg par 4 that breaks right up the hill, is nearly blind all the way. The seventh, a 175-yard par 3 from high off the ledge to a well-bunkered green below, is what the 300 members pay the big bucks for, in this case $150,000 plus property.

The back nine also begins with an uphill par 4 followed by the course's signature 11th hole. Tucked into a small pocket right below the popular peak, and surrounded by monstrous boulders that rival those at The Boulders, this 137-yard tee shot is short and beyond sweet. "The 11th was a tricky area to build in, but it was perfect for a par 3 for obvious reasons," Fazio noted. "With all those great rocks around, it was just an automatic fit."

The par-5 17th hole, a 565-yard dogleg that winds its way left around yet another rock outpost, then down the hill to an oval-shaped green primped by a solo pot bunker, also is a Fazio favorite. "A lot of this golf course looks like no excavation ever took place, like it's all-natural, and that's not something that's easy to do," Fazio said. "Personally, I don't know if I've ever created a course with so much character. Once you play it, it remains in your mind forever. To me, it's easy to see why Estancia didn't miss."

Of course, it helps to have one of the world's top architects, a guy who turns out award winners like he's holing one-foot putts. ⚙

The par-4 fifth hole is charming and challenging.

FOREST HIGHLANDS GOLF CLUB

CANYON: PAR: 71 · YARDAGE: 7,001 · RATING: 66.5–72.9 · SLOPE: 116–131 · SIGNATURE HOLE: 467-YARD, PAR-4 NO. 9

MEADOW: PAR: 72 · YARDAGE: 7,272 · RATING: 67.7–73.3 · SLOPE: 117–130 · SIGNATURE HOLE: 575-YARD, PAR-5 NO. 14

SINCE ITS CONCEPTION in 1987, fabulous Forest Highlands has been one of Arizona's most successful private clubs, which explains its nickname— Paradise in the Pines.

No wonder 180 lots at an average price of $450,000 sold out quickly when Forest Highlands opened up a second course in 1999. Yes, the place is that popular. "I would venture to say that almost every golfer who can afford it covets the Forest Highlands experience," said Jack Grehan, the club's general manager. "Everything has turned out so well up here, from the homes to the courses to the clubhouses."

Denise Martinez, the director of golf at Forest Highlands, said there is another key as to why the club's 800 members can't get enough. "It's nice to have two championship courses that are so different," Martinez pointed out. "Usually, one course dominates a two-course facility. But our members seem to be split right down the middle on which they like best. That's a great situation to be in."

The members at Forest Highlands, which is carved out of the tall pines south of Flagstaff, can thank Tom Weiskopf and Jay Morrish. Weiskopf was the driving force, as he teamed up with Morrish to do the Canyon course, then came back ten years later to go solo on the Meadow. "You couldn't have asked for a better piece of property," Weiskopf said of the first course. "[Developer] Jim Barlett and his partners really delivered, and Jay and I did a good job keeping things natural."

Only one radical move was made, and that came at Morrish's suggestion. "I took one look at that big canyon where the back nine is located, and I was worried about cart traffic and all the elevations," Morrish recalled. "I said to Tom, 'We're going to have trouble making them use all 14 clubs in their bag, so I'd like to do something different here. Otherwise, there's going to be a lot of par 4s that are just a driver and a wedge, especially with that elevation [7,200 feet above sea level].'"

Morrish devised a plan to build six par 3s, five par 5s, and seven par 4s. "I think it worked, because most people never realize that starting at No. 4, every other hole is a par 3 through the 14th."

Ironically, it was a par 4—the 467-yard ninth— that turned out to be the signature hole. The ride starts high on a hillside loaded with wild flowers, then floats through a storybook meadow lined with a babbling brook. The green is accented by a waterfall, pond, and pines. "I remember the first time we hit a ball off that tee," Morrish beamed. "I counted one thousand one, one thousand two, one thousand three, one thousand four, and finally, on one thousand five, it hit the canyon floor."

Weiskopf has his own recollection about the first course. "I remember it finished second in the 'New Private Course' category by a single vote to Shadow Glen, another course we did that year in Kansas City," Weiskopf said, shaking his head in disbelief. "That's funny, because Forest Highlands is now in the top 100 courses [No. 82] by *Golf Digest*, and Shadow Glen is nowhere in sight."

Of course, hosting such prestigious events as the 1996 U.S. Junior Amateur Championship, along with the 1991 Pacific Coast Amateur, goes a long way in furthering a club's national reputation. And to its credit, Forest Highlands also is part of the Arizona golf community, hosting such past events as the Arizona Amateur and the Goldwater Cup.

The addition of the second course has only strengthened Forest Highlands' position among the elite. The Meadow, which is located on a higher piece of ground and offers more spectacular views of the San Francisco Peaks, has twice as many bunkers that are twice as big. More traditional, the Meadow also has more water. "I think it's a little softer course that really flows nicely," Martinez said. "But most important, it's a fun golf course."

Among members' favorite holes are No. 4, a sharp dogleg right that rambles down a steep hill with those awesome peaks in the background; No. 8, a medium iron to an island green; No. 14, a par 5 that also incorporates the peaks as well as a lake down the entire left side; and No. 18, a 575-yard dogleg back up the hill to a sliding green. "I like it as much as the first one," Weiskopf said. "They wanted a course that would complement but not conflict, and it defines its purpose perfectly."

If the truth be known, those with families prefer the Meadow because the course is easier and there are more recreational facilities, such a fitness club. Members without children, and better golfers, probably go more for the Canyon. The food and drink produced by Chef Tony Cosentino and his staff is hard to beat at either retreat. "As a golfer and an architect, I'd put the Canyon Course in the top five of the 30 courses I've done with Jay," Weiskopf said. "Those would be, in no specific order, Forest Highlands, Loch Lomond, The Rim Club, Troon, and Double Eagle. I know which one is my favorite, but I shouldn't say."

But Weiskopf said that if a member at Forest Highlands pressed him, he might reveal his pick. Maybe. . . ."I sold my home up there several years ago, but I'm still up there quite a bit," he said. "Being one of the most beautiful places on Earth, it's hard to resist." ☼

Tom Weiskopf went solo on the Meadow Course.

GAINEY RANCH GOLF CLUB

PAR: 72 • YARDAGE: 5,055–6,786 • RATING: 65.9–75.3 • SLOPE: 115–132 • SIGNATURE HOLE: 492-YARD, PAR-5 №9 (LAKES NINE)

BACK IN 1985, when Gainey Ranch Golf Club made its debut as one of Scottsdale's finest, it was on the northernmost outskirts of the city, far from the madding crowd. Today, Gainey nestles in the heart of downtown, with three mature nine-hole layouts that represent location, location, location.

The nearly 500-strong membership adores the golf courses, which are surrounded by a gated, upscale neighborhood. In many ways, this is Scottsdale's version of a golfing oasis.

Fifty years ago, Gainey Ranch was just that, a cattle operation owned by Daniel C. Gainey, whose passion was Arabian horses and fine wines. Then along came Markland Properties in the 1980s and the rest, as they say, is Arizona golf history. Jim Murphy, the jovial yet highly respected director of golf at Gainey, knows why his club has become so popular. The list is a long one, according to "Murph."

"The number-one reason is it's pretty, which is a prerequisite of all great golf courses," he said. "Second, it's wall-to-wall grass in the desert, and players of all calibers love that because you can hit your ball and find it. The pace of play is always

Water and waterfalls abound at Gainey Ranch.

good, because we let our members and guests take their carts off the path. And the service is fantastic. It's our trademark."

The amenities are pretty good, too. Gainey Ranch is so well thought of that it holds the distinction of being named to *Golf Shop Operations*' list of top 100 pro shops a record 12 times. The Terraces Restaurant also packs in the hungry souls who are spent from a long day of golf. Gainey Ranch is a gracious host, allowing playing privileges to those guests who stay at the nearby Hyatt at Gainey Ranch. The award-winning hotel also has a few great eateries of its own, including the Golden Swan and Sandolo's, where gondola rides on the hotel's lake offer the perfect after-dinner experience. In addition, the golf course also sports a heavy water-park theme, as the Lakes and Arroyo nines are lined with the wet stuff. Perhaps it's not so surprising that they also are the most popular combination.

An early entry into the private Scottsdale golf market, many have forgotten just how good Gainey Ranch really is. But when Club Corp of America adds a course to its portfolio, which also includes prestigious Pinehurst in North Carolina and Firestone in Ohio, there is a sense of arrival.

Gainey Ranch was the creation of Brad Benz and Mike Poellot, two architects with international reputations. The tandem has since gone their separate ways, each rising to revered status in the Orient. It is somewhat telltale that Gainey Ranch has some of that exotic flair.

Of the three nines, the Lakes gets top billing. Having water on six holes always seems to make for an entertaining round of golf. The signature hole is the 492-yard ninth, which brings water into play all the way down the right side, with a bail-out area to the left. The waterfall in the background looks like it belongs in this semitropical environment. Almost as good is the 410-yard seventh hole, which ranks as the number-one handicap. Having even more water

than the ninth hole will do that, as No. 7 has H_2O on both sides and a creek that runs through it.

The Arroyo, while it sounds a little dry, also brings water into play on its signature hole, which again pops up at No. 9. The 555-yard par 5 features water down the left side and a palm-laden green setting that looks more Hawaiian than desert. Once again, there is a close rival, as the par-3 sixth hole is picture-perfect with a waterfall framing the elongated green.

The Dunes is more of a links look with nary a body of water in sight. Instead, lots of bunkers and Buffalo grass give it that Scottish feel, which is a nice change of pace for those who have been dunked earlier. Again, the ninth hole, a 550-yard par 5, is the signature, with a deep wash that divides the fairway proving to be the chief hazard.

"What you get at Gainey is variety, and I think that is of major importance to all great golf experiences," Murphy noted. "Add that into the factors [aforementioned], and we make a lot of golfers very happy."

But even those who blow sky-high and lose a dozen balls in the water can find refuge in the clubhouse. As Murphy pointed out, even though Dan Gainey left the ranch in the early '80s, a part of him remains. "Dan Gainey has a vineyard in California, and we sell his Gainey wines in the pro shop and restaurant," Murph reported. "His chardonnay has won a lot of awards, and his reds are also excellent."

Some would say that the fine wine is a direct reflection of Gainey Ranch Golf Club, which just keeps getting better. ☼

THE GALLERY AT DOVE MOUNTAIN

PAR: 72 • YARDAGE: 5,323–7,412 • RATING: 68.9–74.6 • SLOPE: 122–138 • SIGNATURE HOLE: 725-YARD, PAR-5 № 9

EVERYTHING HAS ALWAYS pointed straight north—or should we say up—for The Gallery at Dove Mountain, a dramatic golf club draped across a tip of the Tortolito Mountains.

First and foremost is its owner, John MacMillan, who hails from way up *north*. One of the most prominent citizens of Minneapolis, MacMillan oversees Cargill Inc., the family's agricultural empire that is the largest of its kind in the United States. Needing an outlet from the real world, MacMillan decided to build a private golf course and do it right. No expense was spared from the lavish $20 million layout to the $10 million clubhouse that exudes Southwestern ultra-chic.

As you might have guessed, MacMillan selected his course site *north* of Tucson on the towering outskirts of Marana. That he went even farther *north* to gain inspiration should come as no surprise. "The vision came during a traffic jam on the way to Desert Mountain," said MacMillan of the now-funny incident that drove him south to The Gallery. "To me, Desert Mountain is the benchmark for golf in Arizona. Those five Jack Nicklaus courses are my favorites among his work. At the same time, I didn't like dealing with all the things it took to get there."

So MacMillan hired a pair of architects with northern roots. John Fought came from Oregon, and PGA Tour star Tom Lehman grew up in MacMillan's home state. "I asked them to create a golf course that I would never grow tired of," MacMillan said of the mission to establish northern exposure near the Old Pueblo. "Then they went and exceeded my expectations."

Fought and Lehman might have been perfect chemistry, as their careers are forged in irony. Fought, the 1977 U.S. Amateur champ, was expected to be a superstar, especially after he earned Rookie of the Year honors on the PGA Tour in 1979. Lehman, who nearly gave up the game at almost the exact time Fought was flourishing, spent over a decade as a struggling pro.

Today, Fought is one of the most respected golf course designers in the industry, while Lehman is among the biggest names in professional golf after winning the 1996 British Open. That life brought them full circle to Dove Mountain is just one of the many tender twists that produced The Gallery.

What Fought and Lehman did particularly well was make a course that is fun to play. With lots of tees and exquisite bunkering reminiscent of the sweeping, finger-style looks of Pinehurst No. 2, The Gallery never lets up. Amazing, since most people think the first hole is perhaps the signature. Fairways that fan out 80 yards wide, and greens that range from 8,000 square feet up to 13,000, keep golfers smiling.

The front nine is a roller coaster as it climbs its way to the fifth hole. The 434-yard par 4 is tucked into a saddle on the mountain, an ideal location for a ranch. Not surprisingly, it once was. The T-Bench Bar Ranch was a 5,000-acre cattle operation homesteaded by Eugene Cayton. The family's old stone well, which dates back to the early 1900s, and a stand-alone cattle chute remain as part of the journey. The sixth hole, a downhill dogleg that dips twice to a green 553 yards away, is so awe-inspiring that MacMillan built his home on the rugged rock outcropping just off the tee. The capper comes at No. 9, at 725 yards one of the most demanding and dazzling par 5s in Arizona.

The back nine is equally rewarding, the pinnacle being the 15th and 16th holes. The 198-yard 15th boasts twin greens, and is a spectacular shot down a rock-encrusted hill. The par-5 16th rambles 550 yards along a lake to a triple-tiered green. The other seven holes are nearly as good, never giving a golfer the same look twice.

No wonder people are flocking to The Gallery, which offers a $35,000 membership, with only a $1,000 transfer fee charged to those who want their money back. Of course, nobody does, which is why a second 18-hole course by Fought and Lehman already has been staked out. Such abundance has allowed MacMillan the opportunity to open the O. B. Sports–managed facility to the public on a limited basis.

But MacMillan is holding a tight rein on the project's density, with homes set 300 to 400 feet off the golf corridors and membership limited to 390 on this 500-acre project. "I've seen so many great golf courses ruined by the housing being packed too tight along the fairways," he explained. "That won't happen here."

The clubhouse, pro shop, and restaurant also are bold statements, with Old World pieces and artwork from such faraway places as Bali, England, and France. Airy and palatial at 28,000 square feet, with just a touch of Frank Lloyd Wright built into it, this temple of golf doubles as—what else?—an art gallery. Add in the far-out palette of colors by Scottsdale interior designer Joski Meskan, who excels in oranges, yellows, and blues, and the dynamic digs will get you even if the divots don't.

"It's my dream come true," said MacMillan, the northern light behind The Gallery of Dove Mountain. ✿

Long views over the Tucson Valley greet golfers at the 197-yard, par-3 seventh hole, which is one of the few forced carries at Dove Mountain.

HASSAYAMPA GOLF CLUB

· ·

PAR: 71 · YARDAGE: 4,695–6,624 · RATING: 71.2 · SLOPE: 134 · SIGNATURE HOLES: 157-YARD, PAR-3 № 16; 206-YARD, PAR-3 № 17

GHOSTS IN THESE PARTS of Arizona have long been associated with the name Hassayampa. One of those spirits still floats in the minds of men, while the other has come back to life, rekindled on the same ground where it originated.

"Faith," as some of the locals refer to her, was a young woman who was jilted on the day of her marriage back in the late 1920s. She had come to the Hassayampa Inn to celebrate her honeymoon, but when her husband failed to return from an errand on that fateful day, she hung herself in a room at Prescott's grandest hotel. There have been "sightings" ever since.

The other tale is much less eerie, and not of the human variety, as this ghost from the past is now embodied in the present. In fact, rarely does the new Hassayampa Country Club evoke a fearful thought, unless it comes on the downswing while teeing off. Thanks to the creative genius of architect Tom Weiskopf, who carved Hassayampa II out of the tall pines and rocky inclines just below Thumb Butte, there are mostly positive vibrations these days.

So what about the ghost? Well, that requires another history lesson that goes back to 1919, when the movers and shakers from Phoenix and Tucson played their summer golf at a little, nine-hole layout also known as Hassayampa Golf Club. Life was good back in those early days, as dinners and dances at the club were worked in around those big-time (at least in those days) 25-cent Nassau games.

Jock McClaren, a Scotsman with roots to famed St. Andrews, had designed the original nine holes. Two different sets of tees allowed for an 18-hole

The par-3 11th hole is backed by Thumb Butte.

experience, which was played out over cottonseed greens. Caddies toted bags for a nickel, and every year like clockwork the club's championship was settled over Labor Day, which concluded the season.

So the migration continued until two unforeseen developments in the late 1960s turned Hassayampa Country Club into Arizona's first "ghost course." Prescott residents struck the first blow, building a rival course called Antelope Hills, which sent local membership scurrying to the other side of town. Then the local water company, which had been the course's lifeline, literally dried up. No water, no golf course.

For over 25 years, the winds whistled through the old, abandoned clubhouse, leaving the ghosts to play their rounds where once there had been fairways. Then in 1996, Weiskopf was hired by Desert Troon Properties of Scottsdale to bring back the memories. Not surprisingly, he took the new course to a level that its forefathers had never known. With a lot of pampering and careful planning, Weiskopf's effort opened in the summer of 1998, almost 30 years from its predecessor's demise.

According to the architect, the latest version of Hassayampa, which is named for a small river in the area, is "purely a members' course, rather than a championship layout. It doesn't have the length to challenge the better players," he conceded. "But they didn't want that. And with this rugged landscape, the elevation we were dealt—canyons, creeks, and outcroppings—I think it turned out magnificently."

There are a lot of ups and downs to Hassayampa, the downs being only geographical in nature. Everything starts at the stately, lodge-style clubhouse, which sits high on the mountain with panoramic views that reach all the way to the San Francisco Peaks near Flagstaff, about 75 miles to the north. In fact, the first eight holes all have some type of downward movement to them, thus bringing about Hassayampa's most difficult stretch of golf. The middle of the course, the ninth through 14th holes, is played out over a meadowlike terrain,

before the closing holes push a player back up the hill, through the pines, and over canyons and creek beds.

Even though Hassayampa is relatively short at 6,600 yards, its tightness toughens it up considerably, especially in the beginning. Three holes—Nos. 4, 5, and 7—are so imposing off the tee spatially that the smart route is to club down and emphasize accuracy. Power doesn't come into play until the ninth hole, but a player must once again scale back when he reaches the 15th, a short, uphill dogleg par 4 to a green nestled into the terrain. Then comes the course's signatures, which are consecutive par 3s over canyons to well-bunkered greens.

True to his mission, Weiskopf left an old-fashioned links course that requires a lot of thought. Perhaps out of respect, the 12th hole, the best par 4 on the course, sweeps past the weather-beaten clubhouse of yore. In every way, the new course has boosted Prescott's pride. The social ramifications of Hassayampa Country Club go well beyond these

storied confines, even to the point of making the Hassayampa Inn once again the "in" place.

The old hotel is a throwback to class, which is obvious with just one step inside the Peacock, where the restaurant and funky old bar are found. Hassayampa's exquisite rooms and suites are filled with antiques, and still look very much like they did when the hotel first opened. Perhaps that is why the bellman beams as he escorts you to your room via an ancient elevator ("lift"). No wonder stars who have stayed here in the past, legends like Clark Gable, Carol Lombard, and Will Rogers, are being replaced these days by the likes of Kim Basinger, Alec Baldwin, and Tom Selleck.

Yes, nothing much has changed at the "old haunt." Every week, or so it seems to the employees, another person asks about the ghost known as Faith. The workers simply smile, try to tell a spooky tale, and chuckle to themselves at the overreactions. The various versions never die, and therein lies the answer to this mystery from the past. ☀

LA PALOMA COUNTRY CLUB

· ·

PAR: 72 · YARDAGE: 4,878–7,028 · RATING: 67.8–75.4 · SLOPE: 116–155 · SIGNATURE HOLE: 538-YARD, PAR-5 Nº 7 (HILL)

JACK NICKLAUS, the Golden Bear, was just a "cub" in the designer business when he pursued the path of golf course architecture to the Old Pueblo. It was a brief stay, as he built 27 holes at La Paloma Country Club in 1984, the same year his Desert Highlands officially opened, and never returned.

As it worked out, La Paloma was one of nine courses Nicklaus built in Arizona, but the only one in Tucson. Having trained under such master architects as Dick Wilson, Desmond Muirhead, and Pete Dye during the late 1960s and early '70s, Nicklaus had just started to go solo when La Paloma popped up on his drawing board. Naturally, La Paloma turned out to be a "Bear" of a golf course in every way.

"At that time in my career," Nicklaus said of the early 1980s, "I had studied under two or three other architects, and my designs definitely reflected

that. I was less experimental than I am now, and I probably only looked at doing [a golf course] two or three different ways, whereas today I'm probably looking at a dozen different ways to do something.

"Personally, I think I started out pretty mellow. What made La Paloma difficult was the piece of land it was built on—washes and canyons and rolling hills. That's true of most golf courses, in that your design is really dictated by the land and what your demands are, because you still have to build variety into that equation."

A few of the members at La Paloma, and many of the guests at the Westin La Paloma Resort, like to refer to Nicklaus as "Jack the Ripper" when they finish playing this twisting tract that winds its way under the Santa Catalina Mountains. They say the tension can be cut with a knife as you make your way through these three nines, which include the Canyon,

LEFT: *Spectacular views of the Santa Catalinas are commonplace.*
ABOVE: *One of three swimming pools at the Westin La Paloma.*

Hill, and Ridge. The names alone are a pretty good indicator of what a golfer can expect at La Paloma. So is the slope, which can be as high as 155.

At first glance, the three nines seem to border on the super-rugged side of things, with lots of shots on the edge or to the edge, greens that are surrounded by trouble, and fairways that are tight and tough at every turn. But then you play it again, and what many feel is an overly penal experience turns out to be a very engaging golf course. This is especially true if you don't try to overpower it off the tee. In fact, for those who simply bag the driver and opt for 3-woods and long irons, life is lovely at La Paloma.

What's good about these 27 holes is that, if you asked three different golfers, they all might have a different favorite nine. The Ridge has two wonderful par 3s in the 199-yard fourth hole and the 171-yard seventh, as both look like they are dressed to kill. The Canyon offers up perhaps the most difficult stretch on the golf course, as the fifth through

eighth holes are extremely exacting. The fifth, a 542-yard par 5 that requires an approach shot over a deep canyon, is three shots for the intelligent player, while No. 8 is the most demanding par 3 on the course at 244 yards.

La Paloma's most famous nine, literally, is the Hill, where the movie *Tin Cup* starring Kevin Costner and Renee Russo, was filmed. The Hill starts slowly,

has a great stretch that runs from No. 5, a big dog-leg par 4 at 467 yards, through No. 7, a 538-yard par 5 that starts high on the hill and also dogs right to a pristine green setting.

The *Tin Cup* folks saw it differently, however, as their filming sites included the fourth, seventh, and ninth holes. It is at the ninth green, the putting surface that sets closest to the clubhouse, where Costner's character, Roy McAvoy, qualifies to play in a fictitious U.S. Open. Ironically, the course was supposed to be in Texas, although the Sonoran vegetation at La Paloma is somewhat hard to distinguish, thanks to some good editing.

The redeeming quality to this golf course is that it gets easier to handle every time you play it. Even though the turf seems skimpy at times, the vistas are always plentiful. La Paloma affords great views of Kitt Peak, the fifth-largest observatory in the country, as well as the landmark known as Finger Rock, which juts up from the Santa Catalinas. Super shots of the Tucson skyline also are everywhere.

La Paloma also is quite popular, which explains why it sports 535 members. The only way to play it from the outside is to get a room at the Westin La Paloma Resort, which can be very expensive. Green fees also will top $200, so be forewarned.

But, hey, you didn't come to lay up at La Paloma. Besides the golf, there's Arizona's longest resort water slide at 177 feet, "the Slidewinder," three additional swimming pools, 12 tennis courts, a health club and spa, sand and water volleyball, and hiking and jogging paths. Three restaurants, including an outdoor cafe next to the clubhouse, are at your beck and call.

In other words, there is something for everyone at La Paloma. Makes you wonder if Nicklaus would even recognize the place. ✿

MESA COUNTRY CLUB

PAR: 72 • YARDAGE: 5,870–6,594 • RATING: 69.4–71.8 • SLOPE: 121–125 • SIGNATURE HOLE: 198-YARD, PAR-3 N⁰ 7

THERE ARE DOZENS of streets in Arizona named Country Club Drive, the vast majority of them having golf courses along the roadway. But only one Country Club Drive is the main drag through a large city, and that would be the street located in Mesa.

Back in the 1940s, Country Club Drive was known as Mesa Avenue. But when a small group of residents got together to build the city's first golf course, Mesa Country Club, the name was changed. The club, which opened December 1, 1949, now sits on Fairway Drive—just off Country Club—and is a monument to the city's past.

The history of Mesa Country Club is rich, although money was always hard to come by for the group put together by the late Lyle Stevens. At the time of the course's conception, Mesa had a population of just 12,000 people, which still was considered significant at that time, as the surrounding communities of Tempe, Scottsdale, and Chandler each numbered 5,000 people or fewer. Today, Mesa tops 600,000 and is the state's third largest city.

Besides Stevens, the early shakers behind Mesa CC were such notables as William Asher, Dr. V. E. Frazier, Tom Freestone, Lew Muegel, Jim Lindsay, and Dwight Patterson, the father of the Cactus Baseball League. Many of those founding fathers are gone now, but the club remains at the upper echelons of the city's society.

Fortunately for Stevens and his small band of golf enthusiasts, they selected the father-son architectural team of William P. and William F. Bell, more commonly known as Billy and Billy Jr. The Bells' traditional, tree-lined fairways made up of classic doglegs, elevated tees, and small greens remain the club's trademark.

Joe Bartko, the latest in a long line of distinguished head pros at Mesa CC that included Dick Kaczsenski, Oren Love, and Dick Turner, has watched the club change through the years. Bartko, the fun-loving pro who is known for his ever-present cowboy boots (Yes, he even has a pair with golf spikes!), said much of the challenge and charm that originally existed at the club still is present. "We've touched it up a few times, but it's still a classic country club," said Bartko, who celebrated 25 years at Mesa CC in 1999. "Gray Madison was very instrumental in restoring some of our bunkers and greens back in the early '70s, and really did an awful lot for this golf course. And Dick Turner added some length to it, because before he got here every par 4 was a driver and wedge, or driver 9-iron."

Mesa CC is unique in that half the golf course, the first seven holes and Nos. 14 and 15, lies on the top level of the mesa for which the city was named.

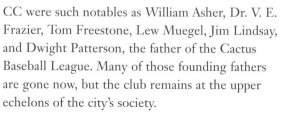

The signature par-3 seventh hole at Mesa Country Club.

The rest are located on the "Lower 40" acres, as the members refer to it. A Salt River Project canal also cuts its way through several holes on the front nine.

Even though the original 100 acres were described in a club history as "worthless sticker bush desert," one would never know it by today's standard. The course, which is lush in terms of trees, bushes, and grass, is one of the few country clubs in Arizona located near the downtown area of a city, sharing that distinction with Phoenix Country Club. It almost wasn't so, as the founding fathers had their choice between that site and what now is Falcon Field.

Through the years, Mesa CC has been a strong member of the golf community, hosting such events as the Arizona Open, Arizona Amateur, Southwest Section of the PGA Championship, and other major events. "The course has always held its own," Bartko noted of the 6,594-yard layout, which is short by today's standards. "Length really doesn't mean strength here, because the greens are small and the fairways tight and tree-lined. Accuracy is the key."

Of course, competition is not really what Mesa Country Club is all about. With excellent clubhouse facilities, a big swimming pool, tennis courts, and an emphasis on junior golf and club play, the aurora is more about family fun than who shot the best score. "This membership is second to none," Bartko noted. "I know that some pros [at private country clubs] take a lot of grief, but the members we've got are so easy to work with that I am truly blessed."

So are those who get to play among these serene fairways and greens. The front nine takes off at the fifth hole, a 520-yard, straightaway par 5 that plays downhill over the canal to an elevated green. The sixth hole, a 380-yard uphill dogleg that makes a hard left to a tiny green, also is a wonderful test. But the best is the 198-yard seventh hole. The par 3, which begins high above the canal, is an incredible

shot that drops 75 feet over water to a small green surrounded by trees.

The back nine is equally good, with several holes playing back and forth over the roadway that enters the club. Falling into that category would be the 154-yard, par-3 16th, which tumbles 50 feet from tee to green, and the 494-yard 13th and 495-yard 18th, both par 5s and both reachable in two shots, provided the ball carries all the way to the uphill greens. "The main thing is getting off the tee in good shape, because you've got to position your ball all the way around the course," Bartko noted.

Positioning always has been big at Mesa Country Club, where the founding members held their ground during some tough times. Believe it or not, it was six slot machines that actually kept the course alive in the early going.

According to the club's history, which was compiled by Bob Scanlan and Dr. Frazier, the income from the slots "was often greater than dues from all other sources, and some say the club could not have survived without that income. They were illegal, of course, but every social club in the Valley had them, and the law made no effort to do anything about them."

One can only wonder how the club's past would have been altered had a planned raid by the Attorney General and U.S. District Attorney's offices come off in 1951. Fortunately, the club's president was tipped off a few hours before the raid. No gambling equipment was found, nor was it ever located again.

"It was assumed they were placed in storage, where they may be yet," was the whimsical way that Scanlan and Frazier phrased it. ☼

MOON VALLEY COUNTRY CLUB

. . . .

PAR: 72 • YARDAGE: 5,278–7,210 • RATING: NA • SLOPE: NA • SIGNATURE HOLE: 412-YARD, PAR-4 NO 9

GOLF COURSE ARCHITECT Bob Cupp had a grand plan when he rebuilt Moon Valley Country Club in 1999. "We wanted to bring it into the twenty-first century," said Cupp of the old Dick Wilson layout that was built in north Phoenix in 1959. "What we've done is bring in all the high-tech stuff, which it needed. And, fortunately, we were able to bring in some length to make it appropriately longer."

But for all of the new, some old also was left in the mix. "I tried to do a little testament to Dick Wilson, who was one of my favorite [architects]," Cupp added. "He was noted for bunkers with long fingers of grass, not sand. And there are a few of those that remain."

Otherwise, this is a new surface of "the Moon," as the LPGA players who tee it up here annually in the Standard Register PING Tournament like to refer to it. Gone are the somewhat boring configura-

tion of holes, as well as the old putting surfaces. In are the new tee boxes, greens, additional bunkers, and recontoured elevations that were designed to provide more movement in what had been a "slow" golf course.

"The concept from the beginning was to redesign the course and, at the same time, add creativity and variety," said Gary Hart, a member at Moon Valley who oversaw the $4.5 million project that took approximately one year to complete. "It needed a massive facelift, so when you looked at the course, it would excite you. What Bob Cupp did was bring out the strategic impact—'how do you play it?'—and the aesthetic value—'how do you feel about it?' It used to be a hooker's course off the tee, whereas now it's balanced between hooks and fades."

Almost every hole has been redesigned, although the routing is basically the same with some minor tweaks. The new greens are composed of L-93 bentgrass, a revolutionary strain that features creeping blades that fill in ball marks and resist heat. Everything from mounding to mowing patterns also has been reworked.

What caused the overhaul of Moon Valley after 40 years of peaceful yet sleepy existence? The rumbling started with the Solheim family, which has owned the course since 1986, when it was purchased by the late PING founder Karsten Solheim.

"The ambiance of the course had changed so much with the [addition] of so many houses," said John Solheim, Karsten's youngest son and the president of PING Manufacturing. "We wanted a great

Moon Mountain frames this north Phoenix golf course.

course for our members, and a great golf course for the [LPGA] tournament. We wanted to keep a little bit of the past, but at the same time bring it up to a higher level."

Moon Valley has 500 members, who also enjoy a large recreational facility as well as a par-3 course called the Moon Walk. For a private club, it emphasizes equal facilities for both men and women, perhaps a reflection of its position as one of the major stops in women's professional golf.

In the beginning, Moon Valley CC was the brainchild of Bob Goldwater, the driving force behind the Phoenix Open and a longtime member at Phoenix Country Club. "There was nothing but desert out there when Dick Wilson started building the course," said Goldwater, noting that the 720-acre project was developed by Del Webb. "I remember Wilson was so impressed with the vastness of the area, which even back then was called Moon Valley because of all the [lava] rock. He ended up making the greens mammoth, with the smallest one being 10,000 square feet."

Solheim said that Cupp plans to reach a happy medium of old and bold. Perhaps the biggest changes, he said, will come at Nos. 2, 8, 9, 15, and 16. "We've changed the tees at No. 2, which will stay a par 3 and share a double green with the eight hole [a par 5]," Solheim noted. "The 15th has gone from an easy par 4 to a challenging par 3, and we've brought the water more into play on the 16th [a par 4]. Same thing at the [412-yard, par-4] ninth hole, where we've brought the green right to the edge of the water. In fact, that hole is so exciting now, that we might have to flip-flop the nines and make it the 18th, because it would be such a great closer."

Ironically, should such a change occur, it would revert the nines back to the way Wilson originally designed them. The new ninth green also is a double green with the practice green. "Actually, the entire golf course looks different, which is what we set out

to do," said Hart, who also works for PING. "I've got to give Bob Cupp a lot of credit because he really did give it a whole new look while at the same time leaving all the good things from the past."

Will the LPGA players who have been competing here since 1987 like it better than the old course? "I'm sure they will," Hart added. "But we didn't build the new course for the LPGA, we built it for our members. At the same time, I'm sure the pros will be more challenged."

Yes, with the strategy changed, and most holes playing differently, this will be a whole new walk on "the Moon." ☀

ORO VALLEY COUNTRY CLUB

. . . .

PAR: 72 · YARDAGE: 5,689–6,964 · RATING: 69.8–77.5 · SLOPE: 121–138 · SIGNATURE HOLE: 441-YARD, PAR-4 №18

MOST OF THE MEMBERSHIP is retired and lives right here in this cozy, little neighborhood, which explains why the practice tee and green are a beehive of activity early each morning. They love Oro Valley Country Club, which literally sits in the shadow of Pusch Ridge and the mighty Catalina Mountains.

Who can blame them? Few, if any, senior communities in Arizona boast such a terrific traditional tract that combines natural beauty with a stern test of golf. Oro Valley Country Club is the work of Robert Bruce Harris, and it's taken very seriously. The members realize that anything less than 100 percent just won't get it done, and their respect is obvious.

Proof they relish every minute lies in the fact that the majority walk these serene fairways and greens, focusing on their golf as the highlight of the day. The quality of the experience makes others envious. "I'll say this about our club: It's very in tune with the game of golf," noted Mike Wilson, the head pro at Oro Valley CC since 1985. "They're mostly in their mid-60s, but still very competitive. They like to practice, and to take a lot of lessons. They're enthusiasm is contagious."

It's always been that way in these parts. The story of Oro Valley Country Club dates to the mid-1950s, when Chicagoan Lou Landon discovered the property in the desert outside of Tucson. The 366-acre parcel, which would soon feature 140 acres of golf and 250 homes, has a history that includes being near the site of the legendary Steam Pump Ranch built by German immigrant George Pusch. There also had been a gold rush nearby, as well as the infamous Tully and Ochoa Wagon Train Massacre of 1872.

Landon had moved to Tucson for its year-round weather and stunning scenery. Being an avid golfer, he had the wealth and foresight to add Tucson's fourth course to the mix, as Oro Valley followed Tucson Country Club, Randolph North, and El Rio Country Club. In 1958, Landon asked Harris to build his first layout west of the Mississippi. Harris, who had built 130 golf courses in East and Midwest, opened Oro Valley CC the following year. Two years later, he designed nearby Tucson National.

Not surprisingly, Oro Valley CC was not an immediate success, chiefly because it was 12 miles outside city limits. But 100 members saw the potential, and today the membership is closed out at 325. It's understandable, as the $17,000 fee is modest for such an incredible playground. "The interesting thing about our golf club is that you could put a

Oro Valley lies in the shadow of Pusch Ridge.

dome over this course and it could look like Chicago, Minneapolis, or a golf course back East," Wilson explained. "All around is the desert, but we look like a traditional golf course. What's amazing is, I've never talked to anyone who doesn't say they appreciate the golf course for its quality and design. In fact, I've heard quite a few people, not necessarily just members, who say Oro Valley is their favorite course in Tucson."

It makes sense. Oro Valley CC has only gotten better over years, with another noted architect, Arthur Hills, adding his artistic touch during a redesign in 1987. Under the guidance of Keith Foster, who would later go on to make a name for himself, Hills' construction crew made several strategic alterations, the most noted being the addition of a lengthy lake at the 18th hole. "The 18th is our signature, and not just because it looks beautiful. It's also a very difficult par 4," Wilson said of the 441-yard hole. "I would say your mind never quits thinking about the lake until your ball is safely on the green."

Of the two nines, the front side is a stroke or two easier because it's essentially flat, with the exception of a multitude of mounds, many of those added by Hills. Typical of the front is the 347-yard, par-4 seventh hole, which is short but exacting. The dogleg right, which is protected by some rather large trees on the corner, is played out on an elevated green that is marked by subtle breaks.

The back nine is dynamite, primarily because of the rolling hills, tall trees and panoramic views of the mountains and wide-open spaces. The best stretch on the course begins at the 10th hole, a big dogleg left to another elevated green. Then it's up the hill 532 yards to the sometimes-brutal 11th green, which is guarded by massive bunkers. The 12th is a short, rolling par 4 to another tough green, this one triple-tiered. The 170-yard 13th might be considered a brief break if not for the par 3 playing

entirely uphill to a partially hidden green. The 14th, a 401-yard par 4, is an awesome tee shot from high on a bluff to a green that is long, narrow, tiered, and guarded by bunkers and trees. The final four holes are nearly as good, although slightly tighter with the exception of the 176-yard, par-3 17th.

Finally, you arrive at the last hurrah, and it is a loud one. Driver or 3-wood or 2-iron off the tee? Any one of the three clubs can get you in trouble, as the water comes into play on the left side of the fairway about 225 yards out. Of course, bail right and there is tree trouble. Only a perfect second shot spells p-a-r, as the water runs all the way to the putting surface and behind the green, where a waterfall tumbles down. Without question, it is among the best closers in Arizona golf. "Everybody thinks it's a wonderful par 5," Wilson quipped. "Of course, it's a par 4, but I let them pretend."

Trust to say, the members know how good Oro Valley CC can be, which partially explains why everyone is so low-key about it. After all, do savvy fisherman tell people about their favorite fishing hole? Absolutely not.

About the only hint of what magnitude lies inside the gate at Oro Valley Estates is a striking obelisk that has stood guard over the entrance since 1960. The white, 25-foot-high column is made up of 50 U-shaped blocks with 150 original designs found in the hieroglyphic inscriptions. Among them are details of the club's activities, as well as life in the desert. The obelisk is the work of Tucson artist James Savage, and is considered a piece of Americana.

In a way, the obelisk is a fitting but humble tribute to Oro Valley Country Club, which, of course, is just the way the members want it. ✺

PARADISE VALLEY COUNTRY CLUB

PAR: 72 • YARDAGE: 5,635–6,686 • RATING: 69.3–75.4 • SLOPE: 127–133 • SIGNATURE HOLE: 517-YARD, PAR-5 NO 15

IN THE WORLD of private golf, pecking orders exist. This is especially the case in Phoenix, where so many elite courses thrive within the greater metropolitan area, with more on the way.

Who is the top club that all those private eyes are watching? Depends on the criterion: caliber of course, social status, wealth, length of wait to become a member, camaraderie . . . take your pick. Still, when it all shakes out, there is a clear-cut number-one club.

In 1957, architect Lawrence Hughes delivered Paradise Valley Country Club, with help from local PGA Tour player Johnny Bulla and the vision of Gray Madison, who had worked on the project since '52. With a prime location nestled between Camelback Mountain, Mummy Mountain, and Marshmallow Hill, PVCC eventually became *the* country club in the Valley, a bastion for the well-to-do.

Of course, there are many other stories of note. Jack Stewart, then owner of the Camelback Inn, traded 180 acres to the club in exchange for 60 memberships and outside tee times for his guests. The Babbitt family chipped in an additional 50 acres, and the spectacular setting was complete. At the time, the community of Paradise Valley had yet to be incorporated, meaning PVCC was a true pioneer.

From the beginning, the club attracted the leaders of the business and professional community, with stature superseding wealth even though the two often are related. Original memberships went for $1,000, or $5,000 if a lot was included. Interestingly, Hughes opted for two parcels of property on the golf course in lieu of a design fee. Had the renowned architect held on to them all these years, his property would be worth at least $1 million.

Today, the $50,000 membership fee at PVCC is modestly priced for most who seek the inner sanctum, which includes 475 golf members and 500 of the social variety. The chief stumbling block is that the average wait to gain such prestige takes about five years or more. Reportedly, there are no exceptions or shortcuts to the rule, which states that everyone seeking entrance into the club is treated equally regardless of their name.

According to head pro Duff Lawrence, the club's position in Arizona golf is understood. At the same time, there is no effort by the members to flaunt or take advantage of it, only to preserve what they cherish. "All who are fortunate enough to play here love this club and course," noted Lawrence, who holds the distinction of being Arizona State University's first All-American in golf. "They really care about it, and it's a big part of their lives. Even though no one needs to say it, in my opinion, weighing all the factors of traditional golf and a private club, I think we're *the* country club in the Valley. We have a lot of well-known members and families, a wonderful location, and the golf course itself."

The role call at PVCC does include some rather famous faces, but even more than that, it exudes variety. Sports mogul Jerry Colangelo rubs elbows

LEFT: *The signature 517-yard, par-5 15th.*

OPPOSITE: *Keith Foster gave Paradise Valley CC a face-lift.*

with former Vice President Dan Quayle, who in turn knows newspaper chief Chip Weil, who often chats with Supreme Court Justice Sandra Day O'Connor. Radio announcer Paul Harvey also is in the loop, along with comedian Leslie Nielsen, baseball Hall of Famer Robin Yount, Cardinals coach Vince Tobin, and golf course developer Lyle Anderson. Hale Irwin, the dominant player on the Senior PGA Tour in the late '90s, also tees it up regularly at PVCC.

Despite such loftiness, PVCC also has been an active participant in the Arizona golf community, hosting numerous state championships. Most recently, it was the 75th Arizona Amateur, where Marty James followed such past Amateur winners at PVCC as Dick Hopwood (1959), Tom Purtzer ('72), and Dennis Saunders ('86). The course record is owned by a current member of the PGA Tour, as local favorite Mark Calcavecchia managed to tame these traditional fairways and small greens with an 8-under 63, eclipsing the record of 64 set by one of his peers, Phil Mickelson.

Not an easy task, as Hughes' testament to time rolls tenaciously over hill and dale, with bunkering, enhanced by Keith Foster, that rewards only well-struck shots. The strength of the golf course is the par 3s, with the par 5s representing the best scoring opportunities. The par 4s are difficult but dramatic. The signature hole, at least in terms of raw beauty, is the 517-yard 15th, a downhill par 5 that sits serenely below Camelback Mountain. The 190-yard 12th hole, a long iron to a postage-stamp green also is excellent. Those seeking a nice stretch of par 4s enjoy Nos. 7, 8, and 9, the last offering coming from 380 yards to an elevated green, engulfed by treacherously deep bunkers.

Of course, the toughest test at PVCC comes long before a player gets to the golf course. Unlike so many of today's private clubs, where money gains immediate approval, this is a study of character. Two members need to stand up as sponsors, and five letters accompany the application. Many who have thought they were a slam dunk to get in, only end up getting slammed. "The club has a nice reputation, but we don't advertise it," Lawrence explained. "It's a bit of a contradiction, being low-key and high-profile in the same breath."

Yes, Paradise Valley Country Club has it all, which is why everyone who is anyone wants to belong there. One thing you'll never hear from the members, however, is "We're number one," even if it's true.

PHOENIX COUNTRY CLUB

PAR: 71 · YARDAGE: 5,858–6,740 · RATING: 70.2–73.0 · SLOPE: 124–130 · SIGNATURE HOLE: 200-YARD, PAR-3 № 15

The first attempt to establish [Phoenix Country Club] was made at the annual meeting of the Phoenix Athletic Club [in October 1899]. While this club was the most active of all clubs, the project of a golf links was tabled and golf faced a dismal future in the city.

— BARRY GOLDWATER

President's Report, 1950

BVIOUSLY, THE MOVERS and shakers of Phoenix at the turn of the twentieth century changed their minds about building Phoenix Country Club. Otherwise, all those great moments at the Phoenix Open would have taken place elsewhere, or perhaps not at all.

Barry Goldwater, the late Arizona senator who served as Phoenix Country Club's president in 1950, put together an eloquent, 50-year history of the club during his term. Even 50 years later, it is fascinating reading. According to Goldwater, the golf club was approved at the very next meeting of the Phoenix Athletic Club, and a nine-hole, dirt course called Phoenix Golf Club was carved out of the desert on the northeast corner of Central Avenue and Roosevelt Street, hosting its first tournament on February 22, 1900.

"This little links kept the golfers of Phoenix happy, but it was obvious that a new location would soon be needed," Goldwater wrote. "The popularity of the game began to spread, and the ladies became interested, not so much because of the golf, but because of the potentialities of social enjoyment.

Phoenix Country Club is an oasis in the center of the city.

This added a reason for moving. . . ."

The second Phoenix Golf Club was christened on January 1, 1901, on "Yuma Road," which today would be near the corner of 17th Avenue and Van Buren Street. Once again, a nine-hole course with dirt fairways and sand greens greeted the membership. "So the club went through the first 10 years of this century," Goldwater wrote on. "It grew in popularity and importance, and kept gaining members until the inevitable happened . . . we had to get more room to grow."

The third site was an 80-acre plot located on the north side of the canal at the end of Central Avenue. Along with the new nine-hole, dirt-desert course came a name change to the Country Club of Phoenix. The clubhouse was built on the south side of the canal, and there were plans to expand to 18 holes. But the second nine never got off the ground, and at a board meeting on October 24, 1919, history again was made. "The Board's recommendation was that the Williams tract of 160 acres on the northeast corner of Thomas Road and North Seventh Street

subtle greens that varied in size, depending on the difficulty of the hole. The pros also liked the way they were treated by longtime head pro Willie Low and his staff. Much of that remains the same, with several strong par 3s such as Nos. 8 and 15; demanding par 4s like Nos. 3 and 17; and two reachable par 5s—Nos. 1 and 18—along with a toughie, the 541-yard seventh. The signature hole is the 15th, at 200 yards a wonderful long iron over water to a two-tiered green. "It's a course that has stood the test of time," noted Ralph Bernhisel, the head pro at PCC. "I suppose that's one of the reasons they host the U.S. Open qualifying here."

Of course, the 600 members enjoy other amenities, too. The men's and women's grills remain a throwback to yesteryear, sitting side-by-side in the stately clubhouse that replaced the original white brick structure in 1960. Locker rooms loaded with history, as well as a state-of-the-art fitness center, also are lodged within.

But PCC's classiest component of all might be the one that Barry Goldwater wrote about in that 1950 report. According to Bob Goldwater, his brother's observation also has stood up to Father Time. "There have been thousands of different people who have added their little touches of personalities to our Club, men and women who have been the leaders in the growth of our state," Barry wrote in conclusion. "As one reads back through the minutes of our meetings through the years, one realizes the tremendous amount of work and worry that has gone into the building of the Club by the men and women who were willing to devote their time to its business, and those people we all owe a debt of thanks.

"The thing that makes us, though, can never be written correctly. It is the friendship that permeates the Club. It is a fine Club! Your interest, and the interest of those who have gone before you, have made it that way." ✺

be acquired," wrote Goldwater. "Once again, the Club was on the move."

Englishman Harry Collis was hired to design the fourth course, which also underwent another name change to Phoenix Country Club. Once those key components were in place at the downtown oasis, the stage was set for yet another storied chapter in PCC's history. Ironically, the Phoenix Open underwent almost as many changes initially as the club itself before it finally became a big-time tournament in the early 1940s. Originally, it was called the Arizona Open in 1932 and '33, and held at PCC, San Marcos, and the Arizona Biltmore. Bob Goldwater, Barry's brother, brought the tournament to PCC in 1934 as the Phoenix Open, but it disappeared from 1936 to '38 due to "a lack of organization."

"I got it going again, although some of the Thunderbirds were ticked at me for doing it," Bob Goldwater recalled of his "one-man meeting" with the Phoenix Chamber of Commerce. "The 'Birds said to me, 'OK, if you want this tournament so bad, put it on,' and I was the chairman for the next 15 years. . . . Goodness, you look at what it was then and what it is now, and . . . Oh, my!"

As Phoenix Country Club grew, so did the tournament, which began alternating between PCC and Arizona Country Club until 1973, when Phoenix Country Club took sole control. Some of the greatest players of all time—Byron Nelson, Jimmy DeMaret, Ben Hogan, Gene Littler, Arnold Palmer, Jack Nicklaus, and Johnny Miller—were among those who won titles at PCC. "The Phoenix Open was always a fun time even though there was a vocal minority at the club that didn't want it," Bob Gold-water said. "At the same time, when it finally left [in 1987 for the TPC of Scottsdale], a lot of people were sad to see it go."

Just like the members, the pros enjoyed the tree-lined fairways; big, traditional bunkers; and

PINETOP COUNTRY CLUB

PAR: 71 • YARDAGE: 5,603–6,458 • RATING: 63.7–69.7 • SLOPE: 115–122 • SIGNATURE HOLE: 175-YARD, PAR-3 Nº 5

IN THIS NEIGHBORHOOD, where Ponderosa pines are accented by cool breezes, Pinetop Country Club stands tall. Since its inception in 1965, the tract designed by Milt Coggins and Gray Madison has always tried hard to be more than the number-two club on the block. Not an easy task when White Mountain Country Club, once known as "Phoenix Country Club North," sits a couple miles down the road.

But give the 375 members of Pinetop Country Club their due. Every season they strive to make their course better, which is why Tucson architect Dave Dubinski was called in most recently to polish this gem. Maintaining it on a daily basis are head pro Jack Pemberton and superintendent Ron Powell.

It is a mission, a love for a golf course, that never ends. White Mountain CC is the furthest thing from their minds. "I suppose that would be a fair assessment," said Pemberton when asked if the difference between the two clubs is that White Mountain is the "old blue blood," while Pinetop is the "new rich." "The courses kind of reflect that. At the same time, that perception has grown less and less over the years. I guess the bottom line is both courses are wonderful country club experiences. I know we couldn't be prouder of our course."

Exactly. There is a lot to puff up any member's chest at Pinetop Country Club, where traditional golf is played out in a soft and serene setting. Not too difficult, the course begins with a straightforward approach, then adds a lot of variety coming home. Along the way, the cardinals and jays chirp, and the sun shines, except for those summer afternoons when the clouds build and thunder brings showers. In every way, it is a good life for those lucky enough to traverse these lush fairways and perfect bentgrass greens. "Everyone who plays here loves this golf course, because there is not one tricked-up hole," noted the easygoing Pemberton. "Good players like it, and so does the average guy, which always is a sign of a good layout. And the greens are always immaculate, which is a tribute to Ron Powell, who has been here since the beginning."

The course opens with four fairly routine holes that capitalize on the tall trees for definition. But by the time most players arrive at the fifth hole, a 191-yard, downhill par 3 to a green backed by the

A lake fronts No. 9 at Pinetop Country Club.

Jackson Tank reservoir, they realize Pinetop Country Club is one of Arizona's treasures. Jackson Tank, which also adds to the ambiance of the sixth tee, is one of the area's landmarks. The reservoir, which acquires water through natural seepage from underground springs, dates back to cowboy days, when the golf course was the site of a large cattle operation.

Naturally, the area's history always has played a big role in the development of Pinetop Country Club. In the early 1920s, the lumber industry was kingpin in these parts, and remnants of the old railroad bed used to carry out the massive logs are recognizable to those in the know. The cattle came later, and Buck Springs Road, the street the club is located on, was once the ol' dusty trail.

Of the two nines, the back is the best. Not that the front isn't just as pretty and playable. It's more a matter of uniqueness, and the back side is loaded with it. In fact, the most memorable stretch of golf at Pinetop Country Club comes in the middle, as the ninth through 11th holes form an "Amen Corner" of sorts. All three holes bring water into play, which was part of Dubinski's renovation when he expanded both lakes and built a cove at the 11th green. The lake at the ninth hole, which also serves as the hazard for No. 18, was enlarged and framed by a rustic, redrock wall.

The bunkering also has been taken apart and redefined by Dubinski. Even though the sandy structures don't come into play that often, they are now dug out deeper and edged into a throwback style reminiscent of those you would find on the East Coast. The soft, tan sand also gives a fresh, natural appearance to the course that helps add an upscale look. The best example is the 175-yard, par-3 15th hole, where the green is simply surrounded by a beach of bunkers. It is safe to say that many big-time golf courses would be jealous of such good-looking hazards.

In many ways, Pinetop Country Club is a mix of coziness and luxury. For instance, the massively regal homes that line the front nine are the most expensive in the area. The back has quite a few of the large, lodge-style layouts, too. At the same time, the clubhouse is an unpretentious chalet, with an interior that caters to golf rather than opulence. Many of the members still work hard, meaning that most of the rounds played at Pinetop Country Club come on the weekends.

Of course, these days, with the course in such top-notch condition the faithful come as often as possible. And being a very active membership, they play lots of tournaments at Pinetop Country Club. "We've got some really good players up here," Pemberton said with obvious pride. "But the golf course also is a fair and fun test for beginners. That's the greatest thing about it. No matter if you hit a driver off the tee, or a 2-iron or 3-iron, you're going to enjoy it. I think that says a lot about the quality of Pinetop Country Club."

It seems to be a theme that constantly moves forward. ✿

PINNACLE PEAK COUNTRY CLUB

PAR: 72 • YARDAGE: 4,952–7,030 • RATING: 68.0–73.5 • SLOPE: 119–136 • SIGNATURE HOLE: 170-YARD, PAR-3 N⁰ 9

VER THE PAST 20 YEARS, private golf clubs in Arizona have become very high profile. The shift in marketing strategy occurred in the early 1980s, when Desert Highlands came on board to much fanfare. But it wasn't always so.

Take Pinnacle Peak Country Club, a traditional desert layout designed by Dick Turner in 1976. Even today, few people outside of the game's aficionados know of PPCC's whereabouts. Ask 10 golfers, and nine would say that it is located next to the well-known landmark of the same name.

They would be slightly off base, as Pinnacle Peak is a good five miles away. In fact, there is an aerial photo that hangs in the administrative offices of the club that was shot just after its grand opening, and there was not a building or a home in the area. Over the years, the neighborhood has exploded, but the mystery that surrounds PPCC remains, thanks to a massive hedge that hides it from those who traverse Pinnacle Peak Road.

Chris Rudi, the head professional at the club over the past six years, understands the low-key intentions of the membership. "It's actually kind of funny," Rudi said. "I'll meet people and tell them that I'm the head pro at Pinnacle Peak Country Club, and they'll say, 'Oh, really. I've heard of that place.' At the same time, few people know where 'that place' is."

Rudi said there are a lot of other aspects of the club that are misunderstood. "First of all, we're not really a country club in the truest sense," he said. "Oh, yeah, we've got the swimming pool and tennis courts that are associated with that definition of a country club, but nobody uses them. We're a golf club, with a group that really loves golf."

While some of the members live around the club in upscale homes that fall just shy of the term "mansion," many live out of state. According to Rudi, those nonresidents might make up as much as 70 percent of the membership. "We also have a lot of members who belong to two or three different clubs," he said. "Even clubs that are right here in the neighborhood, like Desert Highlands, Estancia, and Desert Mountain."

There are several reasons for that, Rudi added. "For one, we're very reasonable to join [$50,000 and no property requirements]," he said. "And it's easy to get a tee time here, because there are only 325 members, where a lot of clubs have upwards of 500. But the biggest deal is that our course is so much more playable than those other [desert] clubs. Even though we're in the desert, and have a little bit of that look, we're very traditional, with lots of grass. In fact, I think we compare very favorably in terms of playability to such courses as Arizona Country Club and Mesa Country Club."

The par-3 ninth hole is the signature at 170 yards.

These days, the conditioning also is impeccable, as PPCC went through a $2.5 million renovation in 1996 that updated almost every aspect of the course. Among the more notable work was a new irrigation system, a redesign and reconfiguration of the bunkering, and all 18 greens were rebuilt and resurfaced. "Our greens have always been our calling card," said Rudi, noting that the surfaces have been switched from bentgrass to a special strain called Crenshaw bent. "They're quick with a lot of slope; tough but terrific."

Of the two nines, the front is the more difficult in terms of scoring. Fortunately, the back nine offers some birdie opportunities, even though it's slightly longer. "It doesn't play that way," Rudi said of the back nine. "I guess that's because the most demanding stretch comes from the third hole through the eighth hole."

Breaking that rugged run is No. 9, considered the signature offering. The 170-yard shot over water to a well-bunkered green is picture-perfect, with a waterfall and flowers adding to the ambiance. Some members might argue that the back nine is just as good, particularly from the 13th through the water-bound 18th.

"It's not a back-breaker by any means, but it can be set up to play very tough," explained Rudi, noting that the winning score in the 1998 Southwest PGA Championship was a respectable 8-under par for 54 holes, "and Scott Watkins had to shoot a course record 66 on the final day just to get that low."

While the clubhouse isn't much to look at, the practice facility is state of the art and loaded with

The McDowell Mountains rise over Pinnacle Peak Country Club.

"range rats." Not bad for a club whose average age is 67. Among its members are LPGA pro Betsy King, and former state amateur champ Betsy Bro, so the guys have nothing on the gals at PPCC.

"Mostly, it's just good golf in a pleasant atmosphere with no glitter or glamour," Rudi explained. "We've got 1,800 trees on the course, and water that comes into play on several holes [Nos. 8, 9, and 18]. And it's very quiet and off the beaten path. Our people really like that."

Which, of course, explains why Pinnacle Peak Country Club remains a secret among the rich and famous. ☼

THE RIM CLUB

Par: 71 · Yardage: 5,212–7,193 · Rating: 67.9–73.4 · Slope: 130–139 · Signature hole: 581-yard, par-5 №13

*At last, we surmounted the Rim, from which
I saw a scene that defied words. It was different
from any I had seen before. Black timber as far as
the eye could see. Then I saw a vast bowl enclosed
by dim mountain ridges and dark lines I knew to
be canyons. For wild, rugged beauty, I had not
seen its equal.*

—ZANE GREY

Initial view of Payson area, 1913

Tom Weiskopf remembers his first glimpse at the land that is now The Rim Club. In many ways, that day in 1994 was similar to the burst of beauty initially taken in by western novelist Zane Grey almost a century ago.

"I walked what is now Chaparral Pines, which was on the north side of the highway, and The Rim, which was to the south, with Payne Palmer and Perry Overstreet, who developed the project," Weiskopf recalled. "The south side was so powerful when you got up high where the vistas and the Mogollon Rim were visible. Both pieces were unbelievably beautiful, but the south was simply stunning. It was so terrific, I never hesitated. "Later on, Jay came up to me and said, 'Good choice.' I was pretty happy about it myself, because earlier in my career, I didn't have that ability to make those kinds of choices."

Little did Weiskopf and Morrish know that The Rim would be their last masterpiece together. "A few months later, Jay faxed me a letter that stated he was basically breaking up the partnership," Weiskopf

The par-3 13th hole boasts an awesome green setting.

said. "I was shocked, hurt, devastated. I couldn't believe he would end one of the great partnerships in golf course architecture in such an impersonal way. Even now, I still can't believe it."

Morrish, who insisted that he and Weiskopf honor their commitment to The Rim, said the break-up was born out of practicality. "My son, Carter, was working with us and wanted to get more deeply involved, and while two of us was great, three was a crowd," said Morrish, who did 28 courses with Weiskopf, many of them highly rated. "Besides, Tom wanted to work more, and I wanted to work less. But my son was the biggest consideration."

So Morrish mapped out The Rim and made his visits every three or four weeks. The contact with Weiskopf, who made weekly visits to inspect strategy, was minimal. "It turned out to be a hell of a great golf course," Morrish noted. "The entire course was designed around the 13th hole, which we saw first during a spring snowstorm. I said, 'This is a golf hole! We need to work our way from here back to the clubhouse.'"

The 581-yard 13th is an incredible journey from high on the hill as the fairway drops down twice to a green framed by two stately pines and a solitary, 80-foot boulder. In the background is the Mogollon Rim and nearby Stewart Mountains. Accenting the setting is an altar-like stone called Spirit Rock, a relic of the land's Native American past.

Oddly, the 13th is Weiskopf's least favorite hole, although he admits the potential is there. "I think it still needs work, because you can take such advantage of the downhill slope, cut off a little bit of it, and with that elevation [5,000 feet] easily hit it on the green in two [shots]," he said. "But I personally feel that holes seven through 18 are the 12 finest consecutive holes that Jay and I have ever designed."

Morrish agrees. "We've always said the course starts at No. 7, but the reality is that there are a lot of great golf holes out there." Among the best of the best: the 533-yard, par-5 ninth is so spectacular that it's tough to leave the tee box; the par-3 12th is a

stylish version of the notorious Devil's Asshole at Pine Valley; and the 18th is a reflection of Payson itself, as it meanders through a meadow filled with wild poppies to a lake-locked green backed by the Mogollon Rim.

Memberships in The Rim started at $75,000 and were limited to 250. Needless to say, the place filled up fast, despite lots selling from $125,000 (don't expect a golf course view) to $750,000. "If it isn't the best new private course for 1999, as well as being in the top 100 in the country, something is wrong," Weiskopf said of The Rim. "It's the best course Jay and I ever did in the United States."

Weiskopf said that his only regret is that The Rim was his and Morrish's final act. "I guess if you have to save the best for last, The Rim was certainly it," Weiskopf conceded. "And while I expect it to do well, the truth is, Jay and I never paid all that much

attention to the ratings. We just lived for a compliment, to hear someone say at the end of the day, 'I really enjoyed that golf course.' Certainly, we're getting that kind of response on The Rim. It makes me wonder what else Jay and I could have accomplished had the partnership stayed intact."

Morrish also reflects on the past with a degree of sadness. "We were a great team, that's true," he said. "We each brought something to the team that was special, uniquely different from the other. Quite frankly, I suspect each of us will never reach that same pinnacle alone."

Weiskopf said, at least from his perspective, it doesn't have to be the end. "If somebody came to me three or four or five years from now, and said that he'd like to bring Jay and me back together to build a special golf course like a Rim Club, I'd do it in a heartbeat," he said enthusiastically. "You bet I would." ⚙

OR THOSE WHO have yet to behold the Stone Canyon Club, just think of those fabulous rockpiles that distinguish The Boulders. Now, multiply the number of boulders by 10. *That's* Stone Canyon.

Proof this is a special piece of property is found in the fact that so many of the top architects in the country wanted to build a golf course on it. Among the heavyweights that sought out the project were Tom Weiskopf and Greg Norman. Weiskopf thought he had the inside track because he had created the nearby Golf Club at Vistoso. Norman liked Stone Canyon so much that he offered to buy the land, but was turned down.

Instead, Stone Canyon Ltd., which essentially is Tempe developers John Beerling and Conley Wolfswinkel, selected Jay Morrish, a former partner of Weiskopf's. With a portfolio that included such Arizona masterpieces as The Boulders, Troon North, Troon Country Club, Forest Highlands, and The Rim Club, Morrish obviously had those "hands of stone." His knack of lacing fairways and greens through the granite proved to be his edge. "Given the terrain, all the boulders and elevation, Jay Morrish just seemed to be the right fit," Beerling said of the decision. "We think it's going to be better than Estancia," Wolfswinkel added point-blank.

Morrish just scoffs good-naturedly. He and Weiskopf actually came close to being the designers of record for Estancia. But, unbelievably, the Estancia project went bust in the mid-1980s. Morrish thinks a better comparison might be The Rim Club, a golf course in Payson that he did with Weiskopf. "I think [Stone Canyon] will set the new benchmark for desert golf in Arizona," Morrish said without a hint of brashness. "The Rim Club was a

great golf course, and I think this one will be right there, maybe a little tougher than The Rim."

Morrish certainly knows which one was the tougher to build. "Trees you can take out," he said of The Rim. "Rocks are much harder to remove, especially when they are the size of a building, like some of these are."

Morrish, who has developed or co-developed over 150 courses, said he knew it was love at first sight when he visited the site in 1997. "Anybody that didn't want this would be crazy," Morrish said, looking out at the rock-strewn hills that lie in the foreground of the Catalina Mountains. "I remember that Troon Golf was managing Vistoso at the time, and they were in charge of finding an architect for the project. [Troon Golf president] Dana Garmany called me—he knew my work from Troon and Troon North—and said they had a site that was marvelous. He said if somebody came in here without the right experience, they might really screw it up. He said I had the right résumé.

"I flew out the very next day and took a look. I was overwhelmed by the site. I think it took 14 seconds to put the deal together." Morrish adds that he is only partly responsible for what has been wrought. "Nature designed the course," he said. "I was just a custodian."

Every janitor should do such a wonderful job. Stone Canyon is punctuated by slightly scary elevated tees from high on the boulder piles; fairways that thread their way through one canyon after another; and Winged Foot–style bunkers that define the fairways while guarding gently-flowing greens.

"I guess if there is one thing that really separates this course it would be that we—my son Carter and myself—made the bunkers much more signifi-

cant than the other courses I've done in Arizona," Morrish said. "I'll probably be criticized for that. But a lot of them are there for protection, to keep a player from going into the desert. That's why they look slightly misplaced. But Alister Mackenzie once said, 'There are no misplaced bunkers, only misplaced shots.' To me, they have purpose."

The bunkering at Stone Canyon is sensational, as many of the fairway versions seem to ripple their way along the edges. Many of the greens' bunkers are of the pot variety, making for a nice mix. With faces that flash up, the bunkering gives Stone Canyon character, much like the bunkering at the nearby Gallery at Dove Mountain.

Morrish works his magic well in tight quarters. And as he mentioned, nature did the rest. "We've certainly got the boulders—but those saguaros. Oh, my! There is a forest of them. And the mountains. . . ." Such surroundings make picking a signature hole impossible. Morrish likes two stretches in particular—Nos. 9–10 and Nos. 17–18.

The ninth is a long par 3 that begins high in the rocky crags, descending about 75 feet to a surreal green setting tucked among the rocks and cacti. "I think we put in 10 or 12 tee boxes on that hillside. Somebody asked me why, and I said, 'Why not?'" The par-4 10th hole also begins from on high, with a long approach shot over water compounded by a small green that sits alone amid an awesome backdrop that seems to include all of Tucson. "I loved the way it turned out. The hole has so much movement."

A theme Morrish carries out to the conclusion: The short, par-4 17th swings its way through a series of bunkers, and the long, par-4 18th might feature the most artistic bunkering of all, as well as

the best view of the Catalinas.

"For [the 18th], you'll want to have your camera in the bag," added Morrish, laughing when someone told him that the owners are thinking of charging a $300 green fee when the on-site Ritz-Carlton Resort opens early in January 2002. The opulent hotel chain plans to break ground in the summer of 2000. But only two or three foursomes will be allowed to

join the members each day, and the only way to get onto the course will be to stay at the Ritz.

Morrish even added a unique oddity to make Stone Canyon a one-of-a-kind layout. "This is the 19th hole," he said, pointing to a small fairway beyond the 18th green. "In Scotland they call it a 'bye hole,' because it was the place where they went to settle bets. But I wouldn't be surprised if the

members and guests who play Stone Canyon refer to it as a 'buy hole,' which basically will mean the same thing. Either way, win or lose, you're buying drinks. . . . I don't think anyone is going to mind." ✿

ABOVE: *Nature's raw beauty surrounds the 18th at Stone Canyon.*

SUPERSTITION MOUNTAIN GOLF AND COUNTRY CLUB

. . . .

PROSPECTOR: PAR: 72 • YARDAGE: 5,408–7,193 • RATING: 68.9–74.7 • SLOPE: 113–131 • SIGNATURE HOLE: 553-YARD, PAR-4 № 18

LOST GOLD: PAR: 72 • YARDAGE: 5,605–7,351 • RATING: 69.2–75.6 • SLOPE: 121–136 • SIGNATURE HOLE: 467-YARD, PAR-4 № 18

HAVING CLIMBED "the Mountain" (Desert Mountain), Jack Nicklaus and Lyle Anderson were in search of new horizons when they came across an 870-acre piece of property in the East Valley near the base of the Superstition Mountains.

It was there that Anderson called on Nicklaus to once again work his magic, the same wizardry the Golden Bear had delivered nearly 20 years earlier when he designed the unique Desert Highlands Golf Club and the one-of-a-kind golf park known as Desert Mountain.

"What was different about this project was that it was a family affair," Anderson said of Superstition Mountain Golf and Country Club, which includes the Prospector and Lost Golf courses. "My sons Taber and Troy were able to work with me on it, and that was a real joy. At the same time, Jack was able to bring in his two sons, Gary and Jackie, to help him do the golf courses. So I guess you could say that Superstition Mountain Golf and Country Club turned out to be a win-win situation for both of us."

Not surprisingly, Nicklaus gives most of the credit to Anderson, his longtime friend and business partner. Even though Nicklaus had co-designed courses with Jackie, his oldest son, this was his first attempt at teaming up with his third son, Gary, who is sandwiched between Steven and youngest son Michael. "Lyle has always been very supportive of everything we've done together, but it was his idea to bring in our boys on this project," said Nicklaus,

who teamed up with Gary on the Prospector course, which opened first, and with Jackie on Lost Gold. "As it turned out, we all had a lot of fun."

Gary Nicklaus, who finally earned his playing privileges on the PGA Tour in 2000, designed the more traditional layout of the two courses, and delivered a very playable tract defined by 87 red-

sand bunkers and 18 relatively large greens. The signature hole on the Prospector is the 553-yard 18th, a par 5 that brings water into play down the entire left side. There is no way out, however, as the right side of the fairway is well-bunkered all the way to an elevated green that also is surrounded by sand.

"I believe in learning under fire, so I just gave

Gary a topo[graphy] map, and said, 'Have at it,'"
Nicklaus said, laughing at the thought. "He had a
few questions, like 'Where do I start,' but I just said,
'What does a train do?' And he said, 'It moves from
front to back.' I said, 'There you go,' and he did it.
When he was done, I critiqued it, added some practicality to it, and we had a very good golf course."

The better players, however, always search for
Lost Gold, a Scottish links-style layout that also
boasts a fantastic closing stretch beginning at the
15th. Built into the higher elevations, the 467-yard,
par-4 18th also earns signature status, although the
175-yard 11th, a picturesque par 3 into the mountain, and the 531-yard 14th, a par 5 that bends
around the mountain, are just as good.

According to his dad, Jackie simply breezed
through Lost Gold, which is laced with 89 bunkers
and fairways that require more exacting shots.
"Jackie is experienced, and he's good," Nicklaus said
with obvious pride. "When I work with Jackie, he's
the lead designer. With Lost Gold, he pretty much
did the entire project, then came back to me when
he was finished and said, "What do you think?'"

Anderson also drew great satisfaction from
working with his sons. "For [oldest son] Taber, it
was his first real chance to oversee a project, and to
his credit, he treated it like it was his baby from the
beginning," Anderson said. "My other son, Troy,
was like Gary [Nicklaus] in that he also got his feet
wet here. He worked on the construction end of it,
and found out what it was like from the ground
floor up."

Not that Anderson and the Bear didn't learn,
too. Having done Desert Highlands and Desert
Mountain, which are both high-end golf developments, this was more of a mainstream effort. Even
though the members at Superstition Mountain also
have first-class amenities, such as an 8,000-square-
foot, stand-alone restaurant and garden patio, this

was more affordable, with memberships that started
at $35,000 and property from the $150,000 to
$300,000 range.

"One of the things I'm most proud of, besides
working with our sons, was that this was the first
time we did everything by ourselves," said Anderson,
whose construction company came together for the
first time to build this $30 million project. "It helps
to have your own people doing the building, and not
just because of the money, because I never get too

concerned about that. To me, it's more about making people happy, like we did at Desert Highlands
and Desert Mountain."

Still, Superstition Mountain will always be
remembered for its "like father, like son" theme.
"What's so great about this is that, as I slowly phase
myself out of the business, I'm bringing my sons
along to carry on," Nicklaus added. "It's a lifelong
dream, because what father doesn't ultimately wish
to be able to work with his kids?" ❁

TERRAVITA GOLF AND COUNTRY CLUB

PAR: 72 · YARDAGE: 5,345–7,242 · RATING: 68.7–74.4 · SLOPE: 129–139 · SIGNATURE HOLE: 550-YARD, PAR-5 NO. 3

FROM THE BEGINNING, Terravita has been a test case for the "good life" that comes with belonging to a big-time country club. Always at the forefront, the north Scottsdale club has grown by leaps and bounds, with a few growing pains along the way.

"Terravita is a very elite neighborhood that sits right across the street from The Boulders, with mountain backdrops that are seemingly everywhere," said Tom Giulioni, the general manager at Terravita. "In every way, it's got a lot of good things

going for it, like a great zip code and wonderful people that make up the membership.

There is one word that Giulioni continually refers to when defining Terravita. "Current," he said. "The membership is very current, and very up-to-date. They pride themselves on being in tune with what's happening now." Proof lies no further away than the Internet, where Terravita's members go surfing (terravitascottsdale.com) for information on club amenities and events.

The Web site is a prerequisite at Terravita, where members can choose from computer classes,

Spanish lessons, investment seminars, cooking exhibitions, and of course, the Terravita Art League, of which noted Scottsdale artist Beth Zink is a member. "We've got 138 of our [1,380] members who are enrolled in the Terravita Art League," Giulioni reported. "They do everything from work with clay to watercolors to oil painting. There's something for everybody."

Yes, members also enjoy an Olympic-sized swimming pool, six tennis courts, a basketball court,

Greg Nash and Billy Casper teamed up at Terravita.

and a wellness center complete with a masseuse and personal trainers on-site. "It's an incredible atmosphere," Giulioni said. "I mean, while the adults are doing laps in the swimming pool, the kids have a lagoon and fountain to play in. And there's also a therapeutic Jacuzzi. It's awesome."

Unbelievably, all the extra perks add up to over $10 million in assets spread out over 10 acres. This is "serious" extracurricular activity. "We have taken social membership to a new level," Giulioni added. "The members really care about the entire package, not just the golf."

Oh, yes, did we mention a superb golf course designed by the noted architectural team of Greg Nash and Billy Casper? Well, Terravita has that, too. In fact, the entire package at Terravita is a story of unbridled success by the Del Webb Corp., which made the project a golden opportunity for those of all ages who love to play the game in a country club atmosphere. Homes and memberships sold at a record pace, and the chic but reasonably priced community was filled in a little over three years. Everyone seemed euphoric over the experience, because for $45,000 and a moderately expensive lot, Terravita was quite attractive. That was especially true when compared to its high-priced neighbors.

"About the only downside to this project was when the members attempted to buy the club back from Dell Web [in 1998]. That turned a little bitter," Giulioni explained. "When everything finally cooled off, the members bought the course, the pro shop and the locker rooms for $6.2 million. To their credit, Del Webb tossed in the clubhouse, pavilion, fitness center, swimming pool, and tennis courts for just $1 more. So it all worked out."

When it comes to Terravita, everything always does. For instance, in the beginning the club somehow managed to finagle a Scottsdale address out of the city. "That was the first step," Giulioni recalled. "Everybody west of Scottsdale Road had been in Phoenix before Del Webb broke that [Scottsdale] barrier with Terravita. You could say that Terravita was [Del Webb's] golden opportunity to take the company from a Sun City template to a younger, newer direction that eventually led to such projects

as Anthem."

Nash, who also built the Anthem Country Club for Del Webb, said Terravita was destined to succeed from the get-go. "More than anything, Terravita was Anne Mariucci's rise to power at Del Webb," Nash said of the company's senior vice president who handles golf projects. "She did everything right, even though she dealt Billy and me a few zingers that really kept us on our toes.

"But as it turned out, Terravita is a very playable, fun golf course with some beautiful holes. At the same time, there were a few—like Nos. 1, 3, and 10—that I'd like to have another shot at. The first hole was boring, the third hole got crisscrossed in the planning stages, and the 10th hole is unplayable as a par 4. To their credit, the members keep fine-tuning the course, so I think that eventually we'll get everything worked out there."

Jim Schreiber, the director of golf at Terravita, says the golf course is very tough from 100 yards in. "The greens are [severely sloped] with lots of undulations, kind of like an Augusta National, which I have played," Schreiber said. "The landing areas, however, are very fair, so it's a little bit of a tradeoff. Of the two nines, the back side is more difficult

because you start out at the 10th with a rugged, 451-yard par 4 that has water around the green. That is the beginning of a tough four-hole stretch."

Schreiber said that despite the demands, the 10th is the signature hole. Nash on the other hand, thinks its No. 3. Giulioni acknowledged the disagreement over which is the course's signature hole, but it's a minor point. "Del Webb always said it was the 10th hole, while the members probably consider it to be [the par-5] third hole, which features a double-dogleg fairway with an ancient ironwood in the center," he said. "But the truth of the matter is that we've got a lot of great holes at Terravita."

Nash said that in any other neighborhood the golf course at Terravita would have been a shining star. But with the likes of The Boulders, Desert Mountain, Desert Highlands, and Troon lying nearby, "everybody is a critic."

"We really would have had to screw it up bad for Terravita not to succeed," Nash said in his easy-going manner. "As it turned out, it was a mixed blessing for everyone involved. The homeowners/members got a terrific golf community at an affordable price, while Del Webb broke all the records [for development] in the process." ⚙

TONTO VERDE GOLF CLUB

PEAKS: PAR: 72 • YARDAGE: 4,791–6,525 • RATING: 67.5–74.1 • SLOPE: 113–140 • SIGNATURE HOLE: 351-YARD, PAR-4 № 5

RANCH: PAR: 72 • YARDAGE: 5,287–6,988 • RATING: 70.1–73.1 • SLOPE: 120–143 • SIGNATURE HOLE: 317-YARD, PAR-4 № 14

A golfer blasts away with Weaver's Needle in the distance.

DAVE RITCHIE never expected to change the face of golf in this small community of retirees that lies along the Verde River. No, Ritchie came to play the game, not to have the business of it bury him. "I moved out here from Michigan in 1974, and planned to just play golf and enjoy life," recalled the president of Rio Verde Development. "But after awhile, I decided I better do something else, because I certainly wasn't getting rich on the golf course."

That was the turning point, not only in Ritchie's life, but also in the lives of those other Midwesterners who followed him to sunny Arizona seeking the good life. First, Ritchie supervised the construction of the Quail Run and White Wing courses in Rio Verde, then he turned his attention to a more elite retirement community called Tonto Verde. "We called the first [development] Rio Verde because of the river," Ritchie said. Along with the larger Colorado River, the Verde is one of only two rivers that run year-round in Arizona. "We picked Tonto Verde for the second, because it was originally in the Tonto National Forest. It was property that we came into through a land swap with the federal government."

There is no comparison between Verdes, as Tonto is much more upscale than Rio. The same could be said of the golf courses. The original Peaks Course at Tonto Verde is charming and petite, while the Ranch Course is a much bigger challenge. The common denominator is architect Gary Panks, who created the Peaks with former partner David

Graham in 1993 before going solo on the Ranch in '99. "The Peaks is a little bit like Sedona Golf Resort in that it's tighter and more picturesque," said Panks, whose Arizona résumé includes the surreal Sedona layout. "The Ranch is more for the better players. It's got a much bigger feel, a more championship quality."

According to Dave Cox, the director of golf at Tonto Verde, those opinions are shared by the members and outside guests, who get to play the courses on a day-by-day, rotating basis. "Those who can't hit it that far really enjoy the Peaks because it's more of a peaceful walk in the desert," Cox noted. "Those who can hit it [far], even if they hit it so far they can't find it, always go for the Ranch."

Tonto Verde has other terrific amenities, like a first-class clubhouse, pro shop, and restaurant. And if 18 holes get to be too much, there is always a well-done putting course that Panks laced through a small lake that lies behind the Peaks.

Of course, with the outstanding variety each course offers, a round of golf is usually on the mind of most of the nearly 400 members. It's reasonably priced golf, too, as memberships go for $35,000 plus property, and green fees are less than at neighboring Troon North and Legend Trail.

The Peaks is so named because of the landmark Four Peaks, which rise above both courses, with the Mazatzal Mountains to the east and the McDowells to the west. For the most part, the Peaks is a tight, desert-style golf course that demands course management over length. The signature hole comes early, as the 351-yard, par-4 fifth hole is lined with water and backed by Weaver's Needle. Be careful, as water comes sneaking into play off the tee and can also prove deadly on the approach. In the opinion of many, however, the ninth and 17th holes are just as picturesque.

Although it's probably more of an illusion than fact, the fairways on the Ranch Course appear to be about twice as wide as the Peaks. The greens also seem gargantuan by comparison. Yardagewise, the front and back nines are almost equal, but hazards and much more movement make the back nine the more difficult of the two. Along the way, you encounter the 14th hole, at 317 yards a very driveable par 4. The 14th, which starts from an elevated tee, then plays down into a well-bunkered fairway and back up to a severely sloping green, also is slightly deceiving. If you can't bust it 240 yards, a 2- or a 3-iron off the tee will prove to be the wiser choice. At the same time, the Ranch is a difficult test from the 11th through 18th holes, and if a birdie is on your mind there is no better time to just "go for it."

That's been Ritchie's philosophy from almost the beginning. After developing Rio Verde and Tonto Verde, his eyes are focused on yet another horizon to the north of Tonto Verde. Yes, Vista Verde, an 830-acre development headed up by Ritchie, is in the planning stages. "I'm not sure Vista Verde will be the final name, but it will have Verde in there somewhere," he said of project, which once again will feature two 18-hole golf courses.

And the architect of choice? "Why, if I have anything to do with it, Gary Panks, of course," Ritchie added. "He's the guy that made Tonto Verde what it is today."

Yes, Panks and a guy named Dave Ritchie, who gave up full-time golf to pursue another course.

TORREON GOLF AND COUNTRY CLUB

PAR: 72 • YARDAGE: 5,372–7,129 • RATING: NA • SLOPE: NA • SIGNATURE HOLE: 377-YARD, PAR-4 № 18

THERE IS an obvious reason why Torreon, the elite golf club cut out of the Sitgreaves National Forest, looks like a painting as the sun settles through the pines late in the afternoon: Robert Von Hagge.

The eccentric golf course architect actually was an artist before his current profession produced 250 golf courses in 33 countries around the world. Von Hagge still sketches his work before it becomes reality. "I don't think I could go anywhere without a picture in my mind first," said Von Hagge, who eventu-ally will complete 36 holes of golf at Torreon. "You can look at all the squiggle, bird's-eye view pictures in the world if you want. But when you actually draw or paint or sketch the hole, suddenly everybody is on the same page."

In every way, Von Hagge is an impressionist. Like a Monet or van Gogh, he lives for the light and the way it affects his subjects, in this case fairways and greens. "The only thing that is eternal in life is light," said Von Hagge, who has designed numerous courses on the French and Italian Rivieras, where those early geniuses of the art world made their reputations. "These beautiful trees at Torreon will come and go, and the water you see here may or may not be here someday. But the light? The light will remain, and that's why we believe that everything on a golf course must be done with vertical expression."

Von Hagge's logic is simple. "Think about it: What separates golf from tennis? It's the visual. You've got to give them something that knocks their socks off. To be a really great golf course, it's got to be strategically put together and it's got to be beautiful, so when someone finishes playing a hole, they'll say, 'Oh, man!' That's what I love about designing golf courses."

Von Hagge refers to Torreon as a candy store. "I'm blessed here," he said of the nearly 1,000-acre project that is being spearheaded by Desert Troon of Scottsdale. "Everywhere you look, we've got these big, enormously beautiful pines. So in a way, that makes it difficult to distinguish each hole, which I'm trying to bring out in a shockingly subtle way."

Torreon, which is a reference to Geronimo's one-time stronghold in Mexico, is a testament to its master's desires. No two holes are the same, as the first 18 holes ramble over the landscape. Only two offerings are basically flat—Nos. 9 and 18—and even those are distinguished by radical design concepts.

"In a few years, when the conditioning matches the variety, I think the members will realize what they've got," said Von Hagge of the first course.

Tee boxes rise like a stairway on the No. 1 at Torreon.

"By that time, we'll be finishing up with the second course, which is going to be a little bit longer and stronger, with less elevation and more meadowlands than the first course. The contrast will be good, as one will complement the other."

In the meantime, the first 18 will have to suffice. "We just opened the first nine [holes], and the reaction was just super," said Terry Duggan, the general manager at Torreon. "What was so fun was the course exceeded their expectations by a mile!"

With memberships that start at just $10,000, and lots that go for $60,000 to $150,000, Torreon might be the best buy in Arizona. According to Sheridan Atkinson, who is in charge of the project for Desert Troon, the affordable price was by design. "We wanted the club to be as good as Forest Highlands or The Rim Club, but more reasonably priced, so it would be attractive to families," Atkinson said of strategy. "The reason we selected the name Torreon was because we want this to be a stronghold, like Geronimo's, for the entire family."

To that end, Torreon will eventually sport its own small town complete with a movie/amphitheater. There also will be a fly-fishing school and trout stream running through the property, as well as a plethora of other recreational activities.

Of course, Von Hagge's two masterpieces will remain the centerpiece. "There's such a fine line between a great golf course and a gimmicky one," Von Hagge noted. "The first time you do Six Flags over Arizona, that's the one they're going to remember. But Torreon has such wonderful green settings, and the paths to get to them are lined with all the natural amenities that God gave us."

The course opens from a spectacular, elevated tee box in the pines, and then spins off for a wild ride through them. Among the holes that the members will grow fond of are: No. 4, a rolling, 554-yard par 5 that teases you with a peek of the flag all the

way from the tee; No. 6, a medium par 3 over a large wash to a green surrounded by seven bunkers; No. 8, a 593-yard double dogleg that plays downhill to a terraced green that falls away; No. 9, a short par 4 that doglegs right around a tree-lined corner to a green situated between two ponds and surrounded by wetlands; No. 12, another long par-5 dogleg that sports 11 pot bunkers; No. 15, a 201-yard par 3 that plays slightly uphill and over water to a two-tiered green framed by boulders; and No. 18, a short, driveable par 4 that plays through the wetlands to a serene green setting.

"I wanted the ending to be special, that's why I gave them a choice [at No. 18]," Von Hagge explained. "It's dicey [to try and drive the hole], but if you're down in your match, and you've got the balls, go for it."

Golfers certainly will. For those who love a challenge, Von Hagge has given them the ultimate in Torreon. He also has put Show Low on the map as one of Arizona's finest summer retreats.

"When I first saw the property, I thought: 'You're going to have to whittle this out of the trees, and make it believable at the same time,'" Von Hagge said of his thesis for Torreon. "I think that's what I'm most proud of in retrospect. It's believable."

Yes, a work of art in every way. ☼

TROON GOLF AND COUNTRY CLUB

PAR: 72 • YARDAGE: 5,082–7,041 • RATING: 68.5–75.6 • SLOPE: 124–148 • SIGNATURE HOLE: 347-YARD, PAR-4 N⁰ 16

UNBELIEVABLY, Tom Weiskopf never had built a golf course when he teamed up with Jay Morrish late in the fall of 1985 to do a project called Troon Golf and Country Club. For the record, Morrish, who had quit working for Jack Nicklaus in 1984, had built only one—the second 18 holes at The Boulders.

Naturally, both were blown away when *Golf Digest* selected Troon as the best new private golf course in America for 1986. "The percentages say that just couldn't happen," said Weiskopf, who ended up creating 28 courses with Morrish before they split up almost 12 years later. "We were just two guys who got together to build a golf course. Usually it takes three to five years to understand each other's ideas and become a great team. Nobody could be that lucky to make the first one a national award-winner."

Troon's sweet success gave Morrish and Weiskopf instant credibility, "and a heck of a lot of confidence," added Weiskopf. "It also allowed us to determine our own path, to be selective about the pieces of property we took on, and to be involved with developers who would allow us to do a great job. Those two factors—the land and the developer—really are the key to any architect's success."

In this case, the developer was Jerry Nelson, who had contacted Weiskopf, who in turn got in touch with Morrish. "I met Jay through Jack, when the two were traveling around doing golf courses like Desert Highlands," Weiskopf recalled. "Ironically, Jerry Nelson had said to me, 'Tom, I'm not a golfer, but everyone tells me you need a name

The 13th hole at Troon is one of the many excellent par 3s.

designer to build golf courses these days. I've got this great piece of property near Pinnacle Peak, and I want to develop it so I can compete with Desert Highlands.'"

Initially, Weiskopf told Nelson that he wasn't qualified to carry out the Troon project. But Nelson insisted, so Weiskopf went ahead with the call to Morrish, who flew out to Scottsdale to evaluate the property. "Jay loved it, and turned to me and said, 'Tom you're the strategist, and I'm the technician,' and that's how we started," Weiskopf noted. "It was give and take, and we really respected each other's opinion."

Morrish also has fond memories of the early days at Troon. "I recall it was Tom's first job, and he spent a lot of time on it," Morrish explained. "I'd show up every two or three weeks, and there would be Tom. He loved it. He'd bring his lunch, and would spend all day with the [construction] crew. I was more the grizzled old veteran after being in the business for over 20 years. "What I remember most was that Troon was a breeze. The developer told us, 'You've got your budget and your corridors, now call me when it's done.' I wish all jobs went as easy as Troon."

Weiskopf also remembers Troon as his school days in golf course architecture. "I asked a lot of stupid questions, but everybody was wonderful," he said. "I was so lucky that Wadsworth was the contractor and Bernie Nichols was the shaper, because in retrospect, they were the best at what they did in the world. The whole thing was way beyond me at first. But it turned out to be a phenomenal experience, so exhilarating. I'd wear my boots, be completely dirty and dusty at the end of the day, and the guys would want to quit at five [P.M.], and I'd say, 'We're quitting already?' Yeah, it was that special. The start of a terrific relationship with a terrific golf course. I couldn't have been happier."

The members at Troon couldn't be happier, either. All the hype had been backed up with graceful fairways that flowed like a painting, and greens

Photos by Tony Roberts

and tee boxes that resembled an artist's palette. Morrish's routing was regal, as it rambled over rock outcroppings and desert washes with purpose and poise. Weiskopf's strategy for shot selection looked like it had been formulated by a master architect rather than a raw rookie.

A thinking person's course in every respect, Troon dazzles those who take it on, with holes like the 296-yard, par-4 fourth, called "Short Four" because you can gamble and try to drive the green with consequences. The sixth, seventh, and eighth holes gives golfers everything they could imagine in a par 4, par 3, par 5 sequence.

The back nine is as good or better. The par-4 14th drops off a sharp ledge, and thus is dubbed "The Cliff," featuring a scary second shot to a well-bunkered green below. The 15th, a 139-yard wedge shot over a canyon to a severely sloping green proves that short par 3s also can be difficult. But the best, many of the members feel, is No. 16, a 347-yard, downhill par 4 known as "Gunsight" because the tee shot must be aimed through the

crosshairs of a boulder pile plopped directly in front of the tee box.

Weiskopf said he only had one minor disappointment with the team's initial work of art, which includes a chic clubhouse complete with panoramic views of the Valley. "I was against naming it Troon. That was Jerry Nelson's idea," said Weiskopf in reference to the fact that his only major championship as a player came at the 1973 British Open held at Troon. "There's only one Troon, and it's in Scotland. But Jerry's spin was it was my first major, and my first golf course. And the bottom line was, yeah, Jay and I built it, but Jerry owned the golf course."

Nelson was the first of many developers to accent Weiskopf's contribution to a project while inadvertently excluding Morrish. "It's such an awesome layout," Weiskopf said, "one that certainly has stood the test of time and only gotten better."

If only the design team of Jay Morrish and Tom Weiskopf could have enjoyed such a fate. But at least they built cherished layouts like Troon before they split. ⚙

TUCSON COUNTRY CLUB

. . . .

PAR: 72 • YARDAGE: 5,737–6,833 • RATING: 69.8–73.6 • SLOPE: 123–132 • 235-YARD, PAR-3 №. 17

IN MANY WAYS, Tucson Country Club is a reflection of its most prominent member, Dr. Ed Updegraff. Honest, respected, revered, traditional, blue-blooded—all of those words describe Updegraff, one of the game's true gentlemen. They also fit Tucson Country Club to a "T."

Built in 1947 by the legendary father-son team of William "Billy" Bell and Billy Jr., Tucson Country Club is golf the way it used to be. There are those, such as Updegraff, who still feel that way. "I'm older,

and I appreciate the older things in life," said Updegraff, who at 77 remains a 5 handicap and plays daily, often shooting his age or better. "Country clubs like Phoenix and Oro Valley and Tucson, they're the old line, the old style, and the most fun to play. Courses like Vistoso and La Paloma and Ventana Canyon—those newer styles—I just don't take to them as much."

Who can blame Updegraff? He won an incredible 27 club championships at Tucson Country Club. And, no, those weren't of *the* senior variety; they

were the club championship. Updegraff's legacy, which included the 1981 U.S. Senior Amateur Championship and numerous Walker Cup teams, was honored in 1998 with the prestigious Bobby Jones Award—the USGA's highest honor. "Dr. Updegraff is a special person," noted Michael Haywood, the director of golf at Tucson Country Club since 1990. "And, yes, I'd say it's fair to compare him to our golf club. Both are the best."

Which is why, year after year, Tucson CC plays a key role in determining the state's best players and beyond. It is the only club in Arizona to have hosted two national championships (the 1982 U.S. Senior Amateur and the 1992 U.S. Senior Women's Amateur) along with 15 USGA qualifiers and six state amateurs. Next up is the 2001 Arizona State Amateur.

Obviously, the members of Tucson CC take great pride in their course's role in the state's golf history. Its storied, tree-lined fairways have witnessed hundreds of great players. Fred Vance, a national golf photographer who also is a member at the club, said he recalls Hubert Green playing in a U.S. Open qualifier there, and making a great shot, as well as quip. "I was shooting for *Golfweek*, and I remember Hubert hit a 6-iron about a foot from the pin at No. 6," Vance said with a laugh. "He turned to me and said, 'If you weren't so ugly, I'd kiss you.'"

There always has been a love affair between Tucson CC and its members. Tucked into the older, northeast section of the Old Pueblo (Tucson), the course winds its way through a small mesquite and pine forest with great views of the Catalina Mountains. Mostly, it's an invigorating walk in the park.

The 235-yard, par-3 is the signature hole at Tucson Country Club.

"The club is steeped in history, but it's also gone through a complete turnaround in recent years," Haywood noted. "At the same time, most of that original flavor remains."

The back nine is tougher, but the front is more fun, chiefly because it offers a player a chance to make birdies. Get them while you can, because the last nine holes can be back-breakers. Especially the closing stretch, which includes two demanding par 4s, the 16th being shorter and tighter, and the 18th being a long shot straight into the clubhouse. Sandwiched between the two is the 235-yard 17th, one of the most difficult par 3s in the state because the lengthy tee shot must be struck to a smallish green that is well-bunkered.

Actually, there is a lot of sand on this course, as only the trees outnumber the 88 bunkers. The greens average 4,800 square feet, which is about half the size of today's more upscale models. But like Haywood said, some changes have been made over the years, perhaps the biggest being a revitalization of the bunkers, tees, and greens in 1997 by architect Keith Foster, who also gave Paradise Valley Country Club a careful facelift.

"Actually, the improvements began about 10 years before that when we built a new, 60,000-square-foot clubhouse," explained Haywood, noting that other changes during that decade involved the practice facilities, irrigation system, and even some turnover in membership. And while its barber shop remained intact, other rooms at Tucson CC did not. "For instance, we don't call it a men's grill anymore," Haywood added. "It's a 'mixed grill,' meaning the ladies are welcome, too."

Obviously, amenities play an important role at Tucson CC, where the membership remains affordable at $30,000. But you need a warm and wonderful place to lick your wounds after taking on this tenacious test from yesteryear. "The course is not overwhelming when it comes to length [6,833 yards]," Haywood noted. "But placement of shots, especially those into the greens, are so important. You just always have to be on your game."

Unlike the grill, the course is one place where the ladies don't get much of a break. "The ladies'

Tucson Country Club has hosted two U.S. Senior Amateurs.

side is very difficult even at a par of 73," Haywood said. "Plus, that's 5,737 yards on a course where the ball doesn't roll much. The soil is soft around here, and it makes for some very long shots into the green."

Updegraff, for one, knows how unforgiving Tucson CC can be. Sure, he has won all those championships on it, but as fate would have it, there was one very big one that got away. That came in 1982, the year of his defense in the U.S. Senior Amateur. That also was the year that Tucson Country Club hosted the tournament. Not surprisingly, Updegraff made it all the way to the finals, where he faced a fellow named Alton Duhon.

"Oh, I remember the last match," Updegraff recalled with clarity. "I was 1-down with one [hole] to play, and he ended up winning, 2-up. Yes, it seemed the whole thing was a little ironic, me losing it on my own home course. "But . . . I was playing a good player, and I had missed some opportunities coming down the stretch. . . . Sometimes things come to you unexpectedly, and at others, when you want them the most, they don't. Golf is unpredictable in that way, which is why we play the game."

And why some of the classiest people in the world, like Dr. Ed Updegraff, form lifelong bonds with courses like Tucson Country Club. ☼

WHITE MOUNTAIN COUNTRY CLUB

Par: 72 · Yardage: 5,746–6,523 · Rating: 67.4–74.9 · Slope: 118–134 · Signature hole: 440-yard, par-4 № 18

SLEEPY AS IT MIGHT SEEM, White Mountain Country Club once was a giant in Arizona golf. Dubbed "Phoenix Country Club North" because many of its members came from the elite club in the Valley, White Mountain ruled the pines of northern Arizona from the late 1950s until 1990, when Forest Highlands in Flagstaff modernized the world of private "summer" golf.

"This has always been our 'other' home, and I think that's the way a lot of our members feel about White Mountain," said Bob Goldwater, one of the original members of the course, which was built in stages from 1956 through 1959. "Over the years, we've made a lot of great friends, and that's made for some wonderful memories. I know that other private clubs up north like Forest Highlands and Hassayampa have come along and made [the private experience] bigger and better. But I love this golf course, just like the other members do."

The history behind White Mountain is interesting but complicated, because many of those involved in its conception have passed on. But, originally, the property was owned by the U.S. Forest Service and leased to the members for $25 to $75 per lot. That changed in the early 1960s during a land swap involving Southwest Forest Industries in cooperation with the New Mexico Land and Cattle Co. In that deal, which resulted in the 1,800-acre parcel that became White Mountain CC, the Forest Service received 16 acres of land near McNary for every one it gave up.

The driving force behind the club, which originally sold memberships for $158 (they go for

The 18th green is a severe test of putting.

$25,000 today), was the Phoenix tandem of architect Milt Coggins Sr. and developer Gray Madison, who later played key roles at Pinetop Country Club and Pinetop-Lakes Golf Course. Initially, Coggins and Madison laid out the first nine holes, which are now the back nine, and superintendent Arthur Snyder oversaw the construction work. A year and a half later, Coggins and Madison, along with Snyder's son, Jack, who would later become a prominent architect, added what now is the front nine.

"I remember it well, because building a golf course in the mountains back in those days was a complicated process," said Jack Snyder, the only surviving member of that foursome. "What I remember most was that when we got ready to do the second nine, Milt, Gray, and I walked the woods and staked it out. Everything was done by pacing it out, but when I put it on paper after surveying it, I realized it wasn't right, so I adjusted a lot of those links."

Snyder said the second nine holes were further

complicated by a forest fire that caused a lot of damage and pollution in the area. "The new nine got a late start that spring, and I remember my wife and I planted a lot of those fairways by hand," he said.

Not that the first nine had been a cakewalk to build. According to Roy Sauve, another founding member, times were different when it came to constructing private clubs. "In the old days, everybody pitched in. It wasn't about writing checks," Sauve noted. "One thing I remember that was very different was that Ol' Milt got everybody to walk the course and pick up rocks, as well as repair fences. Cooperation was the key, even though there were a lot of people involved with the project who had lots of money."

Snyder said one big difference was that several of the White Mountain Apaches were members, as well as a lot of locals. "Some came from as far away as Holbrook to be members, but after a few years that all changed, and it became primarily a club for

those who lived in the Valley," Snyder said. "What I remember most was it was very quiet up there, and that was the big attraction for those who lived in the city."

For the most part, serenity remains a main ingredient in the White Mountain experience, although nonstop development in the Pinetop-Lakeside area has changed the atmosphere slightly. Fortunately, the traditional concept of the golf course remains intact, with stately, pine-lined fairways and beautiful bentgrass greens. Constant elevation changes also add to the character.

The front nine starts out with a straight-forward approach, but by the time a player reaches the 414-yard par 4, an uphill dogleg left over a lily-filled pond, there is the realization that this is special. That perception is magnified over the next five holes, three of them being sensational par 5s. The back nine, which involves fewer shots through the timber, kicks in at the 12th hole, a short, dogleg par 4. The signature hole is the 18th, a 440-yard par 4 over water to one of the state's most severely sloping greens.

It's a perfect ending, as members who have completed their rounds sit on the large outdoor patio enjoying lunch or dinner while watching others three- and four-putt away on the final green. Sometimes it can be comical, as putts take roundhouse routes toward the cup. But scoring is not as paramount at White Mountain as is the emotional shelter that the club seems to provide. "I remember the original clubhouse," Sauve said. "We used to cook hamburgers and hot dogs on a little stove, and it was very informal. It still is [informal] to some extent."

Goldwater said he also cherishes his time at White Mountain, especially the fall months right before the snows shut the course down in late October. "This is a nice, comfortable club for me," he said. "I can't play those big courses like Forest Highlands any more. You've got to be a mountain goat up there." ✿

Hidden Gems

MANY GOLFERS WHO PLAY among Arizona's finest fairways and greens often are unaware of the state's "Hidden Gems" and there are many. Such little-known treasures as Elephant Rocks in Williams, Emerald Canyon in Parker, Antelope Hills in Prescott, and Rio Rico near the Mexican border—to name just a few—also are wonderful golf experiences.

Not only can a golfer find a quiet round of golf, but there are other, terrific times to be had at the 25 courses found in this chapter. Even better, it's great golf at about half the price you would pay at Arizona's better-known courses.

1 ALPINE COUNTRY CLUB *(page 128)*
100 Country Club land, Alpine, 85920
DIRECTIONS: *Two miles east of Alpine (follow signs).*
TEE TIMES: 520-339-4944

2 ANTELOPE HILLS *(page 130)*
19 Clubhouse Drive, Prescott, 86301
DIRECTIONS: *Seven miles northeast of Prescott on U.S. Highway 89, adjacent to airport.*
TEE TIMES: 520-776-7888

3 APACHE STRONGHOLD GOLF COURSE *(page 132)*
Apache Gold Casino, P.O. Box 1210, San Carlos, 85550
DIRECTIONS: *Five miles east of Globe on Highway 70.*
TEE TIMES: 1-800-APACHE8

4 CONCHO VALLEY COUNTRY CLUB *(page 134)*
HC 30, Box 900, Concho, 85924
DIRECTIONS: *Located Between Show Low and St. Johns on Highway 60.*
TEE TIMES: 520-337-2622

5 DESERT HILLS GOLF CLUB *(page 136)*
1245 Desert Hills Drive, Yuma, 85365
DIRECTIONS: *Take Interstate 8 to 32nd Street and follow it to Avenue A, then proceed south one-half mile.*
TEE TIMES: 520-344-GOLF

6 ELEPHANT ROCKS *(page 138)*
2200 Country Club Drive, Williams, 86046
DIRECTIONS: *Take I-40 one mile west of town and follow signs.*
TEE TIMES: 520-635-4935

7 EMERALD CANYON GOLF COURSE *(page 140)*
72 Emerald Canyon Drive, Parker, 85344
DIRECTIONS: *Located along Highway 75, seven miles north of Parker.*
TEE TIMES: 520-667-3366

8 ENCANTO GOLF COURSE *(page 142)*
2705 N. 15th Avenue, Phoenix, 85007
DIRECTIONS: *Just south of Thomas Road off 15th Avenue.*
TEE TIMES: 602-253-3963

9 FRANCISCO GRANDE RESORT AND GOLF CLUB *(page 144)*
26000 Gila Bend Highway, Casa Grande, 85222
DIRECTIONS: *From Casa Grande, take Highway 84 west 5 miles.*
TEE TIMES: 480-836-6444

10 GOLF CLUB AT JOHNSON RANCH *(page 146)*
433 W. Bella Vista, Queen Creek, 85242
DIRECTIONS: *Highway 60 to Ellsworth Exit, south to Hunt Highway, east to Bella Vista.*
TEE TIMES: 480-987-9800

11 KINO SPRINGS COUNTRY CLUB *(page 148)*
187 Kino Springs Drive, Nogales, 85621
DIRECTIONS: *U.S. Highway 82, six miles east of Nogales south on Kino Springs Drive (follow signs).*
TEE TIMES: 800-732-5751

12 LAKE POWELL NATIONAL GOLF COURSE *(page 150)*
400 Clubhouse Drive, Page, 86040
DIRECTIONS: *From Flagstaff, take U.S. Highway 89 130 miles north to Page.*
TEE TIMES: 520-645-2023

13 LONGBOW GOLF CLUB *(page 152)*
5400 E. McDowell Road, Mesa, 85215
DIRECTIONS: *Northeast corner of Higley and McDowell.*
TEE TIMES: 480-807-5400

14 OAKCREEK COUNTRY CLUB *(page 154)*
690 Bell Rock Boulevard, Sedona, 86351
DIRECTIONS: *Take I-17 to Highway 179, north to Bell Rock Boulevard, west to golf course.*
TEE TIMES: 520-284-1660

15 PINETOP LAKES GOLF AND COUNTRY CLUB *(page 156)*
4634 Bucksprings Road, Pinetop Lakeside, 85935
DIRECTIONS: *One and a half miles south of Pinetop off Arizona Highway 260.*
TEE TIMES: 520-369-4531

16 RANCHO MAÑANA GOLF CLUB *(page 158)*
5734 E. Rancho Mañana Boulevard, Cave Creek, 85331
DIRECTIONS: *Two miles north of Carefree Highway on Cave Creek Road.*
TEE TIMES: 480-488-0398

17 RANDOLPH PARK MUNICIPALS *(page 160)*
600 S. Alvernon Way, Tucson, 85711
DIRECTIONS: *Take 22nd Street east to Alvernon, north one-half mile.*
TEE TIMES: 520-325-2811

18 RIO RICO RESORT AND COUNTRY CLUB *(page 162)*
1550 Camino a la Posada, Rio Rico, 85621
DIRECTIONS: *From Tucson, take I-19 south to the Rio Rico exit, then east on Pendelton Road to golf course.*
TEE TIMES: 520-281-8567

19 SAN IGNACIO GOLF CLUB *(page 164)*
4201 S. Camino del Sol, Green Valley, 85614
DIRECTIONS: *From Tucson, take I-19 south to Continental Road exit, south on frontage road to Camino Encanto, then west to Camino del Sol.*
TEE TIMES: 520-648-3468

20 SAN MARCOS GOLF RESORT *(page 166)*
100 N. Dakota Street, Chandler, 85224
DIRECTIONS: *Take Chandler Boulevard east past Alma School, then south on Dakota Street.*
TEE TIMES: 480-963-3358

21 SILVER CREEK GOLF CLUB *(page 168)*
2051 Silver Lake Boulevard, White Mountain Lake, 85912
DIRECTIONS: *From Show Low, take U.S. Highway 60*
east eight miles to Bourdon Ranch Road, proceed north
about seven miles.
TEE TIMES: 520-537-2744

22 TUBAC GOLF RESORT *(page 170)*
P.O. Box 1297 , #1 Otero Road, Tubac, 85646
DIRECTIONS: *From Tucson, take I-19 south to exit 40,*
south on frontage road to archway entrance.
TEE TIMES: 800-848-7893

23 TURQUOISE VALLEY GOLF COURSE *(page 172)*
1791 Newell Street, Naco, 85603
DIRECTIONS: *Eight miles south of Bisbee on Naco Highway.*
TEE TIMES: 520-432-3091

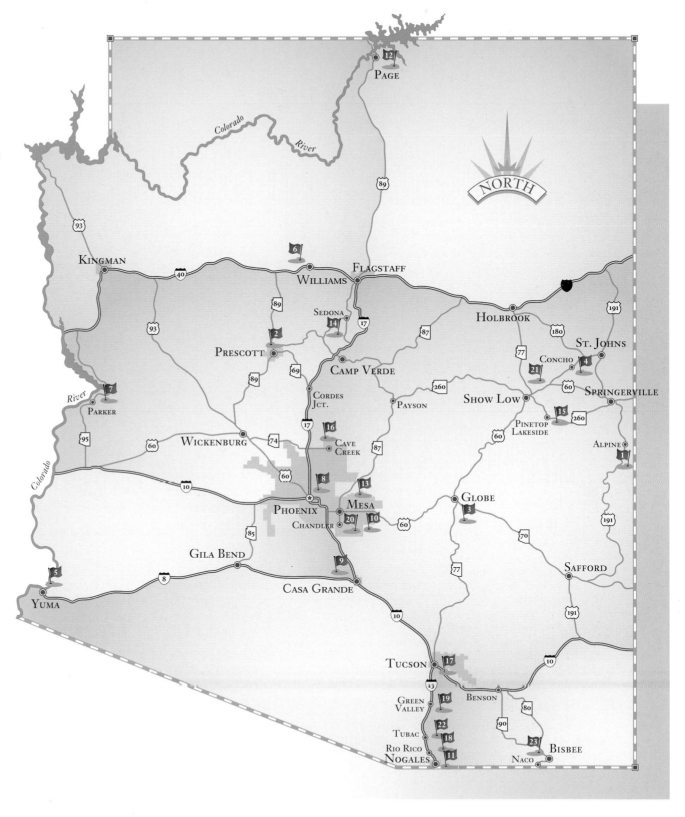

ALPINE COUNTRY CLUB

Par: 70 • Yardage: 4,936–5,288 • Rating: 65.7–67.1 • Slope: 107–108 • Signature hole: 139-yard, par-3 №8 • Green fees: inexpensive

YOU MIGHT THINK that labeling little Alpine Country Club as one of Arizona's greatest golf courses would be a stretch of the imagination. However, when you consider its elevation, environmental stewardship, great cuisine, and atmosphere, it becomes obvious that its worthy attributes distinguish these "wild" fairways and greens from others around the state.

• At 8,200 feet above sea level, it has the greatest elevation of any course in Arizona. Want to hit a 300-yard drive or 150-yard wedge shot with ease? Alpine CC is your place.

• For those who care about wildlife, no course takes greater care of its native inhabitants. The gophers keep digging holes, and the elk bed down nightly. Even the starter, a dog called Tramper, hails from the animal kingdom.

• Great food? Alpine CC has it, which is why even the nongolfing public often frequents the club's restaurant, Las Escondida.

• And if you love a laid-back atmosphere to play golf, no place is, well, greater than Alpine Country Club.

• Oh, yes, just up the road in Greer lies the greatest clincher to this deal. (More on that later.)

"We don't have a head pro," noted Diane Billings, who along with her late husband, James Shelley, bought the tiny tract in 1996. "Shoot, we don't even have tee times. Up here, it's just show up and play."

One thing is certain about Alpine Country Club: There is no golf course turf quite like it in

Fly-fishing is a major attraction at the nearby Greer Lodge.
OPPOSITE: *Alpine CC offers enchanting pine-lined fairways.*

Arizona. "To my knowledge, we've got the only natural fairways in Arizona. That means we don't have an irrigation system," Billings says with a laugh, shaking her head at the gopher holes and elk dung that have brought more than one golf ball to a screeching halt.

"As far as the gophers go, it's like the movie *Caddyshack*. We can't get rid of them. I've thought about putting in an irrigation system, but about 200 elk think they own the course. I don't know how they would like it if we disturbed their beds. So we

leave things as they are naturally."

The 70 or so members, and a smattering of public players, don't seem to mind the somewhat subpar conditions. Billings, who refers to herself as "general flunky and ball picker-upper," views it as part of the ambiance. "We keep it pretty natural around here," she said, noting that Alpine CC stays open from about the middle of April until the middle of October. "I always tell everyone, please ignore our gopher problem and the elk (dung). But that's the beauty of Alpine Country Club."

If beauty truly is in the eye of the beholder, then some will love the quaintness of Alpine CC, which is located in the White Moutains south of Springerville, about five miles west of the New Mexico border.

Certainly, they'll like Tramper, who greets everyone with a wag of the tail at the first tee. "He just showed up one day," reports Billings while establishing the fact that Alpine's front nine was built in 1963 and the back nine added in 1984.

Then there is the first hole, a 267-yard, par 4 that has a green that is essentially surrounded by trees with the exception of about a 10-yard opening in the front. When was the last time you drove a par 4? Play then proceeds through four more par 4s, three par 3s and a 426-yard par 5 on the front nine. The signature hole is No. 8, a 139-yard par 3 that is beautifully backdropped by a small grove of aspens. Even though the tee boxes are pretty much devoid of grass, and the kicks are sort of crazy in the fairway, most people don't hesitate to pay the $10 green fee. Besides, the bentgrass greens are actually pretty good.

Don't expect as much from the back nine, which one member referred to as a "goat track." Still, it does have a great closer in the 480-yard, par-5 18th.

The final fairway provides the setting for "Dick Jr.'s Happy Hour," an old picnic area and barbecue pit. As you exit the green, another sign reminds you to "Have a good day!" Up here, they mean it, and despite a few complaints from some of the club's elders, Billings always keeps her cool.

"Oh, they fuss about everything," she chuckles. "I'll hear 'em out there knocking balls around in the pines like a bunch of woodpeckers, but they love it. And they're right: Of the two nines, the front nine is the good one."

There are other things to like about Alpine CC, especially Las Escondida, where cook extraordinaire Yvonne Palacios serves stacked New Mexican enchi-

ladas, terrific chicken flautas, genuine green burros, and the best homemade chips and salsa around.

"Las Escondida means 'the hidden,' and we really are out here in the middle of nowhere," Palacios explains. "But in a way, that's the best thing about Alpine: We're away from it all."

For those in the know, Alpine CC is only part of the secret to serenity. The other half of the equation lies about 45 minutes north in the small hamlet of Greer, which is only about 10 miles away from the golf course as the crow flies, but becomes much longer by road because of a mountain terrain that separates the solitude of the two sanctuaries.

"In terms of playing and staying conditions,

I guess we're kind of at the opposite end of the spectrum from Alpine Country Club," said Bob Pollock, who teaches fly-fishing at rustic and remote Greer Lodge, another of Arizona's hidden treasures. "For instance, we have guests from all over the world that come and stay with us, simply because you really can get away from it all while enjoying the finest accommodations in an awesome atmosphere.

"On the other hand, I've played golf down at Alpine Country Club quite a few times. And you know what, I enjoy it every time, even if it's not quite as good as the golf up in Pinetop or Show Low."

Like Billings mentioned, it's the beauty of it all. ✿

ANTELOPE HILLS

· ·

NORTH: PAR: 72 · YARDAGE: 6,183–6,778 · RATING: 70.1–76.4 · SLOPE: 122–132 · SIGNATURE HOLE: 515-YARD, PAR-5 № 5 · GREEN FEES: INEXPENSIVE

SOUTH: PAR: 72 · YARDAGE: 5,570–7,014 · RATING: 67.8–72.7 · SLOPE: 114–127 · SIGNATURE HOLE: 200-YARD, PAR-3 № 11 · GREEN FEES: INEXPENSIVE

ANTELOPES DON'T PLAY here any more; they moved north to Chino Valley. All that roams Antelope Hills these days is golfers, who come in herds to play the vintage North Course and the fledgling South.

For those who have not traversed these grounds, Antelope Hills offers two distinct golfing experiences.

The North Course is the only layout in Arizona where nearly every fairway is lined with stately elms, a tree indigenous to the East rather than the Southwest. Built in 1956 by one of Arizona's architectural pioneers, Lawrence Hughes, the North embodies traditional values, especially its gracious greens, which invariably slope from the back to the front, making putts above the hole pure misery. But what would you expect from the same man who created pristine Paradise Valley Country Club the following year?

The South Course, which was added in 1993 by another well-known architect, Gary Panks, has given Antelope Hills a solid one-two punch, since the South is more modern and mound-driven. Trees hardly exist, although the few that dot this gentler landscape give definition, as do several big bodies of water. Of the two courses, the South seems more suited to the beginner's game, although it can be testy when moved all the way back to 7,014 yards.

The South Course gives Antelope Hills a one-two punch.

"We were concerned when we first opened the South that everybody would want to just play the North Course," noted Jim Noe, the general manager of the municipal tracts that attract 99,000 players each year. "But as it turns out, it's been pretty even. I guess there is such a contrast in courses that there's something for everybody."

That might be true for the locals, but not for those who travel in from around the state. The North long has been held in high esteem, hosting such long-running tournaments as the Smoki and the State Father-and-Son, as well as the Players' West Tour for those women who aspire to the LPGA. It would be fair to say that the North is twice as charming and offers more of a challenge. Not that the South is an inferior tract; it's more like the standard set by the big sister was just so high. "Yes, the North Course is so good that most people don't realize it's a muni," Noe admitted. "At the same time, our players are very satisfied with the South. It's a great complement to the North, and every year it becomes a little bit more appreciated."

Perhaps it could be said that Hughes got the better piece of land to work with. Brushed out over a hillside just east of the otherworldly Granite Dells, with panoramic views every which way but east, where the little airport of Love Field lies, the North Course at Antelope Hills is a classic collection of 18 holes. The uphill ones play tough, the downhill ones offer birdies, and putting often is the key, as slick surfaces that run either up or down oftentimes wreak havoc. Oh, yes: Stay out of the trees!

Naturally, the North is not exactly as Hughes left it. Several changes have occurred, the foremost being the course begins on what originally was the eighth hole, an adjustment that came about when a new clubhouse was erected several years ago. According to Noe, accepting what was originally the seventh hole as today's closer was a mental block for some of the regulars, who had been playing the course since the late 1950s. "But I hear less references to that [rerouting] subject these days," Noe

added. "[The old No. 7] is not exactly a pushover at 417 yards to a fairly tricky green. Plus, we might do some tinkering to the 18th, maybe put a lake in and bring it right up to the edge of the green."

Still, it's the feel of the course, not the routing, that makes the North so special. Strolling down those shady fairways can be a treat, like playing golf at an old country club. Enhancing the effect, a new state-of-the-art irrigation system has produced lush, wall-to-wall bluegrass. The soft, seaside bentgrass greens also are killer, sometimes literally.

Once upon a time, the back nine was considered the stellar stretch, but the rerouting has moved up the better holes. Two outstanding runs typify the North to a "T"—Nos. 2–5 and Nos. 9–11. For the most part, Hughes made the par 4s rugged and the par 5s reachable. The par 3s are a nice variety, ranging from 132 to 213 yards, with 160- and 171-yard decisions tossed into the mix. It's pretty hard to beat the signature fifth hole, a short par 5 that swerves its way through an elm forest, although Nos. 3, 4, 9, and 10 come close.

There are other things to like about the Antelope Hills complex, such as the new clubhouse, which sits adjacent to the South Course, about 100 yards west of the North. Functional, fun, and roomy with a sports bar atmosphere, the "go-to" selection is a Vienna hot dog and draft beer.

Of course, many visitors just grab a refreshment and then head for town, where Prescott offers many hearty restaurants and watering holes, including the famed Whiskey Row district, which dates to the turn of the twentieth century. Need good food? Try the Hassayampa Inn or The Rose for classic cuisine, or Murphy's Irish Pub for burgers and seafood. Just want to drink? The Bird Cage is the toast of Whiskey Row, while the Cadillac Saloon plays the best music to drink by.

Just be careful. Too much imbibing on "the Row," and you won't feel like teeing off the next day where the antelope once played. ☼

APACHE STRONGHOLD GOLF COURSE

PAR: 72 • YARDAGE: 5,535–7,519 • RATING: 70.4–74.9 • SLOPE: 123–138 • SIGNATURE HOLE: 675-YARD, PAR 5 NO. 15 • GREEN FEES: MODERATE

EW GOLF COURSES in Arizona have been built for such a noble cause, which is not to say that recreational opportunities and profits didn't factor into the making of Apache Stronghold. But when your people are suffering from unemployment and the social ills that go along with it, as the San Carlos Apaches were in the early 1990s, the only way out seems to be through education, leadership, and vision.

Thus, given the success of its Apache Gold Hotel and Casino, the San Carlos Nation opted to turn those profits into yet another venture that would ultimately provide a more diversified workplace on the reservation. And as sometimes happens when good things go forward, the Apaches got more than they bargained for.

"The course has become an enormous source of pride for the Tribe," said Ed Gowan, the executive director of the Arizona Golf Association, which played a key role in the development of Apache Stronghold, along with maverick architect Tom Doak. "The Apaches asked us to be their advisers . . . and to make sure that no bad decisions were made. I guess our real purpose was to make them aware of all their options."

But the original leap into the golf world was the sole decision of the Apaches, who showed great character by turning their backs on the material benefits that could have been enjoyed from the profits of their casino. With an unemployment rate of almost 70 percent, wisdom played a huge role in pressing forward with the 18 holes. "Our goal from the beginning was to get our people involved in the golf course," said Homer Stevens, a spokesman for the Tribe. "We trusted our people, even though we

realized that it would take a little longer to complete the project because of our lack of experience."

To that end, 80 members were hired in the construction process and, according to Gowan, "ended up doing 99 percent of the work." Over 50 of those workers have been retained to maintain and service the course since it opened in the spring of 1999.

Gowan and the AGA, however, were responsible for finding Doak. "Tom has a free-flowing philosophy that allows for the course to be built randomly, or to be built around what is there, rather [than] tearing it apart," Gowan said. "He just seemed like the right guy for the job given the topography of the land."

Perhaps the greatest feature of the course, which sits at 3,600 feet above sea level, is the setting itself. Surrounded by the Chiricahua, Aravaipa, Superstition, and White mountains, the views are expansive and free of houses. "This is the way the land was in the

ABOVE: *Apache Stronghold is surrounded by mountains on all sides.*
OPPOSITE: *The 16th green (foreground), and 17 in the distance.*

beginning, and it is the way the golf course will stay in the future," Stevens said.

According to legend, Apache Stronghold was a mystical region in which the Apaches could walk invisibly among their enemies. A sculpture of an Apache warrior on horseback overlooks the ninth green, serving as a reminder of the tribe's storied past. As a tribute, Apache artists have painted images on the tee and yardage markers. The pictures of dream catchers, hummingbirds, and dancers have symbolic meanings that are tied to the "holy ground." "Everything that has been done here is to preserve our past and our future," Stevens added. "It is about honor and pride."

Doak certainly did his part in achieving those goals. Known for his "minimalist movement" style of construction, he simply draped the first dwarf, bluegrass fairways in America across these gently rolling hills, with dominant bentgrass blanketing the greens. In every way, the course seems to flow naturally, creating tee boxes and green settings that are free and easy, although don't think for a moment that this course is a pattycake. It isn't especially when played all the way back to a whopping (whipping?) 7,500 yards.

For Doak, the blueprint of this 400-acre project was easy. The Apaches actually gave him carte blanche in selecting his site on the 2,000-square-mile reservation—as long as the golf course started and stopped at the casino. "We simply laid out the golf holes where the contours of the ground were most interesting, but with tees and greens as close

together as possible," Doak said. "Many of the fairways on the front nine are isolated in their own valleys, surrounded by 20- to 50-foot hills covered in sage and mesquite trees. The back nine uses distant mountains as a backdrop for several greens."

The course actually has three distinct stages. The first five holes ease you into the layout, playing up, down, and around the sand hills. What's good about this initial stretch is the variety and character, as Doak brings a little bit of everything—a split fairway, blind tee shot, short par 4, long par 3, big and small greens, and lots of risk/reward—into play. The fourth hole, a par 4 into a saddle green, is a wonderful ride, as is the dogleg par-4 fifth, which is driveable but quite penal. The middle of the course is tougher, as the 10th through 13th holes are long and tight. The closing stretch takes you all over the place, the prime example being the dramatic, dogleg par-5

15th, which drops off a hillside and then rambles for 675 yards.

Some might say that Apache Stronghold is a good golf course but not great, which is half true. It does not have the conditioning or the pomp and circumstance of some of Scottsdale's golf, but still is a player's golf course. And for those who consider themselves hackers, it has the unique atmosphere of the Wild West. In other words, there is something for everyone at Apache Stronghold.

Especially for the Native Americans who call this course home. With golf programs now being implemented into the tribe's schools, and a caddie program in the formative stages at the course, hope and optimism are once again running rampant on the reservation.

Blame it on Apache Stronghold. ✿

CONCHO VALLEY COUNTRY CLUB

Par: 72 • Yardage: 5,878–6,656 • Rating: 67.9–70.0 • Slope: 114–128 • Signature hole: 175-yard, par-3 № 18 • Green fees: inexpensive

Jack Snyder has built 25 golf courses in Arizona, touching nearly every corner of the state. Still, the Phoenix architect was not quite prepared for what he found in Concho Valley, a small community located between Show Low and St. Johns, midway up the eastern edge of the map.

"It was back in the late '60s, and I remember popping up over this hill, and there it was—a beautiful, sweeping plain that spread out forever," Snyder recalled. "It was way out in the middle of nowhere. I remember thinking: 'No one will be able to find this place if we build a golf course out here.'"

As it turned out, Snyder was right about his first impression, but dead wrong about his second. Cozy little Concho Valley Country Club, which Snyder ended up constructing in two, nine-hole phases some 20 years apart, was truly out in the "boonies," but that was exactly why its followers adore it.

Chris Bennett, who has held every job imaginable at Concho Valley Country Club over the past 18 years, said the secret is finally out. "The locals love it, but so does everybody from Phoenix and Tucson," said Bennett, who serves as general manager these days. "I guess the reason Concho Valley has become so popular is that you really can get away from it all, especially in the summer when it's cooler up here."

Dee Hornbake, the perennial women's club champion at Concho Valley since who knows when, has witnessed the club's transition. "There was a time when we had the course all to ourselves, which was wonderful," Hornbake explained. "Now we're so busy in the summer, we have an 800 number and

take credit cards."

Even though the present has almost caught up with Concho Valley, there are a lot of signs of the past, such as the club's tree-covered entrance over a small wooden bridge. Further proof lies just off the ninth fairway, where the ruins of an old cowboy homestead are found. The final piece of evidence comes wafting from the kitchen, where New Mexican enchiladas and tacos have long been the club's standard of excellence. "No one knows for sure, but we believe [the homestead] dates back 100 years," Bennett said. "The members don't even notice it anymore, but most people from the city

still find it curious. They ask a lot of questions about it, but no one knows the answers."

Nor do they care. Not when a small community like this has such a good course to chase that little white ball around on. "Everyone likes Concho Valley because it's user-friendly," Bennett said. "The beginners and the average guy really enjoy it, and there's still enough of a challenge out there for the good players. You take Silver Creek, which is only about 20 miles from here [to the west], and it's beautiful and a very challenging golf course. But the average guy, he's going to shoot a really high score there. Not here."

The fall season comes to Concho Valley Country Club.

Which is not to say that Concho Valley is a pitch 'n' putt. Just the opposite. Snyder, who constructed the first nine in 1970 and came back to complete the 18-hole layout in 1991, molded together a solid, traditional tract. "The course was originally designed to be an 18-hole layout," recalled Snyder, who got the Concho Valley job because he had laid out the first nine holes at Show Low Country Club. "As it turned out, the original nine was what today is the first through fifth holes, and the 15th through 18th (holes).

"I remember we used a lot of cinders from that old volcano mountain nearby [Cinder Mountain]. The cinders helped to elevate the fairways and get them out of the marshland, up a little bit higher so they wouldn't be under water when the snow melted."

Snyder said the first nine was built for about $10,000 a hole, while the second nine jumped to $600,000. The second nine also had a little bit more length to it, "Because some of those macho boys up there thought the first nine was too short. But of the two [nines], I like the first one the best. It's really stood the test of the time as a traditional golf course with some very good-looking holes."

Even though No. 1, a short par 4, requires a lay-up shot off the tee due to a marsh that fronts the green, Nos. 2–5 are wonderful offerings. The second hole, a 380-yard par 4, is gifted with a small stream that lines the right side. The tree-covered tee box and green at the third hole also are special, as is the huge dead tree at the par-3 No. 4, and the big, greenside bunkers and mountain backdrop at No. 5, a long par 4.

Then a player slides into the 1990s version of the course with no real telltale signs. The seventh and eighth holes are very good, but Nos. 10 and 11 suffer slightly because they are played through a wasteland area with no real definition. Coming home, the course is strong from No. 13 on. The last hole, a 175-yard par 3 up the hill to a well-bunkered, rolling green, is the best short hole on the golf course.

Snyder, for one, holds fond memories of Concho Valley, even though he hasn't seen the course for several years. "I still own a lot up there on the ridge overlooking the course," Snyder said. "I remember that on clear day, I could see the San Francisco Peaks all the way up in Flagstaff and the mountain ranges over in New Mexico. That was the thing about Concho Valley: You could always see for miles and miles and miles."

Still can, as Concho Valley is far away from the pollution associated with Phoenix and Tucson. "It amazes me they got enough people to play the course in the beginning," Snyder added. "But now I guess it's pretty popular with the summer visitors and the townspeople. . . . I'm very proud of it."

Yes, not bad for a little golf course "out in the middle of nowhere." ☼

A brilliant sunset ends the day at Concho Valley Country Club.

DESERT HILLS GOLF COURSE

PAR: 72/73 • YARDAGE: 5,694–6,800 • RATING: 68.8–72.4 • SLOPE: 113–122 • SIGNATURE HOLE: 186-YARD, PAR-3 № 17 • GREEN FEES: INEXPENSIVE

HARD AS IT MIGHT SEEM to fathom, Desert Hills Golf Course played a small role in PGA Tour history. That's right, this municipal facility found in the southwestern sands of Arizona, was one of the launching points for the Ben Hogan Tour.

It all came about in February 1990, when the Hogan Tour, which later became the Nike and today is the Buy.Com, played only its second tournament ever at Desert Hills. Even though many Yuma residents still remember their efforts as the "first-ever Hogan Tour event," PGA Tour records indicate the Yuma stop followed a Hogan tournament held the week before in Bakersfield, California. "I'm not sure if we were the first scheduled, or became that after the southern California event was canceled by snow," said Mike Logsdon, the head professional at Desert Hills. "However, most people remember our tournament as the inaugural."

Don King, who was head professional at Desert Hills at the time and the tournament's director, also recalls the Hogan happening as "first-ever." "Actually, the only thing I remember for sure is that I didn't sleep for four months," said King, who served at the course for 19 years. "I also remember it was very exciting for the entire community, who really got behind the event. We had 300-something volunteers, and everyone really embraced it. They backed it as much as they could for a little town like Yuma."

Called the Yuma Open, its first champion was Rick Pearson, who slipped by Sam Randolph by 2 strokes. Pearson was followed to the winner's circle by P. H. Horgan III, Paul Goydos, and Ron Streck. Interestingly, the runners-up during those years also included Randolph, Olin Browne, Steve

Lowery, and Chris DiMarco, who along with Horgan, Goydos, Pearson, and Randolph, all went on to earn their cards on the PGA Tour. "The first purse was $150,000, and Pearson earned $30,000 as our first winner," King said. "But, unfortunately, we couldn't keep up with the financial demands of the Tour, and we had to back off in 1994. But it was fun while it lasted, and even today many people in Yuma miss it."

Who can blame them? Entertainment options are limited in this small desert community, which is best known for its nearby sand dunes and as the location of the Yuma Territorial Prison State Historic Park. Thank goodness they still turn out in droves to play golf at Desert Hills, which in 1994–95 was honored by *Golf Digest* as "The Best Municipal Golf Course in Arizona."

"Everybody liked to come out to the tournament because they could watch some low scoring," said Logsdon, noting that Roger Poland's 10-under 62 shot at the 1991 Hogan event remains the competitive course record. "We'd set the course up easy, and they would shoot lights out, because that's the way the [PGA Tour] wanted it back then, so they could draw spectators. But that's not the way the course usually plays. You can really tuck the pins if you want to, and with the hilly lies, this can be a very tough golf course."

Information about who designed Desert Hills also is sketchy. Everyone agrees that the course was built between 1971 and '72, and opened in 1973. But beyond the construction crew and a few locals, such as the club's original pro, Jimmy Russell, the actual designer remains somewhat of a mystery. City records belonging to the Yuma Parks and Recreation Department report the architect who signed the contract as David W. Kent. But Kent's name and the course itself do not appear in the book *Architects of Golf,* which is the most complete record of golf courses in America. Only a course near Green Valley shows up under the name Desert Hills.

"Well, that's one thing I'm certain about—we're the original Desert Hills in Arizona," noted Logsdon, whose point is made by the fact that Dave Bennett built the Green Valley version in 1978. "Having two Desert Hills in the same state certainly has caused us problems. They'll get our merchandise and we get their bills. But there is no trademark or copyright on the name, so I guess they can use it, too."

Nobody seems to care when they tee it up on these rolling fairways and big greens. Every day the course is packed, which is why Desert Hills does 75,000 rounds a year. Proof of the course's popularity also is backed by the fact that Desert Hills was chosen over the more prestigious Yuma Country Club as "The Best Place to Play Golf in 2000" by the *Yuma Daily Sun,* with Yuma CC getting honorable mention. "Actually, we've got so many regulars here, we're almost like a country club," Logsdon conceded. "They like the condition of the course, the challenge, and the new [clubhouse] facility. Plus, we cater to their whims just like a private club does."

The landscape is fairly sparse, dotted with palm trees, yuccas, three lakes, a creek, and distant views of the Laguna and Picacho mountains. Pilot's Nob, an area landmark, and Yuma's monstrous baby-blue water tower can be seen from almost any hole. Of the two nines, most agree that the front side is the more difficult. That's excluding the last four holes on the back, as the closing stretch features a 594-yard par 5, two par 3s that go 253 and 186 [over water] and an uphill, 392-yard dogleg par 4. "Each side has a lot of character, but the course is tougher than it looks," Logsdon said of the layout that is a combination of desert and traditional golf. "We keep it wet, and there are so many shots up the hill. If you want to hit it 280 [yards], then you better drive it 281."

Afterward, everybody gathers at the Putter Inn, the course's restaurant that features a sports bar atmosphere. Tall tales from the day's round always go better with a Desert Burger (bacon, cheese, and homemade barbecue sauce) and a bread bowl filled with the chef's special chili.

These days, about the only semblance of professional golf is the Players' West Tour for women. Of course, a few dollars still change hands.

"They love their golf in Yuma," said King, who now works in Phoenix in the insurance business. "The biggest game in town takes place each Saturday and Sunday at Desert Hills, where a bunch of scratch amateurs play a skins game. It's great golf, even if it's not quite the level they once played during those Hogan events."

ELEPHANT ROCKS

· ·

PAR: 72 · YARDAGE: 5,309–6,700 · RATING: 67.7–70.8 · SLOPE: 119–128 · SIGNATURE HOLE: 194-YARD, PAR-3 № 18 · GREEN FEES: INEXPENSIVE

IKE MONUMENTS TO TIME, the elephant-shaped boulders made out of huge chunks of lava have stood guard over the entrance to Elephant Rocks, this pristine little golf course on the edge of Williams. Their presence seems to shift conversation into overdrive.

"How did they get here?" "Are they prehistoric?" "Were they made by ancient tribesmen?" "Do you suppose aliens left them?"

As it turns out, the unpretentious pachyderms are the gift of yesteryear, when the railroad into Williams was known as a cross-country connection rather than just a steam engine heading for the Grand Canyon. The elephant-shaped boulders were gathered from around the country in the early 1900s and hauled to Williams by railroad workers, who deposited them one at a time on the shady lane now known as Country Club Drive. "For those who haven't played here, 'The Rocks' really grab your attention," noted John McCahan, the club's head pro. "The locals love 'em, too, but they're used to them so it's not quite as big a deal."

Actually, there is a lot more to like about Elephant Rocks than the entryway. Way more. And if the truth be known, more is on the way after Gary Panks recently added nine new holes to the original nine, which have been around since 1922. "For the past 10 years, we've been making a lot of changes, and all of them have turned out pretty good," McCahan noted. In 1989, "we only had nine holes of golf and sand greens. Today, you'll find 18 holes and the most beautiful greens in Arizona. At least the original nine [greens] are, and the new nine will get that way with a little time."

Time always has been on the side of players at laid-back Elephant Rocks. There is no hurry to play quickly, not with the soft breezes blowing through the pines, and the course looking soft and supple. "It's a whole different world up here," said McCahan, who spent much of his time in the fast lane of Pinnacle Peak Country Club before he decided to kick back at Elephant Rocks.

Originally called Williams Country Club, the name change came in 1990, when those beautiful bentgrass greens were sewn. "Everyone talks about 'The Rocks,' so it was a natural," said McCahan, who reluctantly takes credit for the name switch.

Actually, the entire area once was known as Elephant Rocks Park, thanks to the railroad guys, who lugged in the two-ton boulders. The course was carved on the hillside shortly after, and dang f the railroad gang didn't do an awesome job. "Obviously it goes without saying that Gary Panks is a great golf course architect," McCahan explained. "But you look at what those railroad workers did back then, and I'd have to say they were equal to the task. Most people are shocked

Elephant Rocks is a favorite local pastime.

when they find out who did the original nine."

In a way, the two nines offer a sharp contrast. But by mixing them together, the differences becomes less noticeable, and maturity will reduce it even more. Basically, the new makeup goes like this: The first five holes are original, then the new nine kicks in. The result is the closing stretch—old Nos. 6 through 9—is the same as it's always been, and that's a wonderful thing.

"I think most of our members have struggled with the new nine a little bit, although I also think they're starting to get used to 18 holes," McCahan said. "The new nine is more demanding, with more fairway bunkers and length. Even though it doesn't have as many trees as the original nine, the ones it does have are tougher than hell."

At the moment, the new nine, which includes three par 5s, is not comparable to what came before it. The old nine has some incredibly sweet, serene settings:

• The third hole is a 150-yard, postcard par 3, complete with a small pond bordering the right side and a lake in the background.

• The fourth hole, a 416-yard par 4, streaks straight up the hill through the pines to a green that is slightly tucked to the right. A big fairway bunker guards the entrance, as does a large tree that sits alongside the green.

• The 17th hole, formerly the eighth, is a fabulous par 5 that rolls over hill and dale some 518 yards, with the final 100 yards playing straight up the hill. Along the way, there is a 200-year-old juniper that sports a large, gnarly knot. According to local lore, more than one bottle of bourbon has been stashed inside the treasured tree's small opening. Nothing like a nip coming home!

• The 194-yard 18th, the old No. 9, is almost worth the green fee alone. From amid wildflowers high on the hill, your medium to long iron drops 80 feet to the green below. Every round of golf should end so spectacularly.

"Given a little time, I think the new nine will catch up to what we've already got," McCahan said. "I know [the new nine] has a lot of Gary Panks in it. In fact, it reminds me a little bit of Silver Creek in Show Low and Sedona Golf Resort, two of his best courses."

Unfortunately, the new nine won't be quite as free and easy as the old one, mainly because 250 homes will be built along its fairways in a devel-

opment called Highland Meadows. "Yeah, but we're not changing the name of the golf course to Highland Meadows," McCahan assured. "We really love our golf course's name."

They should. Elephant Rocks is Arizona golf history. That's obvious just by walking into the old clubhouse, which also was built by the railroad guys back in the Roaring Twenties. On its dark walls are some antiquated photographs of the club's forefathers, and a rustic fireplace that is made up of rocks that were hauled in from such Arizona outposts as Bumble Bee, Granite Dells, Cathedral Rock, and the Petrified Forest. "It's a great place to kick back and have an Elephant Beer," said McCahan, who keeps the refrigerator stocked with the namesake brew.

Of course, as good as the Elephant Beer is, nothing will ever overshadow those stone sentries that stand guard at the club's entrance.

"It's funny, but sometimes when the light hits them just right, they do look just exactly like elephants," McCahan added. "There's five or six of them like that. I guess if you use your imagination, you could say it's a small pack."

One that will keep luring you back. ◎

The boulders at Elephant Rocks resemble a miniature Stonehenge nestled among a stand of Ponderosa pine near Williams.

EMERALD CANYON GOLF COURSE

PAR: 72 • YARDAGE: 5,582–6,627 • RATING: 68.1–71.5 • SLOPE: 117–131 • SIGNATURE HOLE: 147-YARD, PAR-3 Nº 5 • GREEN FEES: INEXPENSIVE

THOSE WHO VENTURE WEST to one of the furthest golf outposts in Arizona, are rewarded with Emerald Canyon, a raw and rugged layout that combines traditional, desert, and mountain golf in a most unusual way.

Located in the foothills of the Buckskin Mountains just above the Colorado River, Emerald Canyon can tan your hide. At the same time, few courses in America offer the fun and fantasy of playing golf in an arena that might be best described as the wild, wild West personified. Yes, cowboys would love this place. "Difficult but incredibly beautiful," said Steve Benton, who has been the head professional at the La Paz County–owned facility since 1991. "One thing you can't say, though, is the course lacks character."

No kidding. In fact, one tour of Emerald Canyon and most people scratch their heads in disbelief. How did Tempe architect Bill Phillips, who designed this tight tract in 1989, ever get grass to grow on all of this lava and sandstone? Just as puzzling: How did Phillips ever get in position to build these tee boxes and green settings on the cliffs and canyons that make up Emerald Canyon? "Truly, an amazing feat," Benton concurred. "But it grows more popular every year, which I guess is why we got a four-star rating from *Golf Digest* [in 1999]."

Yes, remote little Emerald Canyon joined 14 other big-time courses as the places that *Golf Digest* readers most like to play when they visit Arizona. "I was surprised when I saw us listed with courses like Grayhawk, Vistoso, Ventana Canyon, Sedona Golf Resort, Legend Trail, Las Sendas, the Ravens

Architect Bill Phillips carved Emerald Canyon out of the rocks.

and a lot of other high-dollar courses," Benton said. "So I did a little research, and figured out that those courses average about $125 to play, whereas our green fee averages about $45."

Does that make Emerald Canyon the best value in the state?

"Boy, you could almost say that," Benton added. "I know that Lake Powell National up in Page also was on that list, and I was surprised that Papago was not. But we're about $15 less than Lake Powell, so maybe we are the best value in the state."

Benton knows only too well why Emerald Canyon's following grows annually. "There's not another course in Arizona that has our landscape," he said. "You play between canyon walls, through the boulders, up on top of cliffs, over canyons and ravines, and all of that time, you get beautiful views of the Colorado [River] and the mountains. "Plus, we've got such a friendly staff, which has been together now for years. People tell me they like to come back, see the same faces, because they really do feel like they're at home."

Not bad for a golf course that looks like it belongs on another planet, or possibly the moon.

"Yeah, we look a little lunar," Benton laughed. "But these days, if you don't get a tee time a week in advance during peak season, you don't play."

Which would be a shame, considering Emerald Canyon has so many one-of-a-kind experiences. The course starts out with three solid holes that really don't prepare players for what they're about to get into. But once you drive through the tunnel to the fourth tee, buckle your seat belt. "Yeah, we like to say, 'That's where the course starts to get interesting,'" Benton said with a devilish grin.

The fourth, a 282-yard straightaway par 4, is driveable. But even an errant tee shot will land in the fairway in what has been labeled "the Land of Ricochet Rabbit." You see, because of the steep canyon walls on both sides of the fairway, missed shots come bounding back into play. Same thing at the 147-yard fifth hole, although this time a shot across the canyon to a green tucked on the side of a cliff needs to be, if anything, long. Yep, the ball will carom off the back wall and rebound onto the green. And so it goes, as the 397-yard sixth hole also has "trainer walls" that keep a golfer upright.

As good as that stretch is, and for that matter

the entire 18 holes are terrific, the next-best run through the rocks occurs at the 15th through 17th holes, although this time you're mostly up on top. Once again, the journey begins with a drive through that notorious tunnel to the 15th tee, where a player is greeted by a 397-yard par 4 with more canyon walls left and right. The 16th, another of those 300-yard, driveable par 4s, also features the ricochet motif. But nothing quite prepares a player for the 17th, a 588-yard par 5 where the approach shot drops an awe-inspiring 150 feet to the green below.

"The course is only 6,600 yards," noted Benton, who annually hosts the well-regarded Parker Open. "But it's much more difficult than that—way tougher. Sure, you'll make some birdies, because four or five of the par 4s you can reach off the tee. But you'll also make some double bogeys and even a triple [bogey] or two. There's just so much trouble you can get into out there."

Not to mention off-course activities, as the new Bluewater Resort and Casino is where most visitors to Emerald Canyon choose to hang out when they don't have their golf spikes on. "You would think you're in [Las] Vegas, they did such a good job with it," Benton said of the 200-room complex which features an indoor water slide for kids. "It's quite the place."

Just not quite as sensational as Emerald Canyon Golf Course. Like Benton said, there is pleasure in the penalties. No wonder the club's official T-shirt, which depicts an exasperated golfer hacking his way through cactus, rocks, rattlers, tarantulas, and Gila monsters, is a "must" souvenir.

"We've sold thousands of them," said Benton of the T-shirt that states: "I survived the Emerald Canyon Golf Course!"

Indeed, there is a lot of truth—and satisfaction—in Emerald Canyon's self-deprecating humor. Of course, there is only one sure way to find out. Like Benton says with a certain amount of glee: "Once they come, they always come back for more." ✿

ENCANTO GOLF COURSE

PAR: 70 · YARDAGE: 5,867–6,386 · RATING: 67.9–73.7 · SLOPE: 112–118 · SIGNATURE HOLE: 219-YARD, PAR-3 № 14 · GREEN FEES: INEXPENSIVE

TIME HAS PASSED it by. All that remains of Encanto Golf Course is a traditional tract that greets and treats golfers the way it always has; the way they once were. Or so it seems.

Back in the 1930s and '40s, Encanto was special. At least it was to the average guy, who thought golf belonged to the rich and famous of the times. Not only did Encanto do away with that notion, but it also paved the way for minorities and women to play the game. In every way, Encanto gave more than it received. Still does.

What is hard to believe is that so many have deserted the municipal's traditional fairways and greens for more modern versions. Consider: Once Encanto did nearly 100,000 rounds per year, and as many as 85,000 just five years ago. Today, according to head pro Jim Farkas, the forgotten, 6,386-yard layout located near the corner of 15th Avenue and Thomas is lucky to do 65,000. "Lot's of competition," Farkas concluded. "But for those who still come out to play with us, they find a heck of a good golf course."

Farkas said no one knows for sure who designed Encanto, although the opening date was 1937. But according to *The Architects of Golf*, it was William P. "Billy" Bell, who also designed the Arizona Biltmore, and Mesa and Tucson country clubs. Bell was a classic designer, and even though Gary Panks did a little touch-up work in 1978, altering Nos. 1, 5, and 9, most of Bell's original routing is intact.

What most have overlooked is the dynamic role that the course played in the Valley's golf history. Remember, Encanto was introduced by the City of Phoenix during a time when country clubs (Phoenix and Arizona) and resort courses (Biltmore, San Marcos, and the Wigwam) ruled. Public golf did not exist. "The property was originally the Norton farm, and the farmhouse still stands by the 18th green," Farkas noted. "[Dr. James Norton] sold it to the city with the stipulation that it must be used for a golf course."

Encanto once was a big-time hit, hosting many exhibitions involving the great players of the day. Farkas said the old-timers still talk about the match held in 1941 between England's Harry "Light Horse" Cooper; Jimmy Thompson, considered to be the John Daly of his day; well-known pro Lawson Little; and Frank Madison, the head pro at Encanto. "I've still go the scorecard," said Farkas, pointing to Thompson's then-record, 6-under 64. "It was one of the biggest exhibitions of its time, and came during the week of the Western Open at Phoenix Country Club."

Perhaps the biggest character ever to call Encanto home was the notorious golf hustler, Titanic Thompson. According to Joe Pennington,

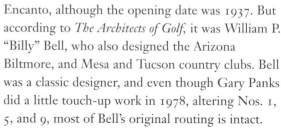

The Phoenix skyline rises above Encanto.

142

good to us over the years, which was great because it's a heck of a good layout."

The back nine is a tad more challenging and consistent than the front, especially from the 13th hole to home. The signature offering is the 219-yard, par-3 14th, which features a monstrous bunker on the left. But if the truth be known, all of the par 3s are excellent at Encanto. Another thing to like is the greens, which come in every size and shape, including numerous turtleback configurations that definitely hold a player accountable.

But mostly, Encanto is a good walk not spoiled, and reasonable at less than $20 to walk. (Riding really is a sin on this flat layout!) And when you drop into Mulligan's Restaurant after a round of golf, a burger ($3.50) and a beer ($2) are cheap by today's standards. Even a bucket of balls only costs $2. "A lot of these guys play here every day, so they know each other, and they know how good this course really is," Farkas added. "I guess some people think its time has passed, but I really don't think that's true."

Just don't compare yourself to PGA Tour player Jonathan Kaye, whose nickname is "the Encanto Kid." Kaye rewrote the course record in 1997 with a 12-under 58, which included eight straight birdies to end his round. "Truthfully, I love Encanto, and I always have, ever since I played it as a kid," Kaye confided. "I guess you could say I'm a 'muni guy.' But say what you want, it's still a great old golf course."

Always has been . . . always will be. ⚙

who has been playing the course since he was a kid in the 1940s, Thompson brought a reputation to Encanto that the city was not fond of. "Golfwise, everything happened at Encanto back in those days, at least for the average guys," said Pennington, who played golf for Arizona State University in the early 1960s. "Titanic, I was told, came to Encanto after being 'urged' to leave Tucson. He took a room over at the old Westminister Apartments near what now is St. Joseph's Hospital, and he was over at the course nearly every day, betting people on everything from playing golf left- and right-handed to how long he could hold his breath under water.

"I remember there was a lot of action in the back room of Encanto back in those days. At nights, a lot of big, black cars would pull up in the parking lot, and the city really frowned on that. But that was Titanic. He would play anybody for anything, and usually had it all fixed his way before he ever went into it."

Pennington said he also remembers watching an incredible exhibition at Encanto involving Julius Boros. He also recalled seeing Jesse Owens and the Mills Brothers play golf, and watching legendary boxer Joe Louis hit balls near the ninth fairway. "Encanto was the only course where minorities could play in those days," he said. "It also had one of the first women's clubs [1944], and that was important, too. But desegregating golf was perhaps its biggest claim to fame."

So it was a natural that in 1946 the Desert Mashies made Encanto their home. The Mashies, a predominantly black organization that emphasizes minority involvement in the game, were the pioneer group to champion equality in golf. Bill Dickey, another longtime Phoenix resident who grew up on Encanto, joined the Mashies in 1958, serving as president on five occasions. "Those were tough times to be a black golfer," Dickey recalled. "There weren't a whole lot of courses back in those days, but there was only one where we could play. I guess you could say that Encanto has been pretty

FRANCISCO GRANDE RESORT AND GOLF CLUB

· ·

PAR: 72 · YARDAGE: 5,507–7,594 · RATING: 69.5–74.9 · SLOPE: 112–126 · SIGNATURE HOLE: 193-YARD, PAR-3 № 3 · GREEN FEES: INEXPENSIVE TO MODERATE

THE LONG HAUL starts at the very first tee at Francisco Grande Resort and Golf Club, and it never lets up. When a course's shortest par 3, 4, and 5 run 181, 424, and 535 yards, respectively, you know you're in for a "long" day. Of course, that is the way Horace Stoneham wanted it when he hired architect Ralph Plummer to build Arizona's lengthiest layout—7,594 yards!—back in 1964.

At the time, Stoneham was the owner of the San Francisco Giants, who held their spring practices each year at Francisco Grande, a namesake resort Stoneham had built in 1961. The unusual request to Plummer, a Texas designer whose work included Colonial Country Club and Preston Trail in the Dallas area, was the result of Stoneham's desire to create recreation for the Giants' "big hitters."

Among those sluggers Stoneham had under contract at the time were Hall of Famers Willie Mays, Willie McCovey, Orlando Cepeda, and Juan Marichal, one of the best-hitting pitchers ever to play baseball. Their photos still grace the walls of the Fanny Granny Lounge, along with many of their teammates. Also in that storied past were actors John Wayne, Dale Robertson, and Gale Gordon, along with singer Pat Boone. That Hollywood four-some, whose photos also appear on the wall of fame at Franny Granny's, showed up often when the Giants were training at Francisco Grande.

"The place has a lot of memories, and no doubt that's part of the charm," said Tim Alai, the head professional at Francisco Grande. "Plus, it's very quiet, with no homes or traffic around us. It makes for a very peaceful and relaxing stay."

According to Alai, winter visitors migrate on an annual basis from Iowa, Minnesota, the Pacific Northwest, and Canada. The course also is quite popular with the locals, who live five miles west of the resort in Casa Grande.

Not surprisingly, most people don't play Francisco Grande all the way back. The majority prefer the white tees at 6,451 yards, while the ladies get a break at 5,507. Of the two nines, the front side is tighter and probably the more difficult unless length is a factor. "You've got out of bounds on the front, and it's all on the right, which means it gets a little scary for the slicers," Alai said. "There also are two lakes [Nos. 3 and 5], some elevation, such as a blind tee shot at the fourth hole, and the doglegs are more subtle, which brings the trees into play."

But, as Alai pointed out, you better be dialing long distance on the back. "That nine is more straightforward . . . than the front," he said. "But by the time you get to those last four holes, whew. . . ." That would be the 477-yard 15th, 181-yard 16th, 472-yard 17th, and 473-yard 18th. And, yes, those 470-yard-somethings are all par 4s. In fact, when you add up the yardage of the last four holes—1,603 yards—it's almost a mile. And no par 5?

Other holes of note include the 636-yard No. 2, which thank goodness does not play uphill, and No. 3, a 193-yard par 3 that is considered the signature hole because it plays downhill to a green backed by water. "You wouldn't necessarily think that the water comes into play a lot on the third hole," Alai noted. "But because the tee is elevated, and it plays a club or two less going down the hill, people manage to find the water more than you might think."

Yes, this place is full of sudden surprises. Just getting here is a bit of a shock, as you drive through flat desert terrain until arriving at the eight-story-high resort, which simply juts up in the middle of nowhere. "People like the isolation, although Casa Grande is right down the road, and we're only 45 minutes from Phoenix and about an hour from Tucson," Alai said.

Francisco Grande is reminiscent of The Wigwam Resort in Goodyear, which also sits on the edge of the desert. "Franny Granny" is dotted with mature pines, palms, and eucalyptuses, and both it and The Wigwam are throwbacks. The chief difference is that Francisco Grande is not nearly as upscale since Stoneham packed up the Giants and moved their spring training facilities to Scottsdale in the mid-1970s.

Alai called Francisco Grande "the total package," because everything you really need is right here. "We're not Troon North or Ventana Canyon, but we have a lot to offer," he said. "The golf course is traditional and solid, the resort is nice at about half the price you would pay in Phoenix or Tucson, and we've got a very good restaurant and a fun lounge."

Alai knows his 101-room resort. For instance, the penthouse suite, and there are two of the 1,200-square-foot "apartments" on the top floor, go for just $250 a night. Golf is usually less than $50, and the restaurant serves up the best filet mignon in the Casa Grande area.

Even though the Giants are long gone, as well as the California Angels (1979–82) and the now-defunct USFL Arizona Wranglers (1984), who also used the facility at one time, Francisco Grande lives on. The old stadium, which once bustled just to the south of the resort, is a mere shell, as only the steps and coaching tower remain. Thank goodness for those old photographs, which feature the fading faces of "the Boys of Spring."

Yes, once upon a time, they all teed it up at Francisco Grande, a true "hitter's ballpark." ☼

Francisco Grande is a "hitter's ballpark" at 7,594 yards.

GOLF CLUB AT JOHNSON RANCH

PAR: 72 • YARDAGE: 5,367–7,141 • RATING: 68.3–74.6 • SLOPE: 119–137 • SIGNATURE HOLE: 372-YARD, PAR-4 № 15 • GREEN FEES: MODERATE

THERE ARE THOSE who claim that the Golf Club at Johnson Ranch lies on some mighty lonesome terrain. And once upon a time, they were right.

But these days, despite being located in the middle of nowhere, the word is spreading about what the locals refer to as "JR," a fairly upscale golf facility and housing development found on the outskirts of the tiny farming community of Queen Creek. "Actually, the biggest challenge still is finding us," conceded Chuck Curtis, the director of golf at Johnson Ranch, a 2,200-acre project that includes an 18-hole championship golf course, an 18-hole executive course, a little nine-holer, and, eventually, 3,000 to 6,000 homes. "Getting people out here is no easy task. Proof of that lies in the fact that everybody who calls for a tee time wants directions."

The 30-minute-to-an-hour trip, depending on which part of the metropolitan Phoenix area you depart from, seems to get more remote as you go. The landscape looks particularly barren once you exit Queen Creek due south. But with the beginning of the Santan Mountains, relief in the form of great golf is soon on the horizon. "The Golf Club at Johnson Ranch is challenging, loaded with character, and the price is right," Curtis noted of the moderately priced layout. "Everybody that plays here seems to enjoy it, because most of 'em come back."

Johnson Ranch is the legacy of George Johnson, a Phoenix developer whose accomplishments include El Conquistador in Tucson. Johnson Ranch was built in 1997 by Kenny Watkins, who made it his first—and to date, only—work of desert art. "I'm a good learner," said Watkins, who worked with such architects as Greg Nash, Keith Foster, Arthur Hills, and Bob Cupp on the construction end of the golf business before attempting to design his own. "They all taught me something, but I just try to keep it simple. To me, it's all about playability."

Watkins said it was that same basic philosophy that spurred Johnson's decision to erect "the Ranch" in such an isolated locale. "I think the reason George picked this spot to build Johnson Ranch was he wanted to bring affordable housing and affordable golf to the public," Watkins explained. "For what you get in a house or a round of golf, it's a good deal."

But despite all the goodness, Johnson sold out to Sunbelt Holdings a little over a year later. Sunbelt stepped in in a big way, hiring its partner, In Celebration of Golf, to run the operation. "Sunbelt is so committed to the project, and the course is so good, that I think in time we can match some of

Johnson Ranch is located near the small town of Queen Creek.

almost like two different kinds of golf courses, and people like that. Believe it or not, they like being out in the middle of nowhere because it's relaxing. Plus, what's cool is, it really is a ranch."

Mosey on down the road a bit, and you'll find an equestrian center where people board their horses and occasionally jump them through hoops in a small arena. And right across the road are "horse properties," where the equines actually live with their owners on one-acre lots. Stick around long enough, and more than one horse and rider will come galloping down the dusty trail.

In Celebration of Golf has picked up on the theme. Inside the clubhouse at Johnson Ranch there is a family room of sorts, complete with cutouts of John Wayne and Hopalong Cassidy. An old, western-style billboard posts news that reflects the week's play in review. Even though the chili is not served from a chuck wagon, it's hearty and the favorite of the regulars. Of course, the "Gimme," a jumbo Vienna hot dog, also rates high when loaded with fixin's.

Not surprisingly, the parking lot fills up early in the morning at Johnson Ranch, despite the rather remote location. "Most of our play right now, I'd classify as resort guests, although there are so many [recreational vehicle] parks in the area, that we get winter visitors, too," Curtis noted. "And if you looked at this area closely, you'd realize there are a lot of small courses from here to the [Superstition] freeway. But we're not one of those golf courses. In fact, I wouldn't be surprised if someday this course goes private, because it's that good. Really, it's just a matter of time."

Someday, no doubt, the brand "JR" will be known far and wide. ☼

those courses in north Scottsdale," said Curtis in a rather bold prediction. "If we can get them out here, more will come because the course is so striking."

Johnson Ranch starts slowly, in that the front nine won't blow you away unless the winds are howling that day on this treeless plain. At the same time, there is not a bad hole on the course, as Watkins did a good job of making the flat-as-a-pancake front nine strategically interesting, and if nothing else, solid. The variety also is very good from the get-go, as the first hole, a 606-yard par 5, has some eye-catching water features. The fifth, a demanding, 460-yard par 4 into the Santans, also is superb. "The front nine? I used everything I could to form backdrops for those holes," Watkins said. "I must have moved the fairways three or four times before I was done. But, thank goodness, I got some

help from Mother Nature on the back."

Absolutely, as the 10th through 16th holes are either into or off of the sandhills that are the start of the Santans. Signature hole? Take your pick from Nos. 12, 13, 15, or 16. All are good, but the 372-yard, par-4 15th, an uphill shot into a well-guarded green tucked tenderly against the base of a small mountain, certainly is the most photogenic. In reality, the picturesque par-3 17th and the water-guarded, par-5 18th also are quite worthy. No wonder the back nine at Johnson Ranch is reminiscent of the final nine holes at Las Sendas, an upscale Mesa course that is much more visible and expensive.

"I think the front nine plays real long and challenging," Curtis said of the dramatic difference between the two sides. "The back nine is more scenic and requires more course management. It's

KINO SPRINGS COUNTRY CLUB

PAR: 72 · YARDAGE: 5,368–6,445 · RATING: 67.7–70.1 · SLOPE: 110–126 · SIGNATURE HOLE: 345-YARD, PAR-4 № 13 · GREEN FEES: INEXPENSIVE

TO UNDERSTAND KINO SPRINGS Country Club, one must enter another world and era. That would be the 1950s and the glittering past of the late Stewart Granger, the English-born actor/playboy who starred in such Hollywood films as *King Solomon's Mines*, *The Prisoner of Zenda*, *Beau Brummel*, and *Bhowani Junction*.

As hard as it seems to imagine, the swashbuck-ling Granger, who was a leading man for such star-lets as Elizabeth Taylor and Ava Gardner, and was later married to the Oscar-winning Jean Simmons, loved cowboys and the West despite his European roots. So he built a rustic retreat called Yerba Buena Ranch along the Santa Cruz River Valley. It was there Granger raised a rare type of cattle called Charolais. At least, most people think the all-white cows were what the actor tended to best, despite the translation of Yerba Buena, which means "good herb" or "good weed."

Granger's unique ties to Arizona also included a tight friendship with actor John Wayne, who pur-chased a spread next door to Granger's. Since Wayne never developed his ranch, he often stayed

The par-3 No. 7 is backed by the Mule Mountains of Mexico.

in the "John Wayne Cabin" at Granger's place, which is part of the lore of the Yerba Buena. As tales go, the two stars often held frolicking poolside parties with young starlets such as Taylor and Gardner at Granger's ranch, thus Wayne needed a place to crash.

In the early 1970s, Granger said goodbye to southern Arizona, and the ranch was sold to developers. In 1974, renowned architect Red Lawrence was hired to build Santa Cruz Country Club, with Granger's ranch house being preserved as the clubhouse.

Actor Stewart Granger on a movie set in Hawaii.

Somewhere along the line, the course was renamed Kino Springs Country Club, and Granger's somewhat infamous bedroom became the pro shop. Also undergoing a remodeling was the actor's dining room, which was converted to a bar and grill that now serves up longneck beers, as well as red-hot salsa and chips. Still intact is Granger's cowboy-theme library, complete with a hidden bar, as well his rustic family room, much as the actor left them. Old photographs featuring Granger and his fellow movie stars still hang from the knotty-pine walls.

Too bad Granger never had a chance to play Kino Springs Country Club. Judging from his fun-loving past and appreciation for the countryside, he would have relished these idyllic fairways that streak through rolling hills below three nearby mountain ranges—the Tumacacoris, Santa Ritas, and San Joses. The Santa Cruz River, which springs up just to the west of the golf course, adds to the sleepy atmosphere.

"Kino Springs is one of Arizona's best-kept secrets," noted Ron Heraty, who spent time as the director of golf here before moving up the road to Rio Rico. "At 4,000 feet [above sea level], the weather is just incredible; never too hot or cold. The setting is breathtaking, and the course is always tranquil. I'm not sure why, but we don't get much golf traffic down here. Even in peak season, we probably do just 60 to 80 tee times a day. I guess it adds to that peaceful feeling."

One can only hope that Kino Springs remains as pure and pristine. In every way, it is one of the state's most serene places to play golf, with the wind whispering through the trees as the birds chirp happily away. Occasionally, an afternoon storm blows through the valley just to shake things up. Life is good.

Kino Springs starts out like it plays, relatively easygoing. But by the time a player reaches the fifth hole, the "A" game must be in place or it's going to be a very long round of golf. "The first four holes are just a warm-up, mostly because they are wide open," Heraty explained. "But from the fifth hole on, it really takes off, as the next nine holes play down, around, and through a canyon."

Demanding but very cool, that pretty much sums up the midsection of Kino Springs. It is a wonderful roller coaster, as numerous tee boxes and greens are steeply elevated, helping a player to map out the free-flowing fairways below.

Several holes stand out, such as the 150-yard seventh, an exacting short shot down into a small valley to a green framed by mesquites and pines and backed by mountains; the demanding, 413-yard 11th, where the fairway buckles twice before arriving

at the green; and the gorgeous, 345-yard 13th, without question the course's signature hole and the epitome of the entire hill-and-dale stretch.

The par-4 12th hole is all or nothing.

At the same time, a player must deal with the sixth hole, where overhanging trees off the tee make any drive difficult, to say the least. No wonder that par 5 wears the No. 1 handicap tag despite stretching just 501 yards. And speaking of tough tee shots, Lawrence just dares you to find the extremely tight neck at No. 12, where laying up seems the only option other than driving the ball 295 yards to the green below. (Hey, you didn't come to lay up, right?)

But then the course smoothes out, and from the 14th on it's clear sailing, much like the first four offerings. Still, don't let up or the 435-yard 18th, a 90-degree dogleg right, will get away.

"Mostly, it's a fun golf course that seems to roam on and on forever," Heraty noted. "It's easy to get a false sense of security at the start, but you've got to be able to play a little if you're going to score."

There is more than a little irony in Heraty's statement, as judging from the old black-and-white photos, Granger also knew how to play a little. ⚙

LAKE POWELL NATIONAL GOLF COURSE

· ·

PAR: 72 · YARDAGE: 5,097–7,064 · RATING: 68.0–72.2 · SLOPE: 122–132 · SIGNATURE HOLE: 212-YARD, PAR-3 № 13 · GREEN FEES: INEXPENSIVE TO MODERATE

STANDING OVER A PUTT on the 13th green at Lake Powell National Golf Course requires a lot of self-discipline. There is a tendency to lose your grip and gaze out aimlessly at the brilliant surroundings. The landscape is a rainbow of blue, green, red, silver, amber, and black. The colors mix like paint on an artist's palette.

In every way, this is "Surreal City." Either that, or golf on Mars. "The scenery is unbelievable,"

conceded Kenny Slavens, who gave up a career as a stockbroker to become head pro at Lake Powell National. "If you haven't seen this golf course before, it will blow you away."

Several factors add to the voltage. For instance, there is the two-hour journey north from Flagstaff on Highway 89. It is an eye-popping trek through the Navajo Nation, where redrock mesas and sweeping cuts of sandstone provide most of the distractions. The terrain intensifies in terms of beauty as

you arrive at Page, the home of Glen Canyon Dam and Lake Powell, the second-largest man-made lake in the United States.

Oddly, Lake Powell National sticks out like a sore thumb in this bizarre, northernmost outpost of Arizona. It takes a few moments to sink in, but finally it clicks as to why these remote links are so special. Yep, this is the first green grass you've run across in the last 100 miles. No (expletive)! "It's kind of amusing, because the golf course is located in the desert, yet it's not a desert golf course," Slavens noted. "We've got the only green grass around, which makes us really jump out at you."

To fully understand Lake Powell National, a small history lesson is required. The canyon-rich landscape remained undisturbed until the mid-1950s, when a large contingent of geologists, engineers, and construction workers began building the federally sponsored dam, which capped the Colorado River and created Lake Powell, a 186-mile-long waterway made up of 96 major canyons and 1,960 miles of shoreline. The original idea was to provide water storage for the thirsty Southwest, but in the past few decades the area has become a recreational haven for boaters and fisherman.

"It's true, most people that visit us don't realize we've got a great golf course up here, too," Slavens said. "At the same time, we have so many visitors, that the word is getting out. In fact, some people come back every year to play this golf course. They tell us it's their favorite layout in the world."

Certainly one of the most unique. Most observers are dazed and confused by their initial view. How in the world did Tempe architect William Phillips ever get grass to grow on these barren rocks when he laid out Lake Powell National in the early 1990s? "I was told it wasn't easy," Slavens

ABOVE: *You can see forever from the 13th green.*

OPPOSITE: *The par-3 15th hole drops 175 feet.*

reported with a smile. "I heard they had to use a lot of dynamite, and it took several years for the grass to grow in."

Today, the course is lush, thanks to the constant nurturing of Superintendent Dennis Dulaney and the watchful eye of John Jacobs Golf, which manages the course owned by the city. In every way, Lake Powell National defies the conditioning normally associated with a municipal layout, which is one of the reasons that *Golf Digest* gave it a four-star rating in 1997 and '99. "We hear that a lot, that the course is immaculate," Slavens reported. "It's also a very fair test of golf."

Lake Powell National opens innocently enough, with an adventure through the lower elevations of the golf course. A player can even get a break at No. 1, a 529-yard par 5 that runs along a huge redrock outcropping called "Mesa of the Dead" by the Navajos. The break comes because yanked shots, or

those with too much draw, can actually ricochet back onto the fairway. The highlight of the front side is the par 3s, which go 202 yards at No. 2 and 234 yards at No. 6. Both are demanding yet dazzling.

Hopefully, a player is in the groove by the time the back nine rolls around. Once again, a soft start greets you at No. 10, then it's up the ridge, where the golf is great and the views greater. The 11th through 13th holes are an inspiring stretch, the final offering a 212-yard par 3 to a green that appears suspended in air. In the distance lies Wahweap Lodge and Marina, which oftentimes resembles the Newport Yacht Club during the summer. The 14th is another creative offering, although if you go back to the championship tee, 504 yards seems extreme for a par 4. The 15th also is memorable, as a sign warns golfers: "Caution! Cliff Edge!" Beautiful, as the 198-yard par 3 drops 175 feet past a craggy edge to the green below. It's a three-club difference, and ball marks oftentimes go so deep that it takes a pitchfork to repair them.

The closing stretch also is dynamic, as the 16th drops down to a green appropriately framed

by the Mesa of the Dead (there is no recovery this time due to a deep wash); the par-5 17th rambles for 665 yards, down a hill and over a creek—twice; and the 18th climbs its way to a tenacious, triple-tiered green. Without question, it is an exhausting stretch of golf.

Naturally, recovery is tied to food and drink, as well as conversation about the creativity and the rainbow of colors that surround the golf course. Most players enjoy a beverage inside the National's comfortable, Southwestern-style clubhouse. Later on they'll head for downtown, where the Dam Bar & Grill will help soothe the soul. There is some truth to the slogan that hangs in this popular watering hole: "Best food and drink by a dam site!"

"We have a lot of fun up here," Slavens said of the small town of 8,500 that attracts over 4 million visitors each year. "Most people come for the water sports, but eventually they discover the golf is pretty good, too."

Oftentimes that realization comes with a shock as supercharged as those generated at the nearby Glen Canyon Dam. ☼

LONGBOW GOLF CLUB

. . . .

PAR: 71 · YARDAGE: 5,554–6,778 · RATING: 65.7–71.8 · SLOPE: 113–128 · SIGNATURE HOLE: 541-YARD, PAR-5 Nº 16 · GREEN FEES: MODERATE

THEY COME BUZZING in like bees, darting and stopping, then racing off again to join the swarm. Guaranteed, at least once during your round at Longbow Golf Club, they will grab your attention. No matter how hard you are concentrating, your eyes will dart toward the dark objects in the sky.

It's not like *Apocolypse Now*. But the AH-64 D Longbow Apache helicopters always make their presence known on the layout designed by Tucson architect Ken Kavanaugh. That's because Boeing, which makes these $100-million aircraft, is located just across the street from the golf course on the corner of McDowell and Higley Roads.

Kavanaugh, who also has designed such spectacular layouts as Gold Canyon Golf Resort near Apache Junction and the Oregon Golf Club near Portland, said the giant helicopters never bothered him one bit when he built the course in 1997. And, despite a modest budget ($6.7 million), he likes the way Longbow turned out.

"Actually, I like all of my golf courses for different reasons, and what I like best about Longbow is that it's the most walkable desert layout I've ever done," he said. "It's golf the way it's meant to be played, which often is not the case in the desert. Plus, and this was a huge consideration, it's playable. You're not going to get beat up. For example, the Oregon Golf Club, which I did with [PGA Tour star] Peter Jacobsen is one of my least favorites. I think it's just too hard."

Obviously, Kavanaugh is a straight shooter, just like Longbow, which by the way, demands a lot of accuracy. Even though the course is named after the Longbow helicopter, those who play golf with the skills of Robin Hood, the rapscallion known for his longbow, will do well here.

Longbow was constructed on gently rolling desert dissected by arroyos, and even though it's not as exciting as some of Scottsdale's chic courses, it's interesting. There are some good views of the nearby Superstition Mountains, as well as an up-close-and-personal with Red Mountain. Even better, the native vegetation and wild flowers, along with a good deal of water, make Longbow mighty attractive. "Remember, this is Mesa, not Carefree," Kavanaugh cautions those with higher expectations. "But for the land we were dealt, I think we gave them a pretty darn good golf course."

According to Cal Berreckman, the director of golf at Longbow, those who play here rarely complain. In fact, most feel they get a lot for a moderate green fee. "As it's matured, it's really come on," Berreckman said. "The course does what all great golf courses must do: It builds to a climax. Everyone loves the closing stretch of holes, especially the 16th through 18th."

Don't be perturbed if the first few holes at Longbow don't grab you, because the course does get off to a somewhat slow start. It's also quite tight from Nos. 3 through 8, and if it's the first time you have been through that stretch, the numbers might be a tad high. Especially if you've played the tips, as the fifth hole is a brutish, 489-yard par 4. "I'm not going to apologize for that one, because seriously, I think the U.S. Golf Association is lagging behind when you consider the technology that is being employed in today's game," Kavanaugh said, a reference to USGA's preference that any hole over 480 yards should be a par 5.

But a return visit to Longbow will help straighten you out considerably, especially on the back side, which boasts a multitude of looks. While Berreckman mentions the 16th through 18th as the best stretch, many feel that the par-3 15th should be included in that mix. That hole, which rivals any of the par 3s at Troon North or Grayhawk, is a testy 190-yard shot directly into Battleship Rock, the most notable landmark in the Superstitions. The 16th, a 541-yard, uphill par 5 also is quite memorable, as the greenside bunker sweeps down to the water, literally creating a beach complete with white sand.

"Most people don't pick up on it, but, yeah, we used three different types and colors of sand on the course," said Kavanaugh, who came up with the unusual concept in order to tie the different shades of sand into the various colors of the landscape. "One of those sands was white, which does look a lot like a beach."

We can hope all those Longbow helicopters that sweep the course each day won't get confused and strafe the beach, assuming that it's a target area. Nah, that would never happen because Boeing just builds them and refers all the battlefield testing to the military, which locates its gunnery ranges much farther out in the desert.

Besides, the nearly 5,000 employees who work across the street enjoy the course so much they would never allow such a mistake. It's their safe haven during lunch, as many prefer hitting balls on Longbow's range to eating a sandwich. Boeing employees even get a discounted green fee, which means that most prefer birdies to "whirly birdies."

At Longbow, there's a good chance you'll get both. ✿

Ken Kavanaugh created sweeping bunkers at Longbow.

OAKCREEK COUNTRY CLUB

PAR: 71 · YARDAGE: 5,916–6,854 · RATING: 67.8–71.0 · SLOPE: 117–128 · SIGNATURE HOLE: 185-YARD, PAR-3 № 4 · GREEN FEES: MODERATE

THE DEBATE LINGERS about who actually created Oakcreek Country Club. Was it the legendary Robert Trent Jones Sr., or was it his talented son, Junior?

"What I've been told is, the back nine was the original nine, and it was done by Robert Trent Jones Sr. in 1967," said Gary Pearce, who has been the head pro at OCC since 1992. "Robert Trent Jones

Jr. is credited with the front nine, which opened in '71.

"There's also a rumor that surfaces from time to time that Junior did the whole golf course. In the book that Robert Trent Jones Jr. wrote about golf course architecture, he lists six courses that were collaborations between him and his father. Oakcreek is one of those six listed."

Turns out there is a little truth to all of the above. Or at least it's possible that all three theories

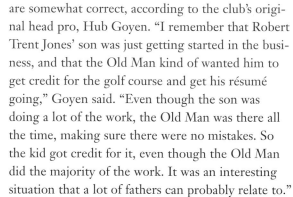

are somewhat correct, according to the club's original head pro, Hub Goyen. "I remember that Robert Trent Jones' son was just getting started in the business, and that the Old Man kind of wanted him to get credit for the golf course and get his résumé going," Goyen said. "Even though the son was doing a lot of the work, the Old Man was there all the time, making sure there were no mistakes. So the kid got credit for it, even though the Old Man did the majority of the work. It was an interesting situation that a lot of fathers can probably relate to."

One thing, however, is crystal clear: Oakcreek Country Club's traditional fairways and greens have stood the test of time, like the vast majority of the approximately 700 courses done by father (550) and son (150). All of their Arizona gems glisten, like the Gold Course at the Wigwam and Rio Rico, done by the father, and the son's Raven at Sabino Springs and Las Sendas.

If Oakcreek was shared genes, the experiment turned out grand. Now, a little respect seems to be in order. "I tell you, people don't know how good that golf course really is," said Goyen, who served as head pro until the mid-'70s. "I know that I always missed it after I was gone."

But Goyen, who served similar stints at Elden Hills, Pinnacle Peak Country Club, and Western Skies, said he left a little of himself behind. "I remember I traded a fellow who owned a nursery there some golf for 1,300 Mondale pines, and I personally planted those seedlings all over the golf course," said Goyen, who can be found at Apache Creek these days. "They're now 30 to 40 feet high, and I smile

Sedona's redrocks frame the signature fourth hole.

every time I see them. I'm sure the members curse me for it, but back then, the course was wide open, and I did it to get some definition into the holes."

For those who have never played Oakcreek Country Club, it is a special place, with peaceful, tree-lined fairways; fantastic bunkering on every fairway and green; elevated putting surfaces that roll with subtleties; and tee boxes that stretch out as much as 100 yards. Several bodies of water add to the ambiance.

"It's a great course that's only going to get better," said Pearce, noting that a renovation project is under way through RTJ Jr.'s office in Palo Alto, California. "It's just a gradual facelift that will restore some bunkers, take out a few trees, and install concrete cart paths unobtrusively. "No holes will be redesigned because that would be a travesty. But we will possibly add some water, like extending it from the 13th to the 16th by way of a babbling brook."

As it sits now, Oakcreek has a fantastic front nine, with Nos. 4–7 being the heart of the golf course. Especially spectacular is the 185-yard fourth hole, a par 3 backed by the red rocks and framed by greenside bunkers. The green is big and sweeping, and as always, stacked. The par-4 ninth hole, a daring 450-yard dogleg left to a green accented by water, also is exquisite. The back nine is a little bit calmer, with the 12th, 14th, and 18th holes stand-ing out.

As good-looking as it is, don't be deceived. Oakcreek CC is plenty difficult, and demands course management and well-struck shots at every turn. No wonder it was an early site of the Arizona Open, and has hosted the majority of the state's major championships.

Pearce agrees with Goyen in that most folks don't realize that Oakcreek is a hidden gem. Part of that, he said, is because the course is hidden behind Highway 179 in a quiet neighborhood made up mostly of the club's 335 members. "Most people can't figure out how to get to the course," Pearce conceded. "They see one of our holes [No. 14]

off the highway next to the Wild Tucan, but the roads getting back to [the clubhouse] are kind of complicated."

The other reason Oakcreek gets overlooked is surreal Sedona Golf Resort. The two courses, which lie less than a mile from each other in the Village of Oakcreek (both claim Sedona as their hometown), give the area a strong one-two punch. But which is 1 and which is 2? "Our profile is low compared to the Golf Resort," Pearce admitted. "But we're not out there spending money to get attention like they are. We're probably not as picturesque or dramatic, but from a playability standpoint, I think ours is the better golf course."

At the same time, it's not like Oakcreek is looking for players. "We do 50,000 rounds a year, and

we're pretty much maxed out in the winter, although we have some availability in the summer," Pearce said. "What's nice is that our members share the golf course with the public, and our rates are very reasonable."

So are the memberships, which are nonrefundable and cost $5,000 for those who belong to the homeowners association, and $10,000 for those who don't. Annual dues are less than $2,000 a year.

"Our members are really active, playing three and four times a week," Pearce said. "They know what they've got, and they appreciate it like there is no tomorrow."

Thanks to Robert Trent Jones Jr. and his dynamic dad—a classic combination no matter how you slice it. ✿

PINETOP LAKES GOLF AND COUNTRY CLUB

PAR: 63 · YARDAGE: 3,999–4,645 · RATING: 59.3–62.7 · SLOPE: 91–98 · SIGNATURE HOLE: 202-YARD, PAR-3 № 11 · GREEN FEES: INEXPENSIVE

WHEN MOST PEOPLE THINK of executive golf courses, they think small. But Pinetop Lakes is no petite pitch 'n' putt, even though the course plays to a par of just 63.

Built in the early 1970s by Arizona architect Milt Coggins, who also designed the more well-known country clubs of White Mountain and Pinetop, there is a lot to like about Pinetop Lakes, which—unlike its big sisters—is open to the public. In every way, the little "Lakes" has a big course feel, and its conditioning is always picture-perfect.

"There are several things we hear over and over as to why people enjoy our golf course so much," said Lloyd Harvey, the club's director of golf since 1992. "Probably the number-one reason is the spectacular scenery. It seems like it's always beautiful and serene up here at Pinetop Lakes. "I suppose the big

hitters probably won't be that impressed, but the average guy loves our golf course. It's not too tough, and you can get around the 18 holes in two and a half to three hours. The green fee also is another factor, as we max out in peak season at $43, which includes a cart. That's pretty hard to beat around these parts."

Pinetop Lakes is well done. There are two par 5s that go 480 to 512 yards, five par 4s that average 350 yards, and 11 par 3s that range from 134 to 191 yards. At least six holes could be worthy of signature status. "It's just a real fun golf course to play," Harvey said of the tract that winds its way through the pine-lined fairways. "The par 3s are all challenging, and the par 5s are great risk-reward situations because you can reach both of them in two [shots]. The course is always in great shape, and our bentgrass greens are as good as any you'll find around here."

Pinetop Lakes opens with a tight par 4 that doglegs right, then immediately serves up one of its better offerings—the 138-yard, par-3 No. 2, which requires a short iron over water. The sixth hole, a short par 4 that doglegs right through pine goalposts, also is a good-looking hole. Another par 3 over water greets you at No. 8 before the first par 5 shows up at No. 9, a picturesque, dogleg right to an elevated green.

The best stretch on the course comes on the back nine, as Nos. 10, 11, 12, and 13 offer some wonderful variety. Of that group, the 11th, a 202-yard par 3 to a water-guarded green, and the 13th, a 351-yard par 4 that also doglegs its way through two huge pine trees, are probably the best of the bunch. An eagle finish at No. 18 is realistic if you cut across the corner on this short par 5.

Pinetop Lakes is a great retreat for the family, as golf is not the only game on the premises. The club also sports some top-notch tennis facilities and a saddle club that offers horseback riders an equally rejuvenating jaunt through the tall trees. In every way, Pinetop Lakes is a recreational haven. "People always enjoy themselves when they come up here, and that makes us all very happy," said Harvey, noting that the club's 225 members are more than willing to share their course with the public.

One of those members, Tammy Wilson, who also doubles as the club's merchandise manager, is reflective of that attitude. "We're real proud of the course, because it's always immaculate," Wilson explained. "The way we look at it, we're just far enough away from Phoenix and Tucson that we have that little extra bit of freedom that really adds to the ambiance."

Many of the visitors that frequent Pinetop Lakes stay at the course-side condominiums. Others stay in cozy cottages nearby, such as The Place in Pinetop, or even farther down the road in the seclusion of Greer Lodge. Dining-wise, Charlie Clark's is number one, although the burgers and beer served up on-site at the Eagle's Nest are very satisfying after a round at Pinetop Lakes.

"I think refreshing is a word that really sums up our golf course," Harvey added. "We've got the cool pines and the cool breezes, and it's not going to take you all day to make your way around our golf course. People really like that. I'm sure there is a perception that we're an 'executive golf course,' but I always tell people not to be swayed by that. I know most executive golf courses are limited by size, which means a few bad holes. But I can honestly say that we don't have a bogus hole on our golf course."

No doubt Coggins, who constructed 18 golf courses in Arizona before he passed away in 1994, would have been proud. His little layout in the pines certainly has stood the test of time. Beautifully. ✿

RANCHO MAÑANA GOLF CLUB

PAR: 70 • YARDAGE: 4,436–6,004 • RATING: 64.8–72.6 • SLOPE: 114–131 • SIGNATURE HOLE: 397-YARD, PAR-4 Nº 4 • GREEN FEES: MODERATE TO EXPENSIVE

MIKE ALLRED REMEMBERS the first time he gazed out on the fairways and greens of Rancho Mañana Golf Club, realizing in a heartbeat that a rescue mission was in order.

"I couldn't believe people were actually paying to play golf here. It was in that bad of shape," said Allred, whose family had been looking for a fixer-upper project in the golf industry. "The place was totally undercapitalized and mismanaged. But we also could see what a unique course and setting this was. What we did, essentially, was stop the bleeding and start with the obvious improvements."

If Allred needed inspiration, he got it when one of the regulars at Rancho Mañana gave him a story about the club that had appeared in *The Arizona Republic* just six weeks before his family purchased the property. The headline on the article, which was severely critical of the course conditions, read: "For Rancho, maybe Mañana, [tomorrow]" In the story, Phoenix architect Bill Johnston detailed how he had built the course in 1989 despite having only about 60 acres to work with. Originally called Eagle Creek, Johnston said that only a few minor details, like additional acreage, had kept him from creating a quality product. "I've hung on to that story just to keep reminding myself how far we've come," Allred explained. "Basically, we've rebuilt the place from the ground up. Now it's more or less a matter of perfecting it."

The rebirth of Rancho Mañana is one of golf's great comeback stories. For Allred, whose family also owns Telluride Golf Club and Ski Company, the project went way beyond the $5 million that was spent remodeling and upgrading. "First of all, this is such a beautiful setting," Allred said, pointing to Elephant Butte, Skull Mesa, and the surrounding foothills of the Tonto National Forest. "Cave Creek runs right through the middle of the course, and to my knowledge, it's the only riparian area involving a golf course in the Phoenix-Scottsdale area. Plus, when you fully understand the history of this place, well, it's special. It certainly was something my family wanted to get involved with."

Rancho Mañana once served as an outpost for the U.S. Calvary as well as the Pony Express. Riders stopped by daily at the small, brick cantina that still stands on the property. "We're not sure of the actual date of origin, but the cantina was built around the

A saguaro stand gazes down on the signature fourth hole.

Short said that rather than trying to build length into the 6,000-yard tract, width was the key to the overall playability. "If you don't try to overpower it, Rancho Mañana is a fun golf experience," Short noted. "Believe me, it's no pushover. We've had the Arizona Golf Association and the Southwest Tour out here, and 1 or 2 under usually wins it."

Of the two nines, the front side is the more scenic, playing up into and out of the surrounding hillsides. The 397-yard, par-4 fourth hole is the signature shot, running entirely uphill with a wash slashing its way across the steep fairway at the 200-yard mark. "It's probably the shortest, number-one handicap hole in the world," Short said. "It's a bit of a grind making the climb, but the view when you get to the green is just fantastic."

The fourth hole starts a solid run of five tenacious tests in a row, as the fifth, sixth, and eighth holes also provide spectacular views. The seventh hole, a 195-yard doozy of a par 3, drops 200 feet to the bottom of Cave Creek. Hang on.

The back nine has just as much elevation, but is not quite as rapid-fire. The big step forward here came by eliminating several holes that bordered housing eyesores and replacing them with the driving range. The palm trees, water, and subsequent bridges also added to the beauty.

But to hear the locals tell it, nothing tops the tantalizing Tonto Bar and Grill, as guests order up filets, fish, and pasta from underneath dark, hand-carved beams that existed in the days of the dude ranch. "Our chef, Eric Flatt, came from Pebble Beach, and needless to say, the food is exceptional," Allred said with obvious pride. "Everything is fresh and baked on property."

Of course, it's pretty hard to beat the Tonto burger and a cold draft beer after a long day of golf. Certainly that would have been incentive enough for the U.S. Calvary, even if Rancho Mañana no longer needs to be rescued. ✿

turn of the [twentieth] century," Allred said. "The Calvary riders would roll in, drink up, and be on their way. We've got some wonderful old photographs that depict what it was like back then."

In the early 1940s, the area served as a dude ranch called—what else?—Rancho Mañana. The Allred family also has some classic photos from that era, which along with the early black-and-whites from the cantina, grace the walls of the sales office. "Besides re-establishing the golf course at Rancho Mañana, we're also building a private hotel and spa," said Allred, noting that the 56 on-site casitas are selling for $80,000 for an annual, four-week stay. "It's been a slow process getting the course and the hotel up and running, but that's only because everything we've done has been first-class."

Among the improvements: 12 holes were rebuilt, two new ones added and five holes revegetated; fairway acreage was added throughout, transforming the playability of Nos. 2, 3, 4, and 6; a series of mounds were built between the first and 18th fairways to distinguish the two holes; dirt cart paths were replaced with concrete; the clubhouse was remodeled with a Southwestern theme and the footage quadrupled; power lines were buried on the back nine and a split-rail fence added for aesthetic value; an oasis-like setting was created in the middle of the 13th through 15th holes; a new driving range and practice facility were built; the existing snack bar/restaurant was replaced with the chic Tonto Grill. "When I first saw the course, it was a total dump," concurred Andy Short, the director of golf and a lifelong friend of the Allreds. "Now, it's just a short, sweet, pretty golf course."

RANDOLPH PARK MUNICIPALS

. . . .

NORTH: PAR: 72 • YARDAGE: 6,134–6,969 • RATING: 70.0–73.7 • SLOPE: 120–129 • SIGNATURE HOLE: 193-YARD, PAR-3 № 15 • GREEN FEES: INEXPENSIVE

DELL URICH: PAR: 70 • YARDAGE: 5,275–6,624 • RATING: 66.4–72.7 • SLOPE: 111–128 • SIGNATURE HOLE: 135-YARD, PAR-3 № 17 • GREEN FEES: INEXPENSIVE

EVERY CITY in the country should have a 36-hole golf facility like Randolph Park, where you get a little old, a little new, a little bold, and a little true-blue. Yes, there is something for everyone when it comes to teeing off on the North Course or its younger rival, Dell Urich.

"They are the perfect complement," noted Brent Newcomb, golf administrator for the City of Tucson. "You've got the modern game of golf at Dell Urich, and the more traditional one at Randolph North, where you weave your way between the trees."

The story of the Old Pueblo's most popular municipals, the ones that annually do 150,000 rounds of golf, began in 1930, when the legendary William P. "Billy" Bell created the North Course. Among the first 10 courses in Arizona, the North

was the toast of Tucson, and the first of three courses Bell did in the area along with El Rio (1936) and Tucson Country Club (1949). Through the years, the North once played host to the PGA Tour (1979–86) and is currently the home of the LPGA's Welch's/Circle K Championship.

Dell Urich, which was designed in 1961 by Bell's son, "Billy Junior," initially was labeled as the South Course. Unfortunately, the South had waned to the point of being a beaten-down tract until Tucson architect Ken Kavanaugh breathed life back into it in 1996 with a revolutionary design concept formed around a storm-water management facility. The name change was in honor of Dell Urich, a longtime head pro at Randolph Park until his death in the early 1990s.

Like Newcombe, Kavanaugh has only good things to say about Randolph Park's 36 holes of

golf. "Tucson golfers reap the benefits because the courses are a sharp contrast between 1930s golf architecture and that of the 1990s," said Kavanaugh, who has done 14 courses of his own in eight different states. "I don't know of another facility quite like it in Arizona, and that's pretty cool."

Which is the better test?

"Good question," Kavanaugh countered. "Neither course is what I'd call easy, but the North is a par 72, whereas Dell Urich is 70, so it's easier to break 80. At the same time, the North is flatter, and you don't get the uneven lies on it like you do at Dell Urich. I guess the detail that separates them for me is the conditioning. Dell Urich is always in better shape because it's wall-to-wall 419 Bermuda, whereas the North Course is common Bermuda, which needs more water to really look good. Obvi-ously, water is a very limited commodity in the desert."

But water, or the possibility of a lot of it, didn't keep officials from turning Dell Urich into a first-ever golf course/storm-water management facility. The deal, which saw the federal government and Pima County ante up $7.1 million and the City of Tucson kick in $4.7 million, was put together prior to Kavanaugh delivering the facelift. "When the [Army] Corps of Engineering approached all of these different groups about the project, all they wanted was a storm-management facility," Kavanaugh said. "When they told me their plans, I wanted to give them a golf course that stored water."

To his credit, Kavanaugh kept Bell's original routing but redesigned every square foot of the 120 acres it was built on. The chief difference from

The Santa Catalina Mountains are in full view of Randolph Park.

the old course and the new was Kavanaugh added subtle yet bold contouring to reshape the existing fairways, which had been flat. Even though the course now is marked by water-retention basins, they play like elevation changes.

Both nines at Dell Urich have lots of movement along with some rugged par 4s that run over 430-plus yards, including Nos. 7, 8, 12, and 15. But the signature hole is the 17th, a picturesque par 3 over water to a green framed by a 15-foot-high stone wall. Even though it's just a wedge from 135 yards, the short shot always seems to come down to all or nothing with the prevailing wind in your face.

The North might be more demanding simply because of length (6,969 yards vs. 6,624). Of course, all of Bell's traditional designs bring into play large bunkers and greens, and doglegs that were exceptionally well thought out. Adding to the flavor, and frustration, are some huge trees that are approaching

100 years of age. "The only complaint you ever hear about the North comes from the pros each year," Newcomb pointed out. "They think the greens are too hard, but that's just a [lack of] water issue."

Unlike the South, which is consistent throughout, the North tends to build to a crescendo, like most of Bell's designs do. All of the par 5s are fun, especially Nos. 9, 16, and 18. The signature hole, however, is the 193-yard 15th, a long iron over water to an elevated green. Hard as it might be to believe, those four holes all were tweaked by the diabolical Pete Dye in 1978, the only time the course has been touched up since its inception.

There are other things you will appreciate about Randolph Park, like the ability to get a tee time any time you want at a price under $30. Plus, its rather large restaurant is revered by the locals for its daily specials, especially the authentic Mexican-American fare.

"Actually, what I like best about the facility is

The signature par-3 17th at Dell Urich.

it's right in the middle of downtown," Newcomb mused. "You've got all this bustling life around you, and right smack dab in the middle of it all are these beautiful, shady golf courses."

Which course is the most popular?

"Oh, I'd say it's right down the middle," Newcomb estimated. "Most people appreciate both for what they are." Even Kavanaugh, who certainly could be biased if not for his love of the game, agrees with the issue of who's number one. "It's funny, but from time to time, someone will ask me when I'm going to upgrade the North course, and I just laugh," he said. "The North is a classic, and it would be a gross mistake to mess with it. Being older, that's the beauty of it."

And when you combine it with the new, it makes for the best. ✿

RIO RICO RESORT AND COUNTRY CLUB

PAR: 72 · YARDAGE: 5,478–7,119 · RATING: 67.9–72.9 · SLOPE: 120–128 · SIGNATURE HOLE: 439-YARD, PAR-4 № 8 · GREEN FEES: INEXPENSIVE TO MODERATE

THIS IS A SPECIAL PLACE on Earth: rustic and romantic, wild and free.

When you consider that legendary architect Robert Trent Jones Sr. built over 500 golf courses during his illustrious career that spanned nearly 60 years, yet constructed only three in Arizona, Rio Rico Resort and Country Club takes on an even more significance.

A blend of nature, a simple lifestyle, and the all the challenging elements that make the game of golf so great, that's Rio Rico. Few courses can be so rewarding.

When the afternoon sun sets on these 18 holes tucked deep in the Santa Cruz River Valley between the Tumacacori and Santa Rita mountains, there is no better place to be. Bright orange gives way to purple haze, and Rio Rico seems to glow. You ask yourself: "How awesome can it be?"

As it turns out, the surroundings have all the elements of a golfers' haven. RTJ Sr. knew this back in 1971 when he first set eyes on this lush yet semiarid area that is located just 15 miles above the Mexican border town of Nogales. Having already completed his famed Wigwam Gold Course in Goodyear some 10 years earlier, and having built Oakcreek Country Club in Sedona with his son, the old master was not all that unfamiliar with Arizona. But, obviously, he had never seen the likes of a setting like Rio Rico.

"One of the things people always comment on is the beauty of the natural terrain. It is so awesome," said John O'Hara, the new general manager of Rio Rico Resort. "But what is really special about this area is the people. They are wonderful."

For those who have played the likes of such high-end, ultra-chic Arizona courses as Troon North and Grayhawk, Rio Rico is a vast departure. The element of time and Jones' traditional values are why it remains such a classic.

Rio Rico has all of Jones' trademark designs: four sets of tees that range up to 100 yards in length on rectangular-shaped boxes; sweeping fairways that oftentimes dogleg up or down the hill; bunkering that is so appealing that it remains the standard for the industry; and greens that vary in width and depth not only for variety's sake, but because course strategy is based on common sense. Blame it on Jones, a scratch golfer in his youth who went on to become what many regard as the greatest golf architect who ever lived.

"We are blessed," O'Hara said of Jones' imprint on Rio Rico. "When you can offer this type of a great golf experience combined with a four-diamond resort, why would anyone want to look elsewhere?"

Many feel the same way after an 18-hole tour. The front side, which originally was the back nine, is one of the great runs of golf in Arizona, especially the fifth through eighth holes, which play over a hillside and require almost every shot in the bag. The stretch begins innocently enough with a 198-yard par 3 up the hill to a huge, well-bunkered green. Then the ultimate test of skill begins at the 414-yard sixth, a dramatic dogleg that plays down, around, and up the hill to an elevated green. There is no letup at the 484-yard, par-5 seventh, where mesquite-lined fairways and lots of elevation off the tee pose potential problems. But if a birdie is to be made, No. 7 is your best bet.

Not that the No. 8, a 439-yard par 4 that is known as the course's signature hole, is without recourse. But scoring "3" here is highly unlikely, as the mission starts high on a bluff, then drops down through two distinct fairway tiers before a player arrives at a serene green surrounded by water and cattails. The hole is so good, a player just wants to go back and tee it up again.

The back nine also is loaded with a character all its own. Much more spacious and flat, the par 5s are long (535 and 602 yards) and the par 3s are absolutely to die for, both playing over water to greens framed between stately trees. In a way the front and back are completely different, except for the one common denominator: Robert Trent Jones Sr.

"I never met the man, but his work is revered, and people who play the course always seem to come back for more. They love his golf course," said Ron Heraty, the director of golf at Rio Rico. "I've played a lot of golf courses, and few can match up with this one. For the better players, they get all they want. And for the beginners, what better place to tee it up, as the course is not at all threatening off the tee like a lot of desert courses are these days."

There is another neat factor that comes into play at Rio Rico: A feeling that you have just had one of the truly great golf experiences of your life. And the truth is, every visit reveals yet another secret that Jones subtly spliced into this Arizona gem.

So you head for the quaint little clubhouse, where a beer and a burger seem to taste better than you remember. A quiet night in the unpretentious but well-done resort high on the hill above the golf course leads to yet another singular thought that pounds in the brain: Perhaps the time is right to play Rio Rico just one more time?

It is an easy decision, so simple and so satisfying. Yes, heaven can definitely wait. ☼

The Santa Rita Mountains rise up behind the par-5 No. 7.

SAN IGNACIO GOLF CLUB

PAR: 72 · YARDAGE: 5,648–6,704 · RATING: 68.3–71.8 · SLOPE: 116–136 · SIGNATURE HOLE: 522-YARD, PAR-5 Nº 13 · GREEN FEES: INEXPENSIVE TO MODERATE

FROM THE PATIO of serene San Ignacio Golf Club, the Santa Rita Mountains rise to the east, looking like monuments that have been there forever. To the southwest, the peaks and canyons of the Tumacacoris begin their trek toward Mexico. Northward lies the Catalinas and Rincons in all their purple majesty.

Master architect Arthur Hills took advantage of all these breathtaking backdrops when he created San Ignacio. It is a tranquil place, where retirees who have been blessed come to savor the sun and, of course, play golf. Every day they pinch themselves, thanking their lucky stars.

Green Valley will do that to you. How else do you explain this small community of 29,000 people

building seven golf courses to satisfy its needs? Besides San Ignacio, there are several other good ones, like Canoa Hills, Torres Blancas, and Desert Hills. Still, San Ignacio is the championship course, where challenge and charm add up to a great golf experience. No wonder the Arizona Golf Association picks San Ignacio for one of its major tournament sites each year.

"There are so many things to like about this golf course," said Dave Powell, the director of golf, who also happens to be one of the finest players in the Southwest Section of the PGA. "But I think what I like most is that, when you're playing San Ignacio, you're always on your very own hole. It's not like you can look over at some guy playing the 16th hole. It's just you and your foursome, and you can't beat that feeling."

Even though houses line the hillsides above most fairways, Powell makes a point. San Ignacio has a lot of privacy for the area's best public course. In a way, nature is undisturbed as golfers go on their merry way. It's almost like being in Mexico, the laid-back ambiance leading to one perfectly relaxing day after another.

Actually, San Ignacio once was a part of Mexico. But the United States purchased the parcel known as San Ignacio de la Canoa in 1854 as a part of the Gadsden Purchase. For over 120 years it was wild Sonoran desert, then one by one these lush little layouts began to color the landscape green. Arthur Hills added San Ignacio to the neighborhood in 1989.

Mostly, it is a golf course that features an abun-

A tree-lined fairway wends its way to the fifth hole.

dance of movement controlled through mounding and elevations. Sculpted mesquite trees define San Ignacio's tight fairways in random solo fashion, while multiple tiers provide many distinct pin placements on its greens. Conditioning also is at a premium, thanks to superintendent Phil Phillips, who earned his green thumb at another of Arthur Hills' great works, Oro Valley Country Club near Tucson.

But what is really cool about San Ignacio is that much of the terrain and wildlife that existed 150 years ago remain today. The course seems to excel as much as sanctuary as 18 holes of great golf. "You never know what you're going to run into next," Powell explained. "For instance, we've got a pair of bobcats that live over on the eighth hole. They're beautiful cats, and boy, have they got a life. It's a smorgasbord with all the dove, quail, and rabbit they dine on. And the other day we had a mountain lion walk right across the blue tee on the first hole. We've got so many inhabitants that call this place home. The only ones that bug me are the javelina; they just tear the hell out of the turf looking for grubs. But what are you going to do?"

Play golf. Both nines are equal to the task, with the signature hole being the 13th, a 522-yard par 5 that heads dizzily downhill with the Santa Ritas rising up in the distance. Along the way, two lakes keep players hugging the right side of the fairway on their first two shots. Still, there is no way to bail out totally, as a golfer's final approach shot must come back to the left, with luck dodging the water that guards the green. "From the 12th on home to the 18th, those are some picturesque golf holes," Powell noted. "But both nines are so strong, it's like: 'Take your pick.' Three of the best holes we've got are the first, eighth, and ninth. I think the par 3s also are one of the course's strengths. They have great variety and looks."

San Ignacio also has become quite strong in the dining department since Tucson restaurateur Bob McMahon purchased 50 percent of the course from

the original builder, Fairfield Homes, in September of 1999. McMahon, an avid golfer, pledged to raise the standard in San Ignacio's kitchen to rival that of his Tucson eateries—McMahon's Steakhouse, Keaton's, Firecracker, and City Grill. "It's been a great marriage, because Bob's brought in some great restaurant background and some really good food," Powell reported. "We're in the middle of redoing the dining and patio areas, but everybody already has noticed it's special. We never serve a bad meal, and the locals love that."

Accommodations also are outstanding, as the Lodge at Green Valley sits high on hill across from the clubhouse. "The Lodge is one of the best kept secrets in Arizona," Powell said. "They've got 86

golf villas that are priced from $65 to $100 [a day], and that includes a full kitchen, washer-dryer, and all the amenities."

The same could be said of the golf course, which truly is a hidden gem, especially when taking into consideration the green fee, which is inexpensive to moderate. "*Golf Digest* selected us as one of its top 100 courses in the 'Super Value' category," Powell added. "Our peak rate is $60, and most people would pay that amount in a heartbeat for this quality of a golf course."

Not to mention all that beauty, nature—and, yes, fantastic food!—that comes as part of the package at San Ignacio Golf Club. ☀

SAN MARCOS GOLF RESORT

PAR: 72/73 · YARDAGE: 5,296–6,463 · RATING: 68.5–75.9 · SLOPE: 114–117 · SIGNATURE HOLE: 477-YARD, PAR-4 Nº 5 · GREEN FEES: MODERATE

THE STARS don't come out at San Marcos Golf Resort any more. At least not like the celebrities did in the resort's heyday, from the 1920s to the '50s.

But once upon a time, this was the place to be if you worked in Hollywood and wanted to get away from all the glitz and glitter. Such big-name screen stars as Errol Flynn, Clark Gable, Jimmy Stewart, Gloria Swanson, Doris Day, and Joan Crawford were regulars at San Marcos, although "Baby Jane" (Crawford) didn't tee it up. Among

other celebrities who stayed and played were crooner Bing Crosby, dancing dynamo Fred Astaire, and boxer Gene Tunney. Hey, even former President Herbert Hoover and notorious gangster Al "Scarface" Capone cruised the fairways of San Marcos, although not at the same time. Their bodyguards wouldn't allow it, for obvious reasons.

Today, San Marcos still is a relaxing round of golf, as those same cedars that existed way back then give golfers shelter—and fits. The course has gone through numerous changes and renovations, as well as owners. But it keeps on bringing out the players

who cherish a traditional style of golf contested on tree-lined fairways. It's not necessarily what you would expect in the Arizona desert, but that was the only way the game was played when San Marcos Resort came into existence in 1912.

Obviously, the course and neighboring resort are steeped in history, going back to the days of Dr. Alexander J. Chandler, who founded this East Valley community that bears his name. The course, or the first nine holes, were built in 1913, when Will H. Robinson and Harry Collis teamed up on the assignment about a mile east of where the present course it located.

The new (or is that old?) 18 holes were constructed in 1928, and once again Collis was the designer, with help from a fellow named William Watson, whose résumé included such prestigious layouts as Interlachen and the Minikahda Club in Minneapolis and Olympia Fields in Chicago. Two years later, the first grass fairways in Arizona were sewn into the desert. Yep, up until that point, golf in the desert had been played on dirt and sand, although a few courses had a strip or two of grass. It would take a few more decades before irrigation systems became par for the course.

Through the years, celebs and others discovered that San Marcos was a great place to retreat and get away from it all. The course was even valued as a championship track that at one time stretched to 7,215 yards, although that length has been tightened considerably to 6,463 yards. But when former PGA Tour star (there's that word again!) Dave Hill established the course record of 11-under 61 in the early 1960s, it was played all the way back.

A tree-lined fairway wends its way to the fifth hole.

The serene par-3 eighth hole at San Marcos.

For the most part, the original routing remains at San Marcos with some minor exceptions, the most notable being a modern-day irrigation system that has blanketed this serene environment with wall-to-wall grass. Certainly the guests of the past would be somewhat astonished to see the course look this good.

San Marcos opens with three fairly straight-forward holes before it settles into the cedars for a mesmerizing run that begins at No. 4 and ends at No. 8. That stretch produces a short par 5 (477 yards), a long par 4 (472), two solid, dogleg par 4s, and a picturesque par 3 over a reed-filled pond accented by weeping willows. Enjoy, as this is as pure as it gets at San Marcos.

The back nine is more wide open, and features another of those quaint, water-guarded par 3s at No. 13. Check out the cottage between the 13th green and the 14th tee, as the gingerbread architecture reminds one of a California bed and breakfast—another throwback to the good ol' days.

From that point, the back side becomes quite demanding. Need proof? How about back-to-back par 5s to end your round? Whew! The course's driving range, which is equipped with those spongy Cayman balls (they go about half the distance of regular golf balls) hardly prepares you for the climax.

But, for the most part, San Marcos remains a walk in the park. Yes, even the little hot dog stand known as Billy Biloo's still offers up refreshments in the center of the course. And the laid-back clubhouse, which also has the old-time cottage feel, is a friendly and informal place to drink a cold beer. Go ahead, help yourself to the popcorn. It's free.

Fortunately, not all things come to pass, as banquet rooms at the resort still honor the afore-mentioned celebrities. OK, so the Clark Gable and Errol Flynn rooms hardly do the late actors justice. Nothing remains the same, and if the truth be known, it's better than no link at all. Besides, when stepping to the first tee at San Marcos, who can forget the famous footsteps that once walked these fairways?

SILVER CREEK GOLF CLUB

PAR: 71 · YARDAGE: 5,203–6,813 · RATING: 66.2–71.5 · SLOPE: 115–132 · SIGNATURE HOLE: 484-YARD, PAR-4 № 15 · GREEN FEES: INEXPENSIVE

WITH JUST A TAD BIT of imagination, you can almost see them, the cowboys of yesteryear cutting steers in and out of the herd on the hillsides that surround Silver Creek Golf Club, a laid-back course located on what once was one of the biggest spreads in Arizona.

Actually, the place resembles the setting for a John Wayne movie, which is fitting. "The Duke" also owned a ranch in these parts, just down the road outside of Eager. Accented by wild flowers and water—both the namesake Silver Creek and White Mountain Lake lie on the outskirts—this is one heavenly place to tee it up.

Once upon a time, Silver Creek was known as the Bourdon Ranch, spanning 10,000 acres. They roped 'em, branded 'em, and drove 'em off to market by the thousands. But these days only a sign that reads "Caution Cattle" remains along Bourdon Ranch Road as you make your way to the golf course. Seldom do you see a "little dogie" or hear a discouraging word.

Especially for those who play Silver Creek, a superlush layout of rye fairways, bluegrass rough, and bentgrass greens created in 1985 by Gary Panks. No surprise there, as Panks also designed such northern delights as Sedona Golf Resort, Antelope Hills South in Prescott, and the second nine at Elephant Rocks in Williams. Many feel Panks' early efforts at Silver Creek turned out to be one of his best courses ever. It certainly fits into the category of "Hidden Gems."

No one knows this better than Marc Silliman, who has been the director of golf at Silver Creek since the first ball was struck. Silliman hears his customers' reviews of the golf course, and they are glowing. He also knows its character and the

forces that often make it rougher than expected. "Mornings are usually perfect out here. Clear, sunny, and serene," Silliman said, reciting the prevalent weather pattern in these parts. "But the winds tend to gust hard in the early afternoon, when the clouds build. Sometimes it's difficult to even make a par."

Powerful electrical storms often explode in the afternoon, and those who choose to play in them are foolish. It is not unusual for a bolt to come crashing down, igniting a fire among the pine. Throw in the wind, and no wonder there can easily be a 10-stroke swing in your round from morning to afternoon.

Still, the small risk (if you use common sense) is worth the trip to Silver Creek, which comes right at you from the get-go. For instance, the first hole, a 545-yard par 5, plays uphill, twisting and turning until you finally end up with a blind approach shot. Two more tenacious tests present themselves before the 126-yard fourth hole offers respite. OK, so you have to carry the mountain lake that fronts the green at No. 4, no big deal. It's a fun hole, especially when your ball bounds off the rock wall between the water and green, ending up with a birdie opportunity.

Enjoy, as there are not a lot of easy holes at Silver Creek. When Panks scales back on the yardage, he usually cranks up the difficulty of the green. Shelves, tiers, and crowns all are featured on these always-slick surfaces. Needless to say, other parts of your short game are thoroughly examined, as missing a green here usually leads to some type of disadvantage.

Like all good golf courses, Silver Creek has its storied stretch, and in this case it's the 12th through 15th holes, dubbed "Amen Straightaway." It's Silliman's silly takeoff on Augusta National's "Amen Corner," where the Masters is settled each year. "Certainly it's one of the most difficult four-

hole stretches of golf in Arizona," he explained. "If you've got any chance at all of shooting a good score here, that's the stretch that will make or break your round."

The par-3 12th is a brute when pushed back all the way to 244 yards. Only Silver Creek's elevation of 6,000 feet above sea level keeps a player from pulling out the driver. But you'll need the big wood at the 13th, a demanding dogleg left that rambles on for 435 yards. Finding the fairway is key on this hole, because shaggy shots from the rough won't cut it to this green fronted by a big swale and a grass bunker.

Then it gets rougher than a cowpoke's beard, as the par-5 14th weaves its way uphill, stretching 533 yards. It's not the number-one handicap for nothing, as the green sits precariously between a bunker and a rock outcropping. The only bail-out area is short of the green, as an errant approach shot usually means you're dead. Which often is the condition a player finds himself in by the time he reaches the 15th, one of the longest par 4s in Arizona at 484 yards. Yes, the U.S. Golf Association should investigate the length of this hole. It should be a par 5, right?

Silliman only laughs when someone asks what the best score ever shot at Silver Creek happens to be. "The course record is still tied to the late John Denver," Silliman says. "Actually, the record is inscribed on one of his old [LP] records in the hallway."

That would be a 3-under 68 that is gold-plated on *Rocky Mountain High*. The 1970s hit song seems the perfect accompaniment to anyone who could accomplish such a feat. ☼

The 533-yard, par-5 14th hole is the number-one handicap.

TUBAC GOLF RESORT

PAR: 71 · YARDAGE: 5,295–6,839 · RATING: 66.9–72.4 · SLOPE: 113–128 · SIGNATURE HOLE: 575-YARD, PAR-5 № 16 · GREEN FEES: INEXPENSIVE

OWN AT TOSH'S CANTINA, the food and drink are flowing fast and furiously: Ultimate margaritas, burrito rancheros, chicken mole, and the best chips and salsa found north of the Mexican border. Occasionally, golfers wander in from nearby Tubac Golf Resort, hungry for fajitas, which fall a little on the lightweight side when it comes to true Mexican cuisine. But no matter what you order at Tosh's, everything is warm and wonderful. There's not a line out the door for nothing!

Tubac is a cool little community of artsy types. Once they were called hippies, but that's all changed over time. These days nearly 40 galleries dot the town square, offering some really weird stuff, as well as some pieces that are literally world-class. In a lot of ways, Tubac reminds one of Sedona before the Red Rock Capital of the World got too big for its britches.

There is something else that makes this small town very special—Tubac Golf Resort, which was molded out of the rich soil found along the Santa Cruz River Valley. The sleepy little golf course was designed by Red Lawrence, "the Desert Fox," a lofty nickname earned after delivering such Arizona nuggets as Desert Forest in Carefree, and the original nine at The Boulders.

Tubac Golf Resort has much of the same charm that is found in the small enclave it's named after, but with a tad more sophistication. That's obvious (well, maybe not) from the golfers who are sitting on those real leather saddles that serve as bar stools in La Montura, a restaurant that is housed in an old

The tee shot is terrific at the signature 16th hole.

ranch-style hacienda that dates back to the early 1800s. Originally, La Montura was known as the Otero House, and once served as the site of a rendezvous for a 1974 meeting between then-President Ford and then-President Luis Echeverria of Mexico. Now it serves up thirsty players and their partners, who have just had the pleasure of a soothing round of golf. The course has been open since 1960, and has the distinction of being one of several locations used in the filming the golf flick *Tin Cup*, starring Kevin Costner.

History is big in Tubac, as the town's roots date back to 1752 when the Spanish built a presidio, or fort, here. The presidio brought some protection from Apache raids and led to the first European settlement in what's now Arizona. Later, after the United States acquired Tubac from Mexico as part of the Gadsden Purchase, the town became the site of Arizona's first newspaper, the *Weekly Arizonan*. In 1859, the newspaper's editor criticized a local businessman, which resulted in a duel. Fortunately, both men escaped unharmed, but the businessman bought the newspaper and moved it to Tucson. In other

The historic Otero House at Tubac Golf Resort.

words, the town has a lot of character and characters. The same can be said of the golf resort.

For the most part, the front nine is fairly wide-open with the exception of two testy par 3s. One of those, the eighth hole, just might be the course's signature. The long-iron shot from 185 yards must weave its way between two cottonwood goalposts and over a water lily–filled pond. If the big branches on the left don't get you, those on the right have a definite chance. The putting surface is so huge that just hitting the green is no sure indicator that a player will make par. There is a tendency to think Tubac Golf Resort can't get any better than this, but it does.

The back nine is one of the stellar stretches of golf in the state, with a crescendo building from the 12th hole to home. The run starts with a dynamic dogleg to the right over, under, and around a behemoth fairway bunker, as the 12th hole is diagrammed to perfection all the way to a tantalizing green that tilts precariously. The 13th hole features a dramatic tee shot over the Santa Cruz River to a green encircled by a mesquite grove, the novelty being you can lay up or go for it at 305 yards. Then you get back-to-back doglegs, first right and then left, down the hill and up. With Elephant Rock, a local landmark, jutting up behind the 15th green, there is a tendency to think it can't get much better than this. But wait; the rollicking ride is not over quite yet.

The 16th hole is a memorable par 5 that doglegs around mesquites while rambling 575 yards. Play it once and you'll never forget it, and not just because it served as the water hole where Roy McAvoy (Costner) dunked approach shot after approach shot while losing a fictitious U.S. Open. For the record, the *Tin Cup* folks spent $150,000 to have the notorious lake installed. It's also quite well-known that when the *Tin Cup* crew moved its film location to Tucson, they cast kept coming back on the weekends to play Tubac. Yep, you can fall in love with this golf course.

Natural "goalposts" protect the 185-yard No. 8.

The roots of Tubac's ownership, as well as those of many of its guests, are anchored in Los Angeles, primarily because Al Kaufman came from there when he bought the resort in 1988. To this day, it remains a California stronghold, although Arizonans are beginning to see the light in greater numbers. Many come to play the "Trio in Rio," which also includes Rio Rico Resort and Country Club and Kino Springs, both of which lie just outside of Nogales and also were built by Lawrence.

"People love this place so much, we get bookings as many as two, three, four years out," Kaufman conceded. "They relish the fact they can relax and recover from the stress of the city, and still have a lot of fun."

It all starts at Tubac Golf Resort, and ends at Tosh's. There is no separation of the two, only an inner peace. ☀

TURQUOISE VALLEY GOLF COURSE

Par: 72 · Yardage: 5,209–6,758 · Rating: 68.1–71.2 · Slope: 114–123 · Signature hole: 727-yard, par-6 №15 · Green fees: inexpensive

IF TEEING IT UP up at Turquoise Valley Golf Course is like tuning into the Discovery Channel, then touring the nearby town of Bisbee is a trip back in time to *The Twilight Zone.* Either way, a visitor is certain to learn a lot about the history of Arizona.

Both Turquoise Valley and Bisbee are throwbacks to the early 1900s. Bisbee was founded in the late nineteenth century and at one time held the distinction of being the largest city in Arizona. Considering its remote location in the southeastern corner of the state, this was quite an accomplishment for a hard-working community that once produced more copper than anywhere else on Earth.

Turquoise Valley, which technically is owned by the City of Bisbee, originated in 1908 near Bisbee's Warren Section, just to the east of what now is the tiny border town of Naco. Legend has it that Pancho Villa, a leader of the Mexican Revolution, once led his band of hombres over the little nine-hole layout.

In 1936, the course and clubhouse were moved to Naco as part of a project that fell under the Works Progress Administration (WPA). Adding to the lore, several barracks occupied by the troops of General John "Black Jack" Pershing, the military leader who chased after Villa into Mexico, still are withering away just down the street from the present-day site of Turquoise Valley.

The golf course itself had fallen on hard times in past years until a Canadian sheep rancher named Peter Lawson and his wife, Leslie, began playing it during the winter of 1996. The couple became so enamored with the warm, small-town flavor they experienced, that they sold their 760-acre spread in Alberta and took out a 99-year lease from Bisbee to manage Turquoise Valley. Under the Lawsons' laid-back approach, the course underwent a $2 million facelift that renovated the clubhouse and added nine new holes of golf, among other improvements. "To make a long story short, I thought we could screw it up pretty bad and still have a great 18-hole course," Peter Lawson quipped. "As it turned out, the expansion went better than even we expected."

Dick Atkinson, a retired physical education professor who serves as head pro at Turquoise Valley, landed the architectural assignment. Early in 1999, he delivered the new nine just to the north of Greenbush Draw, a 20-foot-deep chasm that divides the course down the middle. "The addition of nine more holes has been dramatic," noted Atkinson of what now is called the back side. "I tried to make the [new nine] user friendly; something for everyone. It must have worked, because not only have more people come out to play it, but they keep coming back more often."

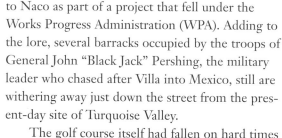

The view is expansive from Turquoise Valley's 11th tee.

There is a wild, expansive look to Turquoise Valley, which has an elevation of 4,600 feet above sea level. In many ways, it is reminiscent of Concho Valley Country Club in northeastern Arizona, as both courses are located on sweeping grasslands backed by mountain ranges in the distance. At Turquoise Valley, the course is bordered to the south by the San Jose Mountains of Mexico, with the Huachucas popping up to the west and the Mules ranging to the north. The area's awesome landscape puts a golfer into such a peaceful mood that even a bad score can be quickly forgotten. (Double-bogey, what?)

Turquoise Valley holds the distinction of being "the oldest continuously operated golf course in Arizona," and also lays claim to another rather large boast. Yes, at 727 yards, the 15th hole is the state's only par 6. It might be even longer in the future. "The boss wanted a par 6 so we could be different," Atkinson explained. "We also wanted it to be the longest hole in the state. I've heard there are several other holes [in Arizona] that are in the 700-yard range, so I think that, eventually, we'll probably take it back to 747 yards, or maybe even 777. Whatever it takes to be the longest."

Of the two sides, the front nine (the old nine), at least at this moment, is more fun to play. With big eucalyptuses and weeping willows that have been around for more than 50 years, plus a fairly traditional layout, it is a solid yet serene test of golf. The new nine is much tighter and somewhat longer, and has more of a desert feel due to a lack of trees. However, Atkinson said he still has some "tinkering to do" with the last nine holes.

Those who play Turquoise Valley don't seem to mind the slight differences in the old and new. In fact, most leave their golf game on the course when they slide inside the cozy little clubhouse called Coyote's Hideout to enjoy a Moosehead or Molson (Lawson's choices of Canadian brews) and some authentic Mexican food. And for those who decide to stay overnight in Bisbee, the good times are just beginning to roll.

Waiting to play host are such ancient hotels as the Bisbee Grand, which opened in 1906, and the behemoth Copper Queen, once noted as "the most memorable pause between New Orleans and San Francisco." Sandwiched into the town's narrow, European-styled streets complete with swinging-door saloons, the two inns are impeccable preservations of the past.

The Bisbee Grand is especially loaded with nostalgia, as each suite is decorated with furniture from the turn of the twentieth century. Or if a visitor really is adventuresome, the Grand offers its eclectic Captain's Suite, which is loaded with mariner antiques and knickknacks from the deep blue sea. A rather odd collection for a mining town, but then again, maybe not. There still is the famed Lavender Pit mine site, which seems so deep it might touch China, as well as underground tours through an old Phelps Dodge mining shaft.

Life moves slowly around here. But after talking with the townsfolk, characters like "Wimpy," "Bear," and "Windsong," and visiting such watering holes as the Stock Exchange and St. Elmo's, it's easy to understand why Bisbee remains so unique. Not much has changed in nearly 100 years. It's as if time has stood still, and no one knows the difference. In every way, Rod Serling, the late narrator of *The Twilight Zone*, would have loved this place. Do you suppose he played golf? ☀

The Bisbee Grand Hotel is loaded with nostalgia.

INDEX

ILL HUFFMAN is an award-winning sports writer who grew up playing golf in Iowa, where golf is sometimes referred to as "barnyard pool." After receiving his master's degree in journalism at the University of Iowa in 1976, he worked as an editor and reporter for *The San Antonio Express-News*, *The Des Moines Register*, and *The Arizona Republic*, where he first began covering the golf beat in 1988. He is a past national president of the Associated Press Sports Editors Association, and has written for numerous national golf publications, including *Golf World*, *Golfweek*, *Golf Digest*, *Golf Magazine*, and *Sports Illustrated*.

Huffman is now the golf writer for the *East Valley Tribune* and *Scottsdale Tribune*, and co-hosts a weekly radio program, *Backspin the Golf Show*, which airs on KGME in Phoenix. He currently serves on the executive board of the Golf Writers of America.

A resident of Tempe, Arizona, Huffman has played 44 of the top 100 courses in the world, but mostly, he's an Arizona golf guy who plays "neighborhood courses" like the Raven at South Mountain, Papago, and Phantom Horse. "I've probably played 90 percent of the courses in Arizona," Huffman adds. "What makes those experiences so unique is that we have so many different kinds—traditional, desert, mountain, and, yes, even a couple that would make for a great cow pasture. It's the beauty of Arizona golf."